Julia Anne Elizabeth Tollemache Roundell

Cowdray

The History of a great English House

Julia Anne Elizabeth Tollemache Roundell

Cowdray
The History of a great English House

ISBN/EAN: 9783337182724

Printed in Europe, USA, Canada, Australia, Japan

Cover: Foto ©ninafisch / pixelio.de

More available books at **www.hansebooks.com**

COWDRAY:

The History of a Great English House.

BY

(MRS. CHARLES ROUNDELL.

With Illustrations

FROM DRAWINGS IN THE BRITISH MUSEUM,

AND FROM

SKETCHES BY THE LATE ANTHONY SALVIN, Esq., F.S.A.

"μέχρι μὲν τούτου ὄψις τε ἐμὴ καὶ γνώμη καὶ ἱστορίη ταῦτα λέγουσά ἐστι."
HERODOTUS, II. 99.
"So far I have set forth the results of my own observation, judgment, and research."

LONDON:
BICKERS & SON, LEICESTER SQUARE.
1884.

To His Excellency

THE RIGHT HONOURABLE

John Poyntz, Earl Spencer, K.G., K.P.,

LORD-LIEUTENANT OF IRELAND.

Dear Lord Spencer,

It is with real pleasure that I avail myself of your permission to dedicate these pages to you.

They relate to Cowdray, one of the stateliest of English houses, and the home of the Montagues. Of that great family you are one of the chief representatives. Few histories of one house can offer so varied a picture of famous and distinguished men.

Believe me to be,

Yours sincerely,

JULIA ANNE ELIZABETH ROUNDELL.

Oeborne, Fernhurst, Sussex,
October 1883.

PREFACE.

THE principal authorities consulted for this history of Cowdray have been Dallaway's History of the Western Division of the County of Sussex, Horsfield's History and Antiquities of Sussex, Lower's History of Sussex, the Sussex Archæological Collections, the Archæologia of the Society of Antiquaries, the Archæological Journals, Lower's Chronicle of Battle Abbey, Thorpe's Catalogue of the Muniments of Battle Abbey, the Gentleman's Magazine, the Annual Register, Collins' Peerage, Grose's Antiquities, the Vetusta Monumenta, Nichols' Progresses of Queen Elizabeth, Elwes' Castles, Mansions, and Manors of Western Sussex, and Foley's Records of the English Province of the Society of Jesus.

Much information has been obtained from the Burrell Collection of Manuscripts and Drawings in the British Museum. Sir William Burrell, Bart., F.R.S., F.S.A., who in 1768 represented Haslemere in Parliament, contemplated writing a History of Sussex. At that time the only history of the county, besides the notice of it in Camden's *Britannia*, was a small volume written in 1730 by the Rev. T. Coxe. Sir William Burrell filled his copy of this history with marginal notes. He travelled over Sussex, taking transcripts from conveyances, settlements, court rolls, and family documents. He visited most of the Sussex churches, making long extracts from the registers, and copying the inscriptions on many of the monuments.

PREFACE.

But before completing his task he was struck with paralysis and became incapable of continuing his work. At his death in 1796 he left all his papers to the British Museum. Sir William employed Grimm, Lambert, and other artists, to make drawings for his work, and these drawings he also left to the British Museum.

The Rev. James Dallaway, F.S.A., Rector of Slinfold, availed himself of the Burrell Manuscripts for his *History of Sussex*. The second volume of this History, in which is contained the account of Cowdray, is extremely rare; for when this volume was nearly ready for publication all but a very few copies perished in a fire at the printer's.

Besides the information derived from books, I am indebted for much assistance in the preparation of this volume to the kindness of living persons. Amongst these my thanks are especially due to Mr. Alexander Brown, agent for the Cowdray estates from 1833 till 1867; to Mr. Richard Fisher of Hill Top near Midhurst; to Mr. Maunde Thompson of the British Museum; to Sir Sibbald Scott, Bart., and to Sir Bernard Burke, Ulster King-at-arms. Mr. Osbert Salvin has kindly allowed me to use the drawings of Cowdray which were taken by the late Mr. Anthony Salvin, F.S.A., about the year 1844.

The drawings for this book have been executed by Miss Beatrice Austin, Church Street, Midhurst.

The *Story of a Curse*, extracts from which I have been allowed to reprint in the Appendix to this volume, was published in the magazine entitled *The Lamp*, and is now out of print. It was written by a member of an old Roman Catholic family in West Sussex. The omitted passages contained historical notices of Cowdray, which are more fully given in the previous portion of my book.

CONTENTS.

CHAPTER I.
THE FIRST LORDS OF COWDRAY . .   PAGE 1

CHAPTER II.
SIR WILLIAM FITZWILLIAM, K.G., EARL OF SOUTHAMPTON .   7

CHAPTER III.
SIR ANTHONY BROWNE, K.G., OF BATTLE ABBEY .   11

CHAPTER IV.
SIR ANTHONY BROWNE, K.G., FIRST VISCOUNT MONTAGUE .   22

CHAPTER V.
QUEEN ELIZABETH AT COWDRAY   .   38

CHAPTER VI.
ANTHONY MARIA BROWNE, SECOND VISCOUNT MONTAGUE .   45

CHAPTER VII.
THE BOOK OF HOUSEHOLD RULES . . .   51

CHAPTER VIII.
COWDRAY DURING THE CIVIL WAR   78

CONTENTS.

CHAPTER IX.
COWDRAY IN THE EIGHTEENTH CENTURY 87

CHAPTER X.
GEORGE SAMUEL, EIGHTH VISCOUNT MONTAGUE . 100

CHAPTER XI.
THE LAST OF THE BROWNE FAMILY AT COWDRAY . 106

CHAPTER XII.
COWDRAY IN ITS GLORY 111

CHAPTER XIII.
THE FIRE AT COWDRAY 126

CHAPTER XIV.
COWDRAY IN RUINS 133

CHAPTER XV.
THE CURSE OF COWDRAY 140

CHAPTER XVI.
THE DOMAIN OF COWDRAY . . . 143

APPENDIX.

THE STORY OF A CURSE.

LIST OF ILLUSTRATIONS.

THE BUCK HALL	*Grimm*	*Frontispiece*
DOOR AND ROOF OF THE PORCH	*Grimm*	. *page* 10
WEST FRONT OF COWDRAY	*Grimm*	28
GARDEN FRONT OF COWDRAY	*Grimm*	,, 28
THE CHAPEL		,, 73
FOUNTAIN FROM COWDRAY	*B. Austin*	92
THE QUADRANGLE, EASTERN SIDE	*Grimm*	,, 111
DO., SHOWING THE GATEWAY AND THE SOUTH GALLERY	*Grimm*	,, 111
WINDOWS OF THE BUCK HALL	*A. Salvin*	,, 123
COWDRAY TWO MONTHS AFTER THE FIRE —*From the Gentleman's Magazine*		,, 131
GROUND PLAN	*A. Salvin*	,, 131
THE KITCHEN TOWER	*A. Salvin*	., 136
THE GATEWAY	*A. Salvin*	.. 136

COWDRAY.

CHAPTER I.

The First Lords of Cowdray.

N the rising ground above the little river Rother, and not far distant from the ruins of Cowdray House, may still be traced the site of the castle of the De Bohuns, first Lords of Midhurst and of Cowdray. The site of this castle was at least four hundred yards in circumference; the dry fosse, the deep trench, and small portions of the old walls may still be seen,* whilst the little field called the Court Green close by shows the spot to which the retainers of the De Bohuns might carry their goods and drive their cattle for safety under the shelter of their lord's stronghold. This plot of rising ground has always been called St. Anne's Hill (the name is now often corrupted into Tan Hill or Thane Hill), no doubt because the castle chapel was dedicated to St. Anne. A very ancient bell, possibly removed from this chapel, still

---

* It is believed that the dungeon and other subterranean chambers still exist in St. Ann's Hill. In the hot summer of 1842 one of the surveyors employed by Mr. Alexander Brown (the steward of the Cowdray Estate) traced nearly all the old foundations by means of the dried-up grass.

hangs in the belfry of Easebourne church, on the confines of Cowdray Park. This bell, which measures 3 ft. 4 in. in diameter at the lip and 3 ft. 4 in. in height, and of which the tone is B flat, is inscribed *Sancta Anna ora pro nobis*.

Dallaway is of opinion that when this old castle of the De Bohuns fell into decay its lords built another house nearer to the river, portions of which in later years were made the first beginning of Cowdray House. It has been thought that the two massive hexagonal towers flanking the main body of the house, which were less injured by the great fire than any other part of the building, were portions of the original structure. It is not certain at what period the De Bohuns removed from St. Anne's Hill to the lower ground, although several of their deeds are dated from Cowdray. The most probable date is the reign of Edward the Third. It is, however, certain that the De Bohuns were a most powerful family. They were the Hereditary Sealers of the King's Briefs, and this office, with that of Serjeant of the Chapel Royal, was resigned by John de Bohun to the King so far back as during the reign of Edward the First.

The importance of the De Bohun family will be seen from the following extract from Camden's *Britannia*, edition of MDCVII.:—" Fluuius autem qui praeterfluit è Septentrionali agri parte scatens, plurimis hinc inde riuulis increscit, inter quos praecipuus est qui praeterlabitur *Cowdrey* Vicecomitis Montisacuti aedes splendidissimas, et ad alteram ripam *Midherst*, quae *Bohunos* Dominos suos jactat, qui pro insignibus crucem coeruleam in aureo clypeo gestârunt, et ab Ingelrico de *Bohun* sub Henrico Primo, floruerunt ad Henrici VII. usque tempora, qui filiam et haeredem Joannis Bohuni Dauidi *Owen* Equiti aurato, filio naturali Oweni Theodori cum opima haereditate in uxorem dedit. Fuerunt hi *Bohuni*, ut obiter adnotem, propter obsoletam verbi antiquitatem, aliquandiu *Spigur[r]nelli Regis*, i. [i.e.] *Sigillatores Breuium*, jure hereditario; quod officium unā cum Ser[v]ientia *Capellae* Regiae Edwardo Primo remisit Joannes de *Bohun* filius Franconis, ut in Charta antiqua ea de re confecta legitur."

There is no doubt that the manor of Midhurst was granted to Savaric de Bohun by Henry the First, and the grant was confirmed by charters of four subsequent Kings, Richard the First, Henry the Third, Edward the Third, and Richard the Second.

John de Bohun fought at Cressy in 1346. On his return he endowed the little Benedictine nunnery of Easebourne, adjoining Easebourne church; and

THE FIRST LORDS OF COWDRAY.

he was summoned as Lord Bohun of Midhurst to the Parliament which sat from 1363 to 1366. John de Bohun's grandson, Humphrey, who died in 1468, left in his will—in order to secure prayers for his own soul and for the souls of his parents—6s. 8d. to each of the vicars, rectors, and curates of the parishes in which he had property. Among those thus endowed were the curates of "Midherst, Esborn, and Farnhirst." It is curious to compare these legacies with the bequests to the members of his household. To each of his gentlemen he left 13s. 4d., to each of his valets 6s. 8d., and to each of his *garçons* 3s. 4d. This Humphrey had two sons; the elder of whom, John, was the father of Mary de Bohun, through whom the property at Cowdray passed to Sir Davy Owen. Humphrey bequeathed to his eldest son his sword and one horse, also one bed "called fedir bed" with its hangings, one mattress, one bolster, one pair of blankets, one quilt, and a brazen pot and plate.

John de Bohun died in 1499, and left no son. His daughter Mary married Sir David Owen (or, as he calls himself, Sir Davy Owen), who was reputed to be the natural son of Owen Tudor. Another account is that he was the son of Henry the Fifth's widow by her marriage with Owen Tudor. This royal lady had died in the first days of 1437, and her husband had been imprisoned in the Tower by the guardians of King Henry the Sixth. In the following year he contrived to make his escape. He was killed at the battle of Mortimer's Cross in 1461.

Whatever may have been the true story of Sir Davy's birth, he was no doubt recognised and honoured at court. In 1487 he was one of the twelve knights bachelor who held the canopy over Queen Elizabeth of York at her coronation; and in 1503, as one of twenty-eight knights banneret, he "attended the fiancelles of Princess Margaret to James, King of Scotland, escorting the bride to Scotland, and carving at the marriage dinner, wearing a very rich chain." This chain may have been the collar of SS., which is represented on his effigy in Easebourne church.

Mary de Bohun and Sir Davy Owen were probably married in 1489; and she must have died before Sir Davy made his will in 1529, as he leaves bequests to his second wife Anne, the sister of Lord Ferrers. But his tomb, with his own effigy, and the effigy of his first wife, must have been previously completed, as in his will he makes provision for the new painting and gilding of both.

Sir Davy Owen in 1529 was called as a witness before the commissioners appointed to inquire into the legal proofs of the marriage of Prince Arthur, elder brother of Henry the Eighth, with Katherine of Arragon. He was a most important witness, as he declared that he saw Prince Arthur married in St. Paul's Cathedral to Katherine, "with his own eyes, being then and there present." The examination was conducted partly in English and partly in Latin, and a transcript of it still exists in the British Museum. In that document Sir Davy is described as "of the county of Sussex, where he has dwelt forty years or thereabouts."

Sir Davy Owen died in 1542, and was buried at Easebourne, underneath a beautiful alabaster effigy. There is, however, no trace of the effigy of his first wife, Mary de Bohun, to which reference is made in his will. Sir Davy himself is represented in complete armour, with his sword at his left, and his dagger at his right side, and wearing his collar of SS. His head with its long hair is uncovered, and rests on his tilting helm as on a pillow.*
"Over the armour of the body is a tabard of arms shaped to the figure at the waist, between the openings of which at the sides are seen portions of the taces below the breastplate, and from them hang the tuilles, under which appears a skirt of mail indented at the bottom. The lance-rest is shown on the breast as if it passed through the tabard. The arms are in brassarts, coudes, and vambraces of plate, and the hands, which are brought together on the breast in an attitude of devotion, are in laminated gauntlets not divided for the fingers. The legs are in cuissarts, genouillères, and jambes of plate, and the feet, which rest on a lion, are in laminated sollerets rounded at the toes and there ornamented with roses: spurs being attached by straps." Sir Davy orders in his will that when his effigy, after being "new gilte and peynted," is "sett up, I wille the iron work that shall be sett about it, be ordered, faconned, and formed after the forme and facon of my Lorde

---

* "The great tilting helm or heaume was actually worn only at the moment of the charge, or while the combatant was in the thick of the mêlée: it was placed *over* the smaller basinet [or iron skull-cap], and it rested on the shoulders. In English monuments this heaume is habitually represented placed beneath the head of armed effigies, for which it forms a befitting pillow." The *taces* [or *faudes* as it was called abroad] was a sort of kilt of armour or iron petticoat: to this a small shield called a *tuille* covering the front of the thigh was fastened by straps and buckles, so as to admit of the free movement of the leg. The *brassart* protected the upper part of the arm, the *coude* or *coudière* the elbow, the *vambrace* or *avant-bras* the lower part of the arm. The gauntlets were made of pieces of iron sewn like scales on strong leather gloves. The *cuissarts* covered the thighs, the *genouillères* the knees, the *jambes* or *grevières* the legs, and the *sollerets*, which were constructed in the same manner as the gauntlets, protected the feet. [*Boutell's Arms and Armour.*]

Daubeney's Tombe at Westmynster, where he lieth, but I wille that it be of more substaunce." This iron work was probably of Sussex manufacture, as the iron works and forges of Sussex, beginning in the time of the Roman occupation of England, were not extinguished until late in the eighteenth century. But not a trace now remains of the iron work which once surrounded Sir Davy's tomb. The iron work, too, around Lord Daubeney's tomb (which exhibited his badge of "two dragons' wings conjoined by a knot or") is all gone, though the tomb itself, like Sir Davy's, remains.

Sir Davy Owen gives minute directions as to his funeral at "Essebourne," which was to be conducted "with laudable ceremonyes, after the degree of a banneret." His helmet and sword, his coat-armour, his banner, standard, pennant, guydon,* and the banners of the Trinity, of the Virgin Mary, and of St. George, were to be borne into the church with his body and hung up there. Mourning was to be given to those present according to their rank. To the church at Easebourne he left valuable silver vessels, mass-books, and rich "altar clothes"—vestments and copes of tawny damask, and of green damask embroidered with swallows, wolves, and red roses. He left also money to finish the roof of the church, "to gylt the Aungels and knottes, and peynt the panes [panels] with rede and blew." To the churches of Farnhurst and Lodsworth Sir Davy gave mass-books, vestments of red and blue damask, and a chalice for each of the value of four marks. All his gifts of altar vessels were to be engraved with his name.

Sir Davy was very liberal to his second wife, leaving her much valuable plate,—"a Basene and ane Ewer of silver of the gretest sort; thre Bowles of silver, pounced with a cover, and a wolfes hede with a rynge in his mouthe upon the cover parcellgilt; a great Bowle pounced with a highe foote dowble gilt, with a Lyons hede with a rynge in his mouthe upon the cover; a gret standynge cuppe dowble gilt with a Crowne downwardes; thre gold goblettes with a cover with my Armes upon the knoppe of the cover of the sort; a Salt of silver and dowble gilt, with a Wolfe upon the cover with roses and sonnes, and the fote a rote of a tree made of silver and gilte; two great Pottes of silver and gilte, nyghe a yarde hygh, of a gallon a pece, dowble gilt turned vice wise; a playne Salt of silver without a cover; a dosene of Spones of silver with knoppes gilte; a gilte Spone with a knop of golde sett with a saffer; a chafynge Dische of silver with a wolfes hede

---

* *Guydon*, a long streamer slit at the end, used at funerals.

therupone." She was also to have "a Crosse of Diamontes and thre great perles, price one hundred markes," besides "haffe the stuffe of householde and of all other things, a dossene of kyne, and tenne great oxene for her wayne." These oxen were much needed in the deep mud of the Sussex roads, for so late as 1724 Defoe saw "an ancient lady, and a lady of very good quality, I assure you, drawn to church in her coach by six oxen; nor was it done in frolic or humour, but from sheer necessity, the way being so stiff and deep that no horses could go in it." Sir Davy also bestowed on his wife down beds and "fedir" beds with pillows and sheets, counterpanes of verder [*i.e.*, embroidered with trees], one of them having "a great Lyone in the middes of golde and silke;" his travelling-beds of black velvet and russet satin embroidered with wolves and swallows, "wyth O and N of golde, and diverse flowers imbrowdred." Another legacy to her consisted of "fyve peceys of Arrays made with imagery of King Henry the V$^{th.}$, Henry the VI$^{th.}$, the Duke of Clarence, the Duke of Bedford, the Duke of Gloucester, with diverse other great men." The arras now in the Guild Hall at Coventry is somewhat similar to this in design, though perhaps a little later in date. But if Sir Davy's widow married again, she was to forfeit all these bequests, retaining only "a hundred poundes in money."

Sir Davy Owen appointed his relative Sir William Fitzwilliam his principal executor, and "for his labor and payne" about the will he was to receive a sum of a hundred marks, and another sum of a hundred pounds. The other executor, "my good lorde of Oxenforde" (the fifteenth Earl of Oxford and Lord Chamberlain), was only to "have for his labour forty poundes."

To this Sir William Fitzwilliam, there having been no issue of the marriage between Sir Davy Owen and Mary de Bohun, Cowdray had been sold in 1528, subject to Sir Davy's life interest.

The original will of Sir Davy Owen is now in the possession of Mr. Alexander Brown. It is written on five skins of very thin parchment, joined together lengthwise, and is signed D. Owen. On the back is the word *Useless*, which was written by Mr. Forster, solicitor to Mr. Poyntz. This will was found in a bundle of rubbish at Cowdray.

CHAPTER II.

Sir William Fitzwilliam, K.G., Earl of Southampton.

SIR WILLIAM FITZWILLIAM may be regarded as the builder of Cowdray House, though much was added by his half-brother Sir Anthony Browne and his descendants.

Sir William was the second son of Sir Thomas Fitzwilliam of Aldwarke in Yorkshire, and of Lucy, daughter and co-heir of John Nevill, Marquis Montacute, brother of Richard Earl of Warwick, the King-maker. Sir Thomas Fitzwilliam had an elder son, Thomas, who was killed at the battle of Flodden Field in September 1513. One of the pictures at Cowdray represented this Thomas and a John Fitzwilliam lying dead, dressed in armour; between them was the cognizance of the family, the trefoil *argent*, "which was sprinkled all over the leaden pipes of the mansion-house," and beneath the figures was the inscription, "In doing their dutys against the Scotts."

Lady Lucy survived her husband, and married secondly Sir Anthony Browne.

Sir William Fitzwilliam was one of the most eminent men of his time; he was created a Knight of the Garter, and subsequently became Lord Keeper of the Privy Seal, Lord High Admiral (in 1523), and Earl of Southampton (in 1537). There was a picture of Sir William at Cowdray, in which he appeared "walking by the sea, holding a staff with a golden knob, his face very fine."

One of the principal points of interest in reference to Lord Southampton is his having acted as gaoler to his aged cousin Margaret of Clarence, whom he kept shut up at Cowdray for many months. This undaunted lady was the daughter of George Duke of Clarence, who was put to death in the Tower in 1478 by being drowned in a butt of Malmsey wine; the sister of Edward Earl of Warwick, who was executed in the same prison in 1499; and the mother of the Lord Montacute who was beheaded on Tower Hill at the end of 1538. She was the niece of Edward the Fourth, and had established her claim to be Countess of Salisbury in her own right. She married Sir Richard Pole, a Knight of the Garter, who was cousin to Henry the Seventh. Lady Salisbury lived at Warblington near Havant, and was a determined Roman Catholic, never allowing her tenants to read the New Testament or any of the books which the King had "privileged." One of her sons, Reginald, who afterwards became the celebrated Cardinal Pole, was rector of South Harting (in the neighbourhood of Midhurst) in the year 1526.

Lady Salisbury had incurred the displeasure of Henry the Eighth, not only on account of her Catholic opinions, but also from the grave suspicion which attached to her of being actively concerned in the promotion of that rising of the Catholics in the North and West which was known as the Pilgrimage of Grace.

Lord Southampton was, therefore, sent late in the year 1538 to arrest Lady Salisbury at her own house, and to take her to Cowdray as the first stage of her journey to the Tower. He was no doubt well aware that his task would be a difficult one, but it appears to have proved even more troublesome than he had anticipated. He went to Warblington on the 13th of November 1538, and conveyed his prisoner to Cowdray. From Cowdray he wrote on the 16th of November: "We have dealed with such an one as men have not dealed withall before: we may call her rather a strong and constaunt man than a woman."

Lady Salisbury must, when at Cowdray, have heard of the execution of her eldest son on Tower Hill, but her spirit was unbroken. A few months later Lord Southampton wrote that he "went in hande with her, but although he entreated her in both sorts, sometyme doulx and milde and now roughly and asperly, she would disclose nothing. Wee suppose that there hath not been seen or herd a woman so ernest, so manlique in continuance, and so fierce as well in gesture as in wordes."

But Lord Southampton had found in his stout-hearted cousin's house conclusive proofs of her guilt. He had not only found "certayne bulls graunted by a bishopp of Rome," which alone were sufficient to ensure her conviction, but he had discovered in her linen wardrobe a tunic of white silk embroidered in front with the Royal Arms of England, and at the back with the device of the Five Wounds of Christ—the well-known badge of the Northern insurgents. This tunic was held up by Thomas Cromwell in the House of Lords when, on the 28th of April 1539, "the Countess of Salisbury and several other persons now in custody were attainted without trial." Lady Salisbury's guilt was now considered to have been fully proved. She was probably kept at Cowdray until the bill of attainder had passed, and was then taken to the Tower. Here she was imprisoned for two years: but neither disappointment, sorrow, nor suffering could cow that brave spirit. Her father had died in the Tower, her brother and her son had been beheaded on Tower Hill; but she "in whose person died the very surname of Plantagenet" remained, in spite of all, firm to the end. Lady Salisbury was executed on the 27th of May 1541. She refused to lay her head on the block, "saying, ' So should traitors do, and I am none.' Neither did it serve that the executioner told her it was the fashion. So, turning her grey head every way, she bid him, if he would have her head, get it as he would, so that he was constrained to fetch it off slovenly." *

Lord Southampton obtained a royal patent to add to his park at Cowdray, and to build there an embattled castle of stone. Part of his work may still be seen in the beautiful square porch at Cowdray House with the remains of its roof of groined stone and plaster ornament. This roof is ornamented with a radiated circle surrounding a pendent Tudor rose: inside the circle are eight double quatrefoils, each within a circle of its own, and in each compartment is Lord Southampton's cognizance,† a slipped trefoil

---

* Lady Salisbury was beheaded on Tower Green, and was buried in the church of St. Peter ad Vincula within the Tower. She had prepared for herself a beautiful tomb in the small chapel to the north of the altar at Christchurch Priory in Hampshire—a priory which had been greatly embellished by the Earls of Salisbury. The commissioners who enforced the Act of Dissolution wrote from Christchurch to Henry the Eighth with reference to this tomb, as follows : " In the church we found a chapel and monument made of Caen stone, prepared by the late mother of Reginald Pole for her burial, which we have caused to be defaced, and all the arms and badges clearly to be delete " [erased].

† In St. George's Chapel, Windsor, Lord Southampton's motto is rendered *Leaulte se provera* on the shield, and *Loyall et sa provara* on the standard. The badge is a trefoil slipped *argent*. In

bearing his initials W. S., alternating with the anchor which marked his position as Lord High Admiral. Over the doorway of the porch the achievement still remains of the Royal Arms with the lion and griffin as supporters, and with Lord Southampton's motto underneath, LOIAULTE SAPROUERA (*Loyauté Se Prouvera*). The letters L. and P., which alternate with W. S. on the door of the porch, were probably intended to represent the first and last words of the motto.

In the year 1536 Lord Southampton received a grant of Easebourne Priory from Henry the Eighth. In a portion of this house Sir Davy Owen appears to have made his home after having sold Cowdray House, and some of the alterations in the windows and other parts of the Priory have been thought by Dallaway and others to be due to him.

Lord Southampton died in 1543. He had married Mabell, daughter of Henry Lord Clifford, and in his will he desired that he might be buried at Midhurst if he died within a hundred miles of the place, and that a "new chapell" should be built there, at an expense of five hundred marks, for the burial of himself and his wife. But as he died at Newcastle-on-Tyne, whilst serving on an expedition against the Scots, his body was not brought back to Midhurst; and no trace of the "new chapell" existed when it was searched for by Sir William Burrell a century ago.

Lord Southampton had no children, and left his estates at Cowdray and in the neighbourhood to his half-brother Sir Anthony Browne.

---

the same chapel may be seen on the knee-piece of the armour of the effigy of the Earl of Lincoln an anchor cabled, being his official badge as Lord High Admiral. [*Villement's Collegiate Chapel of St. George, Windsor.*]

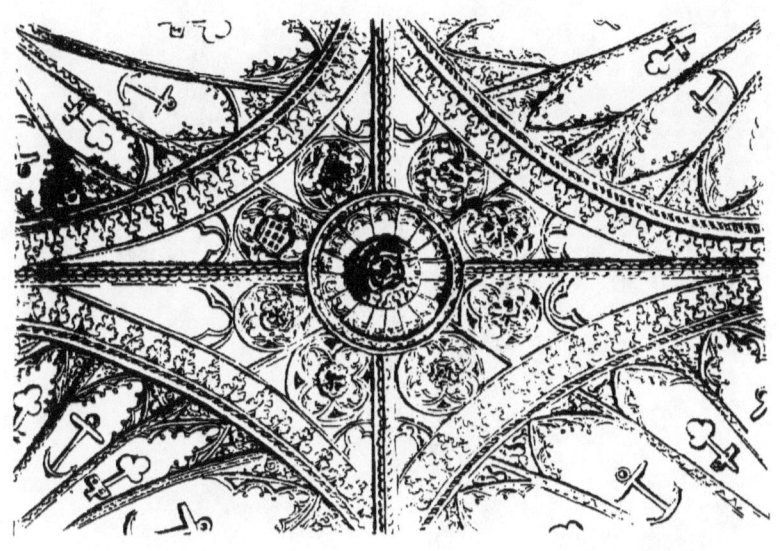

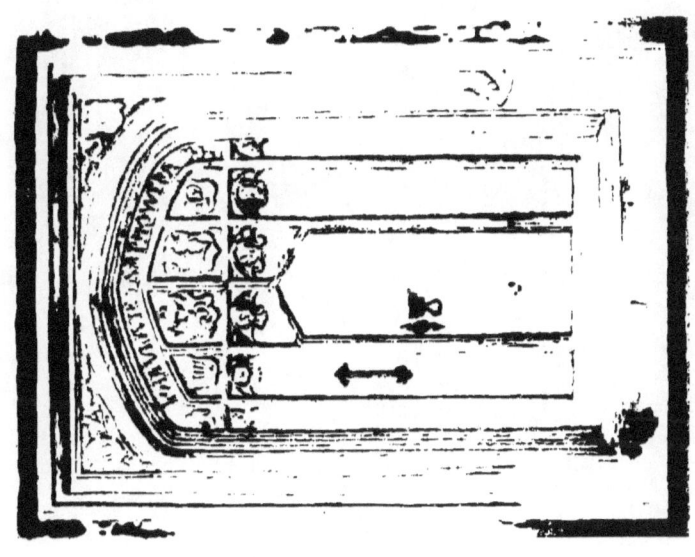

CHAPTER III.

Sir Anthony Browne, K.G., of Battle Abbey.

IN the middle of the fourteenth century Anthony Browne (the younger son of Robert Browne or le Broun, who represented Cumberland in Parliament) settled in London, and in time became a rich merchant. He was created a Knight of the Bath at the coronation of Richard the Second, for he had lent a large sum of money to the King, and had been generous enough to cancel the bond. This Anthony Browne left two sons, Sir Robert and Sir Stephen Browne. Sir Stephen, when Lord Mayor of London in 1439, sent ships to the Prussian coast for cargoes of rye, which he gave away "among the poorer sort of people." In consequence of the scanty harvest of that year, corn in England was extremely dear, costing three shillings a bushel.

Of Sir Robert Browne, brother of Sir Stephen, nothing is recorded. But his son, Sir Thomas Browne, was Treasurer of the Household to Henry the Sixth, and was one of the Commissioners who met in 1458 at Rochester to inquire into the quarrel which had arisen (and which had been fought out at sea) between Richard Earl of Warwick, the King-maker, and the citizens of the free city of Lubeck, "who were under a treaty of friendship with the King." Sir Thomas Browne married Eleanor, daughter and co-heir of Sir Thomas Fitzalan (brother of the Earl of Arundel), and by this marriage he acquired Betchworth Castle in Surrey.*

---

* Betchworth Castle was four miles east of Dorking. The baronetcy of the Brownes of Betchworth expired at the death of Sir Adam Browne in 1688. Sir Adam Browne had been selected

The third son of Sir Thomas Browne, Anthony, married Lady Lucy Nevill, after the death of her first husband Sir Thomas Fitzwilliam, and he thus became stepfather to Sir William Fitzwilliam, afterwards Earl of Southampton. Sir Anthony Browne and Lady Lucy had three children: Anthony; Elizabeth (who married the Earl of Worcester, ancestor of the Dukes of Beaufort); and Lucy (who married Sir Thomas Clifford, the ancestor of the Earls of Cumberland).

At the accession of Henry the Seventh in 1485, Sir Anthony Browne was "made Standard-bearer throughout the whole realm of England and elsewhere," and in the following year he became one of the Esquires of the King's body, and Governor of Queenborough Castle in Kent. In this year, 1486, he was knighted for his gallant conduct at the battle of Newark, where, on the 16th of June, the Earl of Lincoln and Lambert Simnel were defeated. In 1503, Sir Anthony was made Constable of the Castle of Calais, and there in the year 1506 he died and was buried. Twice during the three years of Sir Anthony's governorship of Calais he was, "in consideration of his loyalty, industry, foresight, and care," commissioned to receive the sum of 25,000 francs in gold (the annual tribute paid by Louis the Eleventh to Henry the Sixth).

He was succeeded by his only son Sir Anthony Browne of Battle Abbey, half-brother to Lord Southampton, and the first of the Brownes of Cowdray. This Sir Anthony was knighted after the siege and capture of Morlaix in Brittany in the year 1523, in which year he, with the Earl of Surrey, Lord High Admiral, "convoyed" the Emperor Charles the Fifth from Southampton to Biscay. In 1524 he was made Esquire of the

by Charles the Second as one of the intended Knights of the Royal Oak—that order which was intended by the King "to perpetuate the loyalty of his faithful adherents, but abandoned under the apprehension that it might perpetuate likewise dissensions which were better consigned to oblivion." On the death of Sir Adam Browne's daughter Margaret (wife of William Fenwick), in 1726, the Betchworth estate was sold; and the castle was pulled down about 1830. The crest of the Brownes of Betchworth, a griffin's head erased, was to be seen in perfect condition on the Browne monument in Easebourne church a few years ago. It has since been mutilated by thoughtless visitors to the church, but can still be distinguished. The arms, like those of the Montagues, were *sable*, three lions passant in bend, between two double cotisses *argent*. The motto also was similar, *Suivez Rayson*. Sir George Browne, eldest son of Sir Thomas and brother of Sir Anthony Browne, was beheaded in 1483, having espoused the cause of the Earl of Richmond and Lambert Simnel in their conflict with Richard the Third. One of his daughters named Katherine, married John Poyntz, High Sheriff of Surrey in 1572 and again in 1584. John Poyntz was the ancestor of William Stephen Poyntz, who in 1794 married the last of the Brownes of Cowdray.

Body to Henry the Eighth, and at the Christmas feast held by the King at Greenwich in that year he was one of the challengers in the jousts and feats of arms. From that time Sir Anthony became more and more a favourite with the King. In 1526 he was made Lieutenant of the Isle of Man "and those other islands belonging thereto," during the minority of Edward, Earl of Derby; and two years later he was sent to invest Francis the First with the Order of the Garter, "as also to take his oath that he should not violate the league made with King Henry." In 1533, Sir Anthony Browne was again sent into France, accompanied by the Duke of Norfolk, "the Lord Rochford, brother to the Queen" [Anne Boleyn], and Sir William Paulet, in order to attend Francis the First to Nice, and to "commune with the Pope there, concerning his stay in the King's divorce" from Katherine of Arragon. In 1539, Sir Anthony "obtained a grant of that eminent office of Master of the Horse, with the yearly fee of forty pounds for that service," and in the next year this office was confirmed to him for life, and he was created a Knight of the Garter.

But Henry the Eighth was not content with conferring mere honours on his favourite. In 1535 the manor of Poynings in Sussex had been granted by the King to Sir Anthony Browne in exchange for other lands; and on the 15th of August 1538, he received "a grant of the house and scite of the late monastery of Battle in Sussex, to him, his heirs and assigns for ever."

Only three months elapsed between the surrender of Battle Abbey by John Hammond the last abbot, and the establishment of Sir Anthony Browne and his family in his place. The abbot's lodging, according to the usual custom when an abbey was surrendered to the King's Commissioners, became the residence of the new owner. In this case the chapter-house, the cloisters, and other portions of the beautiful abbey were razed to the ground. Not one stone remained upon another of the magnificent cathedral church, for Sir Anthony Browne was actually able to place his garden on its site, and he planted a double row of yew-trees along what had been the nave of the minster.

Sir Anthony Browne was, as we have seen, much in favour with Henry the Eighth, but an additional reason for his having received so valuable a grant as Battle Abbey may have been his marriage with Alys, the daughter of Sir John Gage, one of the Royal Commissioners who carried out the Act of Dissolution with respect to Battle. Sir John Gage, who was a Knight of the Garter and Constable of the Tower, had the credit of having carried out the provisions of the Act with great severity. However that may have been, in his will he directed that his gold collar of the Order of the Garter should be sold and the proceeds given to the poor who came to his funeral from all the forty parishes in which he had property. He was buried at Firle near Lewes, under a magnificent altar tomb; and the manor of Alciston in the Rape of Pevensey, granted to him as part of the spoils of Battle Abbey, still belongs to his descendants, the Viscounts Gage.

But Battle Abbey was by no means the only grant of Church property which Sir Anthony Browne received. He was given at the same time the Priory of St. Mary Overy in Southwark, where he built a house.* He also received the manor of Send in Surrey, which was one of the "temporalities" of Newark Priory, and later he obtained a grant of the manor of Brede (which included a considerable portion of the town of Hastings), and Godstow, which had belonged to the monastery of Syon. Besides these grants, Sir Anthony, on succeeding, in the year 1543, to the property of his half-brother Lord Southampton, inherited the Priory of Easebourne, the monasteries of Bayham and Calceto,† and the Cistercian Abbey of Waverley in Surrey.

In the year 1540 Sir Anthony Browne was sent to the court of John of Cleves, there to act as proxy at the marriage of Henry the Eighth and Anne of Cleves. He appears to have been much distressed at her appearance, for he says he was "never more dismayed in all his life, lamenting in his heart, which altered his outward countenance, to see the lady so far unlike what was reported." But it was then too late to prevent the marriage, and Sir Anthony acted as proxy, wearing the blue and white suit of clothes in which he was afterwards painted. Alys Lady Browne was selected to attend Anne of Cleves on her arrival in England, and her opinion of the unfortunate bride seems to have coincided with that of Sir Anthony, for she told him that "she saw in the queen such fashions and manner of bringing up so

---

* The Priory of St. Mary Overy had been surrendered to Henry the Eighth on October 27th, 1539, but the church (now called St. Saviour's, Southwark) had been immediately purchased by the parish. In 1545 the site of the priory was granted to Sir Anthony Browne, and among the MSS. belonging to Mr. Cole, F.S.A., is a bill which was sent to the first Viscount Montague for "worke done upon your honor's house at Sent Marie Hoveris" in 1569. Sir Davy Owen had left money to the Prior of St. Mary Overy for masses to be said in that church as a "perpetuall memorye" of his grandmother, who was buried there. In the time of the second Viscount Montague the house at St. Mary Overy was called Montagu Close.

† Calceto is close to Arundel. It was sold by Mr. Poyntz.

gross that she thought the King would never love her." Lord Southampton was not so honest: he, with four hundred English noblemen and gentlemen, was sent to receive Anne at Calais, and he actually spoke " of her excellent beauty, such as I well perceive to be no less than reported." When Henry saw her himself, he complained bitterly of the fate of " princes, who take as is brought them with others, while poor men be commonly at their own choice." No doubt he regretted having sent Holbein to paint Anne's portrait, instead of leaving the choice in the wise hands of Sir Anthony Browne.

Two months later, in March 1540, Alys Lady Browne died, and was buried at Battle.

In 1543 Sir Anthony Browne went to Scotland with the Duke of Norfolk's army, in which expedition "they burnt above twenty villages." In 1544 he and the Duke of Suffolk accompanied Henry the Eighth to France; the Duke being in command of the English army, and Sir Anthony Browne acting as Master of the Horse. Three of the principal pictures at Cowdray represented the chief events of this expedition—namely, the march from Calais towards Boulogne, the encampment of the English forces at Marquison, and the siege of Boulogne. When the surrender of the town was imminent, Sir Anthony Browne was sent by Henry the Eighth to "treat of a general accord" with the ambassadors of the French King; and the English army then returned home. The French, however, were constantly endeavouring to retake Boulogne, and early in 1545 Sir Anthony Browne was employed by Henry the Eighth to raise more troops. "The King confiding in his loyalty, valour, industry, foresight, and care, being Master of the Horse and Knight of the Garter, commissioned him with Sir Thomas Wriothesley Lord Chancellor, Henry Earl of Arundel, and William Lord St. John, Chamberlain of the Household, to levy, array, and try all men able to bear arms in the counties of Surrey, Sussex, Southampton, Wilts, Oxon, and Berks, and to arm them according to their degrees, and to muster them in proper places; and to march all his liege subjects so arrayed and tried (as well men-at-arms and archers, as other horse and foot), by themselves or others by them deputed, to suppress his enemies, as often as occasion shall require."* In the same year Sir Anthony was made Justice in Eyre of all the King's forests beyond Trent, and, finally, he was constituted Standard-Bearer to Henry the Eighth, as his father had been to Henry the Seventh.

* Collins' *Peerage*.

In the last illness of Henry the Eighth Sir Anthony Browne undertook the dangerous task of telling the King of his approaching end. This duty he fulfilled with his usual "good courage and conscience," and Henry valued his old servant to the last. He appointed Sir Anthony guardian to Prince Edward and to the Princess Elizabeth, he made him one of the executors of his will, and he left him a legacy of three hundred pounds.

Edward and Elizabeth were at Hertford at the time of their royal father's death, and Sir Anthony Browne went with the Earl of Hertford to tell them of it.*

A few days later, Sir Anthony took a prominent part in the wonderful procession which conducted "the King's Majesty from the Tower through the city of London, in most royal and goodly wise, to his Palace of Westminster." This took place on Saturday the 19th of February 1547, when Edward the Sixth was rather more than nine years old. One of the great pictures at Cowdray represented this procession. At the meeting of the Sussex Archæological Society held at Chichester in 1853, there was exhibited a letter from the seventh Viscount Montague to the Society of Antiquaries, dated 1785, in which he gives permission for this picture, and this picture only, to be engraved.† John Topham, F.S.A., in the eighth volume of the Archæologia, gives a particular description of this celebrated picture, a drawing of which he exhibited at the meeting of the Society of Antiquaries in 1787.

"The streets through all the way where the King should pass were well gravelled in every place, and railed on the side from Gracechurch Street to the Little Conduit in Cheap, to the intent that the horses should not slide on the pavement, nor the people be hurt by the horses. . . . Within these rails stood the crafts along in their order, to the Little Conduit aforesaid, where stood the aldermen. On the other side of the streets in many places stood priests and clerks with their crosses and censers, and in their best ornaments, to cense the King; and all the way where the King should pass on either side were the windows and ways garnished with cloths of tapestry, arras, cloths of gold and of silver, with cushions of the same, garnished with streamers and banners as richly as might be devised."

The picture represented the procession at the moment of its passage

---

* This incident, together with that of the procession of the young King, has been made use of by Mr. Harrison Ainsworth, in his *Constable of the Tower*, Book I. chapters 1 and 2.

† Page 97.

through Goldsmiths' Row, with the shops set out with cups and beakers of gold, and the master of each shop standing at his door ready to salute the young King as he went by. Maitland, in his *History of London*, says of this Goldsmiths' Row: "It was beautiful to behold the glorious appearance of goldsmiths' shops in the South Row of Cheapside, which in a course reached from the Old Change to Bucklersbury, exclusive of four shops only of other trades, in all that space." But the artist contrived to show the course of the procession all the way from the Tower to Westminster; with the City companies, each headed by its master, and every liveryman wearing his gown and hood. In the background was a view of London Bridge, St. Mary Overy, the palace of the Bishop of Winchester, the Bankside in Southwark, and, far away, the river Ravensbourn and the royal palace at Eltham.

Edward had to witness many pageants and devices on his way, and to listen to much "goodly melody, and eloquent speeches, treating of noble histories, to the joyful welcoming and respect of so noble a King." It is a relief to find that one real diversion had been provided for the little boy. "In Paul's Churchyard there was a rope as great as the cable of a ship, stretched in length from the battlements of Paul's steeple, with a great anchor at one end, fastened a little before Mr. Dean of Paul's house-gate, and when his majesty approached near the same, there came a man, a stranger, a native of Arragon, lying on the rope, his arms and legs abroad, running on his breast on the rope from the battlements to the ground, as if it had been an arrow out of a bow, and stayed on the ground: then he came to the King's Majestie and kissed his foot, and so, after certain words to his Highness, departed from him again, and went upwards upon the rope till he was come over the midst of the churchyard, where he, having a rope about him, played certain misteries on the rope, as tumbling, and casting one leg from another; then took he the rope and tied it to the cable, and tied himself by the right leg, a little beneath the waist of the foot and hung by the one leg a certain space, and after recovered himself up with the said rope and unknit the rope, and came down again. Which stayed His Majesty with all the train a good space of time." Sir Anthony Browne, as Master of the Horse, rode next the King, "leading a goodly courser of honour, very richly trapped." The King, dressed in cloth of silver embroidered with damask gold, buskins of white velvet, and glittering all over with jewels, rode under a canopy borne by knights, and his horse had "a rich caparison of crimson satin embroidered with pearls and damask gold." The procession was of immense length, and Sir Anthony Browne, "guardian of the King's Majesty," must have been as glad as the tired child himself when at last the day was over.

Sir Anthony Browne began to build a wing at Battle Abbey for the reception of the Princess Elizabeth, who was to reside there. But he did not live to finish it, and it was completed by his son. Among the muniments of Battle Abbey is a letter to the steward there, impressing upon him the necessity of watching over the rough-layers (or masons) employed on the works. It appears that the building was being erected by contract, and that the first set of masons, dissatisfied with their wages, had "returned home to their own country." Other masons were to be sent, with "a substantial man as a morter-maker," and the writer urges the steward "that ye woll se them well handelyde in their wages; yf men feell no gayne by their labours and travell, hytt were as goode that they werre gone, for they woll worke none theireafter. As I vnderstonde, the worke ys takyn in greatt by one mann, and he doweth gyve small wages by cause hys owne gayne shulde be the morre."

Sir Anthony Browne also built Byflete House in Surrey: now pulled down.

After the death of Alys Lady Browne, Sir Anthony determined to marry again. His second wife was Lady Elizabeth Fitzgerald, daughter of Gerald ninth Earl of Kildare, and better known as the Fair Geraldine. Sir Anthony was forty-five years older than his bride, for at the time of their marriage he was sixty and she only fifteen years of age. She had been brought up at Hunsdon House with the Princesses Mary and Elizabeth, though Henry the Eighth had remorselessly hunted down and killed nearly every member of her family. There has been a strange confusion with respect to this second marriage of Sir Anthony Browne; and even Horsfield, in his *History of Sussex* (vol. i. p. 529), makes the mistake of saying that she and Alys Lady Browne were one and the same person. He remarks: "It is said that Alice was a great beauty, and celebrated by the Earl of Surrey at the tournaments under the name of the Fair Geraldine." After the death of Sir Anthony Browne, Lady Elizabeth married Sir Edward Clinton, first Earl of Lincoln, and was buried with him in a magnificent tomb in St. George's Chapel, Windsor.

Sir Anthony Browne survived Henry the Eighth, whom he had served with so much honesty and discretion, only one year. He died at Byflete, on the 6th of May 1548. He was buried at Battle under the beautiful altar tomb which he had prepared, and on which the effigy of his wife Alys lies beside his own. The tomb was richly ornamented with colours and gilding, many traces of which still remain: it is in excellent preservation, although the noses of both figures have been knocked off,—a misfortune that is said to have happened within the last thirty years. The effigy of Sir Anthony was described by Collins in 1756 as "a figure of a man in armour, lying on his back, habited with the mantle and collar of the noble Order of the Garter; his head resting on a helmet, and at his feet an eagle (the crest of his family). By him lies his lady, in the habit of the times, reposing her head on a cushion, and at her feet a wolf with a collar about his neck. Underneath are several cherubs, and under them escutcheons of arms curiously cut in marble and painted, but now worn out." The inscription is:

"Here lithe the Ryght Honourable Sir Anthony Browne, Knyght of the Garter, Master of the Kings Majestis Horsys, And one of the moste honourable Prive Cowncel of our most Dread Soverayne Lorde And Valiant Kyng Henry the Eyght; and Dame Alis His Wyfe.

"Wich Alis decesid the 31 Day of Marche Ao. Dni. 1540. And the sayd Sir Anthony decesid the Day of —— Ao. Dni.* On whose Sowls And all Cristens IHU Have Mercy, Amen."

The funeral pageant with which Sir Anthony's body was brought from Byflete to Battle was one of great splendour. Being Standard-bearer of England at the time of his death, the royal Standard was borne before his body; his own banner of arms was borne "between the Standarde and the corps;" at the four corners of the coffin were two pennons and two guydons, and four tapers were carried by four poor men "in gownes and hoodes gornyshed with scoucheons of armes." Sir Anthony's coat of arms, his targe of arms, his helmet, his crest, and his sword were carried in the procession, and the Standard and other banners were to be "holden about the grave untyll the earth be caste uppon hym." The next day at "the masse of the communyon" the armour and the banners were offered to the church with great ceremony, and hung up there. The hook on which the helmet hung remained on one of the pillars of the chancel till the restoration of Battle Church a few years ago.

---

* The blank was left by Sir Anthony when building the tomb, and was never filled up.

The character of Sir Anthony Browne is well described by Lloyd, who says: "Three things facilitate all things: (1) *Knowledge;* (2) *Temper;* (3) *Time.* Knowledge our knight had, either of his own or others whom he commended in whatever he went about, laying the ground of matters down in writing and debating with his friends before he declared himself in council. A *Temperance* he had that kept him out of the reach of others, and brought others within his. *Time* he took always driving, never being driven by his business, which is rather a huddle than a performance when in haste: there was something that all were pleased with in this man's actions. The times were dark, his carriage so too; the waves were boisterous but he the solid rock, or the well-guided ship that could go with the tide. He mastered his own passions and others' too, and both by time and opportunity: therefore he died with that peace the state wanted, and with that universal repute the statesmen of those troublesome times enjoyed not."

The most celebrated portrait at Cowdray was that of Sir Anthony Browne in the parti-coloured suit which he wore when acting as proxy for Henry the Eighth at the marriage of Anne of Cleves. He was represented with " his neck and shoulders bare and very brown ; a monstrous sword ; his breeches strait and slasht, counterchanged, the left side blue and white, the right white; a hat and feather, with a gillyflower in the band, and the George round his neck." The picture was painted on panel, and underneath it was the following inscription :

"Sir Anthony Browne. He lyvinge was all at one time and at his death Master of the Horse to Kyng Henrie the Eyght, and after to Kyng Edwarde the Syxte, Captain of both their Majesties gentilmen pensioners, Chief Standard Bearer of England, Justice in Oyer of all their forestes, parkes, and chaces beyonde the river Trente northwarde, Lieutenant of the forestes of Wyndesor, Wolmar, and Ashdowne, with dyvers parkes and chaces southwarde. One of the executors to Kynge Henrie the Eyght, one of their Majesties' Honourable Privie Councel, and Companion of the most noble Order of the Garter. He ended his lyfe the syxt of May, in the second yeare of King Edwarde the Syxte, at Byflete house in Surrie by hym buylded, and lyethe buried at Battell in Sussex, by Dame Ailice his fyrste wyfe, where he begann a stately howse since proceeded on by his sonne and heyre Anthony Vicecount Mountagewe, Chief Standard Bearer of England, Lieutenant of the forest of Wyndesor with other parkes, one of the Quene Marie's Honourable Privie Councel, and Knight Comptroller of the most noble

Order of the Garter. He had by Dame Ailice, daughter of Sir John Gage, K.G. (Controwler to King Henry the Eighth, and Chancellor of the Dutchy of Lancaster, and after Lord Chamberlain to Quene Marie, Constable of the Tower of London, and one of theyre Privie Counccl), seaven sonnes, Anthony of his proper name, William, Henrie, Francis, Thomas, George, and *Henrie Browne. He had also by her three daughters, Marie, Mabell, and Lucye. His second and last wyfe was the ladie Elizabeth Gerald, after Countess of Lincoln, and of the daughters of Gerald Fitzgerald, Earle of Kildare, by whom he had two sonnes, Edward and Thomas, who both died in their infancie. In this dress he married by proxy Princess Anna Cleves, relex † of Kyng Henrie the Eyght."

This curious picture was in a gilt frame, and was in 1771 covered with glass. It unfortunately perished in the great fire at Cowdray on the night of the 24th of September 1793.

Two portraits of Alys Lady Browne existed at Cowdray, both of which were burnt. Both were full-length portraits: one was taken when she was thirty years of age, and represented her with "her hands clencht, holding a watch, her gloves embroidered with yellow; a book on a desk beside her." In the other picture she wore "a black gown full of long points on the arms, breast, and to the bottom; gold border to her ruff; chain of gold and pearls on her neck."

But there appears to have been no portrait of the Fair Geraldine at Cowdray: no trace of one can be found in any of the catalogues and descriptions of the pictures there which were written before the fire of 1793.

William Browne, the second son of Sir Anthony Browne, married Anne, the daughter and co-heir of Sir Hugh Hastings of Elsing near Southampton, and from this marriage the Brownes of Elsing are descended. Francis Browne married Anne, the daughter of Sir William Goring of Burton near Petworth. Sir Anthony's eldest daughter, Mary, married John Grey, the younger son of the Marquis of Dorset; Mabell, the second daughter, became Countess of Kildare; Lucy, the youngest, married Thomas Roper of Eltham, ancestor of Lord Teynham.

---

* At that time it was no uncommon practice to give the same Christian name to two persons in one family.

† The etymology of the word *Relex* is open to much question. Perhaps it is a form of the word *Relegata*, and it might be rendered *Rejected*.

CHAPTER IV.

Sir Anthony Browne, K.G., first Viscount Montague.*

NTHONY BROWNE, eldest son of Sir Anthony Browne of Battle Abbey, succeeded his father in 1548. Like his father, he was a man of great ability and was deservedly esteemed throughout his long life. He was a staunch Roman Catholic, and never varied from the faith in which he had been brought up: yet he retained the favour of three successive sovereigns during those troubled years in which the religion of the State changed with every change of ruler.

He entertained at Cowdray both Edward the Sixth and Queen Elizabeth, and he was greatly valued by Queen Mary.

Sir Anthony Browne was one of the forty gentlemen who were knighted at the coronation of Edward the Sixth, and he soon afterwards married Lady Jane Ratcliff, daughter of Robert Ratcliff, Earl of Sussex.

In 1552 Edward the Sixth made his only progress, and during his journey he visited three houses in Sussex,—Petworth, Cowdray, and Halnaker. At Petworth the King slept four nights, attended not only by the greater part of the Privy Council and an enormous number of attendants, but also by a considerable armed force. Edward, when at Petworth,

---

* The Register of the Titledeeds of the first Viscount Montague (sold as waste paper) is now in the British Museum, Additional MSS. 31952.

wrote in his journal: "Because the nombre of bandis that were with me this progresse made the traine great, it was thought good they should be sent home, save only one hundred and fifty wich were pickt out of al the bandis. This was bicause the traine was thought to be nier 4000 horse, wich ware inough to eat up the country, for ther was litle medow nor hay al the way as I went."

On July 27th the King with his diminished retinue went from Petworth to Cowdray. In a letter to his friend Barnaby Fitz-Patrick (who had been whipping-boy to the King, and was now serving in the French army), Edward thus describes his visit: "For whereas you al have been occupied in killing of your enemies, in long marchings, in pained journeys, in extreme heat, in sore skirmishings and divers assaltes, we have been occupied in killing of wild bestes, in pleasant journeyes, in good fare, in vewing of fair countries, and rather have sought how to fortifie our own than to spoil another man's. And being thus determined came to Gilford, from thens to Petworth, and so to Cowdray, a goodly house of Sir Anthony Browne's, where we were marvelously, yea rather excessively banketted."

In the next year, 1553, Lady Jane Browne gave birth to a son, on the 22d of July, and on the same day she died. She was buried at Midhurst on the 4th of August, and her effigy is on the Browne monument, which stood in Midhurst church till 1851. The effigy is evidently a portrait, and in looking at it one cannot but feel sorry for the young creature who died so sadly "at the age of twenty years," just as her husband was entering on his long course of prosperity and honour. Lady Jane had had a daughter named Mary, who lived to marry three times. Her first husband was Henry Wriothesley, Earl of Southampton; on his death she married Sir Thomas Heneage; and lastly she became the wife of the Sir William Harvey, Bart., who was "first created Lord Ross in Ireland and afterwards Baron of Kidbrook in England." It is curious that the date of Lady Jane's death, given on the Browne monument, should be 1552. This must be an error, as Edward the Sixth, whose visit to Cowdray is known to have commenced on the 27th of July 1552, could not have been received there when Sir Anthony Browne's young wife had been dead only five days, and still lay unburied.

In 1554 Queen Mary married Philip of Spain, and on this occasion she created Sir Anthony Browne a viscount, "in consideration of the good and laudable service" which he, her "faithful and beloved servant, hath done and still continues to do, as also his nobility of birth, early care, loyalty and honour." Sir Anthony chose the title of Montague, probably because his grandmother, Lady Lucy, was the daughter and co-heir of the Marquis Montacute. His arms were: *Sable*, three lions passant in bend between four cotisses *argent*. Supporters—two lynxes *argent*, ducally collared, chained, and armed *or*. * Crest—on a wreath an eagle displayed *vert*, beaked and membered *gules*. Motto—SVYVEZ RAYSON.†

In the same year Lord Montague was made Master of the Horse, and was sent with Thurlby, the Bishop of Ely, to the Pope in order to make arrangements "for reducing of this realm to an union with the Church of Rome and to the obedience of that See." In 1555 Lord Montague was made a member of the Privy Council and a Knight of the Garter; and in 1557 he acted as Lieutenant-general of the English forces at the siege of St. Quentin in Picardy.

On the death of Queen Mary the whole aspect of affairs as regarded both the policy of the government and the religion of the state was entirely changed. It is much to the credit of Lord Montague that he never allowed the risk of losing the favour of his sovereign to influence him in his religious opinions, and it is also much to the credit of Queen Elizabeth that she respected him for his constant adherence to his own faith, and valued him for the honesty with which he served her.

Lord Montague was naturally left out of Queen Elizabeth's Privy Council, and two years later he was called upon to subscribe to the abolition of the Pope's supremacy in England, and to the recognition of the Queen's authority instead. Lord Montague and Francis fifth Earl of Shrewsbury were the only peers who refused "out of a sentiment of zeal

---

* In the *Baronagium Genealogicum*, by Joseph Edmondson, Mowbray Herald Extraordinary, published in 1732, the original crest of the Viscounts Montague is said to have been a buck proper, collared and lined *or*. This appears to have been a mistake, as Sir Anthony Browne of Battle Abbey had for his crest the green eagle of his mother's family. In 1732 there were forty-nine quarterings on the shield of the Viscounts Montague. The supporters have been variously given as wolves, bears, "neboks," boars with bears' legs, bears with bulls' feet and lions' tails, heraldic tigers, and lynxes. Garter King-at-Arms has kindly examined the Garter plate of the first Viscount Montague (installed in October 1555), and has thus enabled me to give the correct blazon. In the collection of Garter plates made by Garter Leake, the Montague crest is a buck at gaze *gules*, with ducal collar and chain *or*. But the third Viscount Montague is known to have entered the eagle displayed as his crest.

† On the Browne tomb the motto is rendered SUIVES RÆSON.

and honour" to do this. Lord Montague declared that "he for his part had, by authority of Parliament, and in the name of the whole body of England, tendered obedience to the Pope; the performance of which he could by no means dispense with." He added, "that it would be a very disgraceful reflection for England, which was so lately and so well reconciled by the Apostolic See, to make so sudden a revolt from it," and he pointed out that "the hazard would be as great as the scandal, should the Pope thunder out his excommunication, and expose the nation by that means to the resentment of its neighbouring enemies upon the score of this desertion." He and Lord Shrewsbury therefore boldly voted against the proposal. Lord Shrewsbury "survived this uncourtly act of sincerity" only a few months, but Lord Montague lived to find that his honesty had not diminished his favour with his sovereign.

Soon after this, in 1561, Queen Elizabeth sent Lord Montague on a special mission to Spain. Its object was "to satisfy the King of those realms what just cause she had to send an army into Scotland," and to represent to him the risk that he as well as herself would incur if the Guises were allowed to proceed unchecked. She considered that Lord Montague was the most fit person to act as Ambassador on this occasion, as she "highly esteemed him for his great prudence and wisdom, though earnestly devoted to the Romish religion."

Lord Montague was appointed one of the forty-seven Commissioners who sat on the trial of Mary Queen of Scots in the February of 1587. For Queen Elizabeth, according to Camden, "having experienced his loyalty, had a great esteem for him (tho' he was a stiff Romanist). For she was sensible that his regard for that religion was owing to his cradle and education, and proceeded rather from principle than faction, as some people's faith did." She had obliged him to suppress a chantry which he had founded in Midhurst church during the last year of Queen Mary's reign, but her confidence in him was fully justified by his behaviour at the time of the threatened invasion of the Spanish Armada. When, in the spring of 1588, Queen Elizabeth reviewed her army at Tilbury Fort,* "the first that showed his bands to the Queen was that noble, virtuous, honourable man the Viscount Montague, who now came, though he was very sickly and in age, with a full

---

* Copy of a letter to Mendoza, the Spanish Ambassador in France, dated London, September 1588, and found in the chamber of a seminary priest in England. Harl. Miscell. vol. i. p. 149.

resolution to live and die in defence of the Queen and of his country, against all invaders whether it were Pope, King, or Potentate whatsoever; and in that quarrel he would hazard his life, his children, his lands and goods. And to show his mind agreeably thereto he came personally himself before the Queen with his band of horsemen—being almost two hundred—the same being led by his own sons, and with them a young child, very comely, seated on horseback, being the heir of his house,—that is, the eldest son to the son and heir; a matter much noted by many, whom I heard commend the same, to see a grandfather, father, and son, at one time on horseback afore a queen for her services; though in truth I was sorry to see our adversaries so greatly pleased therewith."

Lord Montague, in thus "perilling his whole house in the expected conflict," must have greatly pleased Elizabeth, for she was well aware that many Roman Catholics were at that time having masses said and prayers offered for the success of the Spanish Armada.

Three years after the defeat of the Armada, in the August of 1591, Queen Elizabeth paid a visit of nearly a week to Lord Montague at Cowdray. The curious and minute account of this visit has been often quoted, but as often altered and cut short: in the next chapter an exact copy of it, with the original spelling, is given. Much has been said of the ridiculous and fulsome speeches, laden with compliments, which were made to the Queen on this occasion,—at a time when she was within a month of her fifty-eighth birthday; but if the account of her Progresses is examined, it will be seen that, in foolish expenditure and bombastic addresses, her entertainment at Cowdray was far behind most of those visits which so much impoverished the noblemen whom she honoured with her company.

Lord Montague's second wife was Magdalen, the daughter of William Lord Dacre of Gillesland. On the Queen's arrival at Cowdray she was received by Lady Montague and by her daughter Elizabeth, the wife of the first Baron Dormer of Winge.

Another lady was also staying at Cowdray during the Queen's visit,—Mabell, the sister of Lord Montague, who had married the eleventh Earl of Kildare, brother of her stepmother the Fair Geraldine. The history of this Lord Kildare is most romantic. Henry the Eighth had destroyed the whole of his family, except the Fair Geraldine (whose safety may have been due to her early marriage to Sir Anthony Browne). His father had been shut up in the Tower till he died broken-hearted, and the King had caused his five uncles, and his half-brother, the tenth Earl of Kildare, to be beheaded. The young Gerald was secretly conveyed by his tutor to Flanders, where Charles the Fifth sheltered him and refused to give him up to Henry the Eighth. Cardinal Pole, the boy's kinsman, sent for him, and with him he remained for three years, living in the Cardinal's own house in Rome. After this Gerald served under the Knights of Rhodes in Barbary during a campaign against the Moors, and spent some years with them at Malta and at Tripoli. On his return to Rome he narrowly escaped an end which, to him, would have been more painful than a death on the scaffold or on the battle-field. Whilst he was hunting near Rome his horse jumped into a deep pit which was hidden from view by bushes and underwood. The horse fell to the bottom and was killed, and Gerald, after clinging for a time to the roots of the trees which overhung the pit, became exhausted and dropped on to its body. His dog remained at the edge of the pit, and its howls at length attracted the attention of some of his companions. They drew Gerald safely to the top of the pit in a basket, but not till after the lapse of many hours.

At length Henry the Eighth's death enabled Gerald to return to England. He was one of the "comeliest young men of that age;" and when at a masque he met Mabell, the daughter of Sir Anthony Browne, who was not only beautiful, but "a lady of great worth and virtue," he fell in love with her and married her. This marriage proved to be of great advantage to him. No doubt it was owing to the influence of Mabell's father that Gerald was at once knighted by Edward the Sixth. In the same year, 1552, he was made a Knight of the Garter, and he received back by patent his forfeited estates in Ireland. Queen Mary, in 1554, restored him to his titles of Earl of Kildare and Baron Offaly. Mabell survived her husband, and lived in "the fair house of Maynooth" till her death in 1610.

Lord Montague probably invited his sister to Cowdray to meet Elizabeth, for it does not appear that she was in attendance on the Queen. In fact, though it is recorded that Elizabeth "and the whole Court were magnificently entertained" at Cowdray, no list of the guests has been preserved. Lord Burleigh, however, must have been among them, as he heads a letter, dated August 18, 1591, " From the Court at Cowdray."

The Queen's principal amusement when at Cowdray was shooting deer in the park. She killed three or four, and "Queen Elizabeth's Oak," against which she rested her bow, is still standing. It is a magnificent tree, measuring twelve yards in circumference at a height of four feet from the ground, and stands with several other fine oaks, pollards like itself, in a hollow in Cowdray Park called "The Deer Down Bottom."

Lady Kildare was the only member of the party who ventured to shoot with the Queen, and though she only killed one deer, Elizabeth was so much displeased with her audacity, "that she did not afterwards dine at the royal table." Lady Kildare was however at length forgiven, for in the list of New year's gifts to the Queen in 1599, her offering of "seven buttons of golde of two sortes, garnished with sparkes of rubyes and pearle," was accepted, and a "return in guilte plate, 21 ¾ oz.," was made her by order of Elizabeth.*

It is certain that before the visit of the Queen Lord Montague had completed the additions to Cowdray, which made it, to use the words of Mr. Freeman,† "one of the greatest houses of the best house-building time. . . of the very stateliest architecture, an architecture which is the growth of our own soil, whose associations are those of our own history, and which is surely surpassed by the architecture of no other nation in splendour, in consistency, in practical convenience." No doubt Lord Montague had already caused to be painted the series of enormous frescoes which represented the various scenes in which he himself, his father, and Lord Southampton had taken part whilst serving their sovereign abroad. He had completed the great quadrangle, and he had put up above the door of the beautiful gateway the arms (so often still seen on the ancient firebacks cast at Farnhurst for Lord Montague) of his house, with the lynxes as supporters, the sixteen quarterings, the coronet beneath the helmet on which is the crest of the eagle displayed, and the motto Suivez Raison at the bottom.‡

---

* These New Year's presents varied in value from magnificent jewels given by the great Lords, from the red silk purse containing forty pounds in "dimy soveraigns" given by the Archbishop of Canterbury, to dresses and petticoats offered by poor ladies, to pots of green ginger and of rinds of lemons presented by the royal physicians, and even included "a very fair marchpane" [i.e., a rich cake], "made like a tower with men and sundry artillery in it," from the yeomen of the Chamber, and another marchpane, " with the modell of Powles' church and steeples in paste," from the Surveyor of the Works. Return presents, carefully apportioned in value, were made by the Queen. Lord and Lady Montague always gave the same present,—a purse of cloth of gold from each, containing ten pounds in " dimy soveraigns." In return, Lord Montague received one "guilt cup with cover, of 23 oz." Lady Montague's cup weighed only 18½ oz. ; but the one given to the Archbishop weighed 40 oz.

† *English Towns and Districts*, p. 372. This article was written after a visit to Cowdray from Oeborne. Reprinted from the *Saturday Review*, November 6, 1875.

‡ These firebacks cast for Lord Montague are all alike, and would therefore seem to have been cast at the same time. One is now at Oeborne, and in this the quarterings are (1) Browne ; (2)

WEST FRONT OF COWDRAY.

GARDEN FRONT OF COWDRAY.

Lord Montague's eldest son (whose mother, Lady Jane Browne, had died at his birth) married Mary, daughter of Sir William Dormer of Ethorp in Buckinghamshire,* and had a family of three sons and three daughters. But in the year after Queen Elizabeth's visit to Cowdray he died, on the 29th of June 1592. His widow afterwards married Sir Edmund Uvedale, and on his death she married Sir Thomas Gerard of Bryn in Lancashire.

The aged Lord Montague survived his eldest son only "three months, two weeks, and six days," for he died at a house he had built at West Horsley in Surrey, on the 19th of October 1592. " This year died *Anthony Browne* Viscount *Montacute*, whom Queen *Mary* honour'd with this Title, because his Grandmother was Daughter and one of the Heirs of *John Nevil* Marquis *Montacute;* who tho' he was a great Roman Catholick yet the Queen [Elizabeth] finding him faithful always, lov'd him, and in his Sickness went to visit him." †

Lord Montague was buried at Midhurst on the sixth of December 1592. He had already prepared the beautiful tomb, composed of marble and alabaster, which so long stood in a chapel on the south side of the altar of Midhurst church.‡ At the lower part was a great table tomb, on which were the recumbent effigies of Lord Montague's two wives, Lady Jane Browne and Magdalen Viscountess Montague. Both were of the size of life, and evidently were portraits. They were dressed in robes of state, richly ornamented with colours and gilding. They lay on an altar tomb of great size, and between them (the effigy of Lady Jane being at the north, and that of Lady Montague at the south side) rose another altar tomb on which was the kneeling figure of Lord Montague, also life-size; this effigy also is

---

Albini; (3) Fitz Alan; (4) Fitz Alan of Clun; (5) Warren; (6) Maltravers; (7) Nevill; (8) Montague; (9) Monthermer; (10) Inglethorp; (11) Burghe; (12) Delapole; (13) Bradston; (14) Tiptoft; (15) Charlton; (16) Montague. Some of the lower quarterings are indistinct, as the heat of many fires has worn them away, but all can be traced. This fireback originally came from Cowdray.

* The sister of Mrs. Browne married the Duke of Feria. At Cowdray there was a full-length portrait of " Dame Joanna Dormer, Duquessa de Feria," at the age of twenty-five, "verie pretie."

† Baker's *Chronicle*, p. 380.

‡ The tomb was of considerable height, so that the head of Lord Montague was on a level with the gallery in which were the seats of the boys educated at the Midhurst Grammar School. The weekly amusement of these boys was to put a piece of paper into Lord Montague's mouth. Sir William Burrell remarks that when he visited Midhurst in 1768, the seventh Lord Montague had "lately fitted up a gallery for his own family, south side the church, to which there are stairs leading from his chapel."

an undoubted portrait. Lord Montague is represented in a suit of gilt armour, over which he wears the mantle and collar of the Order of the Garter, all painted in gold and colours. He kneels before a third altar, which is raised on arches, and upon which his helmet is placed. A very old helmet, "thrown aside" on the removal of the tomb from Midhurst church, used to rest on the altar before Lord Montague as well as the sculptured one. This helmet was exhibited at the meeting of the Sussex Archæological Society at Chichester in 1853, and has fortunately been replaced on the monument. It appears to have been inlaid with gold, and was undoubtedly the helmet worn by Lord Montague.* On the panels of this great tomb are large escutcheons, containing divers quarterings rich with colour. The tomb was surrounded by small figures kneeling in pairs. These probably represented the eight children of Lord Montague. Four tall obelisks of Sussex marble rose at the angles of the tomb: each obelisk supported on four balls and surmounted by a ball and by a spear-shaped pinnacle.

On a square of marble inserted in the side of the altar at which Lord Montague kneels is the inscription:

"Here lyeth the Bodie of ye Right Honourable Sir Anthony Browne, Viscount Mountagewe, Chief Standarde Bearer of England, and Knight of ye Honourable Order of the Garter, whereof He was Ancienst at his Death, and One of ye Honourable Privie Councell to Quene Marie, who, as He was Noblye Descended from the Ladye Lucye his Grandmother, one of the Daughters and Coheyres of Lord Jhon Nevill Marques Mountague, so He was Perfectly Adorned with Al ye Virtues of True Nobilitye. And in ye 66 yere of His Age He Ended His Lyfe at His Howse at Horsley in Surrey, ye 19 of October 1592, and in ye 34° yere of ye Raigne of oure Most Soveraigne Ladie Quene Elizabeth. This Honorable Man in ye yere 1553 was Employed by Quene Marie in an Honorable Ambassage to Rome with Doctor Thyrlbie Bishope of Elye, which he Performed to his Great Honor and Commendation: And ye Seconde yere after He Served Quene Marie as Her Majesties Livtenant of ye English Forces at ye Siege of Saint Quentines. In ye yere 1559 Quene Elizabeth sent Him Ambassador into Spain to Kynge Philipp, and Likewise 1565 and 1566 to the Duches of Parma then Regent of ye Lowe Countries. All which He Effected both Wiselye and Honorablye to ye Service of God, his Prince, and Countrie."

---

* In the drawing of the tomb which was taken by Grimm in May 1790, this helmet, with the vizor raised, is placed on the top of the sculptured helmet.

FIRST VISCOUNT MONTAGUE.

The inscription on Lady Jane Browne's side of the tomb is as follows:*
"Here lyeth ye Bodie of ye Ladye Jane Radclyffe, one of ye Daughters of Robert Earl of Sussex, who Ended Her Lyfe at Cowdray A°. D^i. 1552, ye 22 of Julye, And Was of ye Age of Twenty Yeares. And ye First Wyfe of Anthony Viscount Mountague Here Buryed, By Whome He had Issue One Sonne Anthony Browne Esquier Deceased and Here Likewise Buryed. Which Anthony Was Father Unto Anthony Viscount Montague Now Livinge. He had Also by Her one Daughter Marye Browne yet Livinge, who was Married first to Henry Wriothesley Earle of Southampton, And After to Sir Thomas Heneage, Knt., Vice Chamberlain to Queen Elizabeth, and One of the Honourable Privie Councell."

On another tablet is this inscription:—"Anthony Viscount Mountague took to His Second Wyfe Magdalen Dacre, one of ye Daughters of William Dacre Knight, Lord Dacre of Graystock and Gylesland, and Lord Warden of ye West Marches of England foranempste Scotelande. By whome He had Issue Five Sonnes, Philip, William, Sir George Browne Kn^t, Thomas, and Henry. And Three Daughters, Elizabeth, Mabell, and Jane. Whereof Philip, William, Thomas, and Mabell Departed this Lyfe before their Father."

This magnificent tomb, which was one of the most interesting historical monuments in the country, stood untouched in the centre of its chapel in Midhurst church until 1851. At that time increased accommodation was required in the church, and the unfortunate device was resorted to of providing this additional space by the removal of the Browne monument from Midhurst to Easebourne church, on the outskirts of Cowdray Park. Here it was placed in a mortuary chapel at the east end of the south aisle,—a chapel which now forms part of the body of the church. This, the only spot available for the reception of the monument, was much smaller than the chapel at Midhurst in which it originally stood. The effigies of the two ladies, instead of lying as before one on each side of the kneeling figure of Lord Montague, are crowded together on the moiety which alone was preserved of the table tomb. Lord Montague's figure is placed close against a window, and thus one principal side of the monument is wholly obscured.

---

* It will be seen that these inscriptions were drawn up by Lord Montague's grandson, Anthony Maria Browne, second Viscount Montague. He might easily have made a mistake as to the date of the death of his grandfather's first wife.

Nor was this all the damage sustained by the monument. Its removal was unluckily entrusted to persons ignorant of its beauty and historical interest, who only thought of making the tomb fit the space allotted to it. Most of the small kneeling figures were irreparably injured; the alabaster columns remained in a builder's yard till destroyed by the action of the weather, and the escutcheons of arms were removed. The fine old iron-work altogether disappeared (it became the property of the builder in Midhurst, Grist by name, who had the contract for the removal of the monument to Easebourne), and the four obelisks which rose high above the tomb at its angles were left to perish in the open air.

Nothing can now be done to restore the mutilated monument to its original form. But the escutcheons, and two of the kneeling figures, have fortunately been preserved, and these have recently been replaced by Lord Spencer as nearly as possible in their original positions. Lord Montague's original helmet has been cleaned from rust. A brass tablet has been placed by Lord Spencer in Easebourne church, on which is the following inscription:—

"The Monument, in memory of Sir Anthony Browne, first Viscount Montague, K.G., who died 19 October 1592, aged 65, formerly stood over the family vault in the Chancel of the Parish Church of Midhurst. Whence it was removed in the year 1851 to the position in this church where it now stands. The monument is surmounted by the sculptured figures of Sir Anthony and his two wives—the Lady Jane Radclyffe (daughter of Robert, Earl of Sussex), who died at Cowdray 22d July 1552; and Magdalen Dacre (daughter of William, Lord Dacre).

"This tablet was placed in Easebourne Church in the year 1883 by John Poyntz, Earl Spencer, K.G., Lord Lieutenant of Ireland, grandson of the Honourable Elizabeth Mary Poyntz, who died 30th December 1830. She was the only sister of George Samuel, eighth Viscount Montague, who died in 1793."

There was at Cowdray a portrait of the first Lord Montague, "in his coronation robes, his coronet on his head, and wearing an immense ruff." This picture was unhappily destroyed in the fire, and no portrait existed of either of Lord Montague's wives. It is therefore fortunate that the effigies on the Browne monument have been preserved from injury.

A fine full-length portrait of the first Viscount Montague is in the possession of the Marquess of Exeter at Burghley. It was painted by Lucas de Heere. Lord Montague is represented in a rich dress, with the insignia of the Order of the Garter. He wears a cap and holds his gloves in his right hand.

The account of Lord Montague's possessions is curious.* "By the inquisition taken after his decease, at Midhurst in Sussex, the 19th of April, in 35 Elizabeth [1593], the jury found that he made his will the 19th of July, 34 Elizabeth, and died on the 19th of October following; and that Anthony Brown, Viscount Montagu, was his grandson and heir, and of the age of nineteen years the 1st of Febuary last, and was son and heir of Anthony Brown (who died in his father's lifetime), son and heir to the aforesaid Anthony Viscount Montagu, deceased. They also found that he died seized of the manor of Battell, the manors of Barnehorne, Bread, Gateborough, Chiling, Mitchelham; the farm of Maxfield with the appurtenances in Gosling, and Westfield, Gatesborough, Marshes, &c., in Rye and Winchelsea; the manors of Chiting-Poynings and Chiting-Balney; the manors of Loddesworth, West-Horseley, Effingham, and Verdley, and lands and tenements called Tadham; the manors of Lurgershall, Fullam, Saddlescomb, Shulbread, Willinchmere *alias* Linchmere, Verdley *alias* Boxton, Begham, Calceto, Westbrock near Bourne, Levenshot, and North and South Key: the college of Hastings and rectory and advowson of the same; the scite of the priory and demesne lands of the monastery of Welverley [Waverley]; the scite of the demesne lands of the priory of East-borne [Easeborne]; the manors of Wainborowe, Monkenhoke, Neatham, Dockenfield, Worthinge; the farms of Oxenforde, Northolt *alias* Monkton; the rectories of Eastborne [Easeborne] and Farnhurst, and divers lands there; the manors of Poynings-Pearching, Preston-Poynings, and Piggedeane: A capital house called River-Park-House; the manors of Cowdray, Midhurst, Cocking, Lynch, Rustington, Ripley, and Send, and Chapel-Farm, and Fendbarnes; Jury Farm, Newark Priory, and the rectory of Send; all in the county of Sussex: The scite and mansion-house and priory of St. Mary Overies, with the tenements, wharf, and liberties of the same; the manors of Stralford, Clifford, South Bradstone, Downe *alias* Downe-Farm, Blackwell Farm; the Warrenhouse and lands near Guilford Park; the Alms-houses in Foyer Lane, in the parish of the blessed Mary in Guilford; the manors of Pirbright,

* Collins' *Peerage.*

Stockwell, Pitford, Wichambreaux, Clayton, and Stedham, and Oxenford Farm; all in the county of Surrey; and the manor of Levenshothe in the county of Kent."

On the death of Lord Montague his widow seems to have taken up her residence at Battle Abbey, and to have acted there as Lady of the Manor. It is not known whether Battle Abbey was her dower-house, or whether she undertook the duties of Lord of the Manor on behalf of the second Lord Montague. But among the Battle Abbey papers are "Rolls of the First High Court, View of Frankpledge, and Court Baron, holden by Magdalen Viscountess Montague for the Manor of Battle, March 1593." She continued to hold these courts and to receive "the Presentments of the Homage" until the year 1606. The date of her death is not to be found, but as the courts of 1607 were held by Anthony second Viscount Montague, it is probable that she died in 1606.

Lady Montague seems to have resided at St. Mary Overies during part of 1593, and again in 1597, occupying the house built there by Sir Anthony Browne [p. 14]. But she lived principally at Battle Abbey. Her memoirs, written in Latin by her chaplain Richard Smith, still exist in the Grenville Collection at the British Museum. From these, and from a curious "secret information" found among the Burghley Papers, it appears that she, like her husband, adhered steadfastly to the Roman Catholic religion. The informer complains that "since the La. Montague's coming to dwell at Battel religion in that countrey and especially in that towne is greatly decayed." She harboured recusants, amongst whom was one Gray, a priest who had been imprisoned, but who, says the report, "now liveth in my ladye's house, being suspected to doe much harme both with the Deane* and others thereabouts." The anger of the inhabitants of Battle was roused to a great pitch by the conduct of Lady Montague's retainers when the report was spread that the Spaniards had landed at three places in Sussex. The whole town was in "the greatest hurly-burly," but "at the same time my Lad. Montague's people, seeing the towne of Battel in that uprore and miserable state, rejoiced, and shewed signes of joy; in so much that the people fel to greate exclamations and cursinges of them openly in the streates."

Sir George Browne, the eldest son of Lord Montague by his second

---

* John Wytheris, who was Dean of Battle for forty-four years.

wife, knighted at Cowdray by Queen Elizabeth, was the ancestor of the Brownes, Baronets, of Wickham in Kent. From his brother, Sir Henry Browne, the Brownes, also Baronets, of Kiddington in Oxfordshire are descended.

Lord Montague's daughters by his second wife all married. Elizabeth, the eldest, became the wife of the first Baron Dormer of Winge; Mabel married Sir Henry Capel, ancestor of the Earls of Essex; and Jane, the youngest, married Sir Francis Lacon of Willey in Shropshire.

The saying in Baker's Chronicle that Lord Montague was "a great Roman Catholick" is fully borne out by the confession elicited from Robert Gray, a priest. This person was examined by Topelyfe, "the famous persecutor of Papists." At first "he showed himself very obstinate," but on a third examination he said enough to show that Lord Montague both favoured and harboured Roman Catholic priests. The original of the paper in which this confession appears is in Topelyfe's own handwriting. He says: "In his third confession, 29th of August 1593, after warning, and that Robert Graye is told how he hath dissembled in his former confession, and denied that he had spoken with any Jhezewitt or Seminary priest since he did come to the old Viscount Montague's service, now again he is told that it is discovered by letters and by apparent confessions that he hath been in the company of divers Jhezewitts and beyond-sea priests in Sussex, Surrey, in or about London, Bucks, and elsewhere, within these six years; that the names of divers of them be known, and the places of their haunts. At length he sayeth and confesseth that in summer, now three full years last past, he being at Cowdray with his lord and master, Sir George Browne, that now is, Knight, did come to him and did ask him if he would go with him to speak with a learned man, and this examinant said yea. Then they two went together, and Sir George brought this examinant to one Denny's house to Todham,* half a mile from Cowdray, and there Sir George brought this examinant up into a chamber where they found a man sitting in his cloak, of above forty years old, long slender face, black hair of head, and a little beard black, whom since he heard was Father Curry the Jhezewitt.

---

* The fine old manor-house of Todham was demolished early in the present century. Drawings of it are among the Burrell Collection in the British Museum. One of the rooms had a richly ornamented ceiling covered with coats of arms : in another room the same coats of arms were arranged in compartments on the wall.

But of whom he hath heard so at that or any time this examinant doth no way remember. And he and also Sir George Browne had talk with the said Curry about a contract of marriage betwixt Mrs. Constance Cussalde (or Cafelde) and a gentleman. And they talked also of old Garnett's matters. He sayeth that they three tarried together not above half one hour, and so departed, and he did never see Curry the Jhezewitt after nor before, nor never heard from him by letter, writing, or message since, nor ever did hear of him before or since. But once that he heard that the said Curry was at River Park, where Mr. Anthony Browne was living, son and heir to the old lord. . . . He remembereth that when the Lord Montague, his old master, and the Lady Viscountess his wife, were at Wynge with Sir Robert Dormer, about St. James' tide in the next summer before the Queen's majesty was at Cowdray, or a day or two before the Assumption of the Virgin Mary 1590, this examinant's lord and master and lady being at Sir Robert Dormer's (who hath married their daughter Elizabeth) for the space of five or six days, there was during those five or six days there one Mr. Harris, a priest, whom he did hear that he had used much with the Lady Babington. A tall man, blackish hair of head and beard. And this man, during this time, did always (for the time of the Lady Montague and the ladies being at Wynge) dine and sup and lodge in Sir Robert Dormer's house—Sir Robert Dormer and his wife being at home there at Wynge. And this examinant did daily resort into the said priest's chamber, called that Mr. Harris, and conferred with him, the said Harris. And during that time he did never see the said Harris go or come out of his chamber. But that he did twice, upon two several days, talk with the said Harris, and so did the Lady Montague, with my lord, and the now young Lady Dormer their daughter, they all being there in Mr. Harris' chamber. He doth well remember that Harris moved the lord and lady to be good to Anthony Garnett, and they both said to Mr. Harris then, that neither of them both did malice Garnett. Examinant resolutely answered that he would not accuse himself, having been asked if he had said mass there, but he did not deny it, but would not confess whether Harris did or not. 'For if he see an hundred priests say masses he would not accuse one of them thereof.' He confesseth that he hath seen Dowlman and Jackson at Cowdray, in his lord and master's house; and his lord and the old lady did speak with them, both his lord and his lady knowing them to be priests. Dowlman and Jackson did dine in examinant's chamber, and did

FIRST VISCOUNT MONTAGUE. 37

both lodge there at Cowdray one night. And this was three or four years passed. ROBERT GRAY, *Priest.*
" Confessed before me, Richard Topclyfe." *

Robert Gray was no doubt the priest who was sheltered by the widowed Viscountess Montague at Battle Abbey [p. 34].
In a letter to Lord Burghley, also dated 1593, Topclyfe tells him that " Francis Ridcall, the rebel and traitorous priest, late steward to the old Lord and Lady Montague," had fled " from his farm and goods worth £1000 which was near to Woking, Surrey, upon land belonging to Lord Montague." Ridcall first took refuge with Sir Robert and Lady Dormer and Harris, " her traitorous seminary priest." He then went to Edward Bentley, " lately condemned for treason, but at liberty," who had married a niece of Lord Montague. The Bentleys lived in a tower belonging to Lord Windsor in Derbyshire, and sheltered Ridcall in a wood close by. When Garnett and Gray were apprehended, Ridcall fled to the north. Topclyfe adds that he expected to catch him, having seized the father and mother of his guides. But this expectation does not appear to have been realised. [*Records of the English Province of the Society of Jesus,* vol. ii. p. 273.]

* *State Papers,* 1593, vol. ccxlv. 138. Quoted in *Records of the English Province of the Society of Jesus,* vol. ii. p. 430.

CHAPTER V.

Queen Elizabeth at Cowdray.

HE very scarce pamphlet which gave an account of the Queen's visit to Cowdray was reprinted in "The Progresses and Public Processions of Queen Elizabeth," collected by John Nichols, F.S.A.

The Honorable Entertainment given to her MAJESTIE in Progresse at COWDRAY in Sussex, by the Right Honorable the Lord MONTE-CUTE, anno 1591, August 15.
Printed by Thomas Scarlet, and are to bee solde by Willaim Wright, dwelling in Paules Churchyard, neere to the French Schoole. 1591.

The Queene, having dyned at Farnham, came with a great traine to the Right Honorable the Lord Mountague's, on Saterdaie, being the 15 daie of August, about eight of the clocke at night; where, upon sight of her Majestie, loud musicke sounded, which at her enteraunce on the bridge suddenly ceased. Then was a speech delivered by a personage in armour, standing betweene two porters, carved out of wood, he resembling the third; holding his club in one hand, and a key of golde in the other; as followeth:

Saterday, August 15.
THE PORTER'S SPEECH.

"The walles of Thebes were raised by musicke: by musick these are kept from falling. It was a prophesie since the first stone was layde, that these walles should shake, and the roofe totter, till the wisest, the fairest, and most fortunate of all creatures, should by her first steppe make the foundation staid, and by the glaunce of her eyes make the turret steddie. I have beene here a porter manie yeeres; many ladies have entred passing amiable, many verie wise, none so happie. These, my fellow-porters, thinking there could be none so noble, fell on sleepe, and so incurde the seconde curse of the prophesie, which is, never againe to awake. Marke how they looke, more like postes than porters, retaining onlie their shapes, but deprived of sences. I thought rather to cut off my eie liddes than to winke till I saw the ende. And now it is: for the musick is at an end, this house immoveable, your vertue immortall. O miracle of Time! Nature's glorie! Fortune's Empresse! the World's Wonder! Soft, this is the poet's part and not the porter's. I have nothing to present but the crest of mine office, this keie: Enter, possesse all, to whom the heavens have vouchsafed all. As for the Owner of this house, mine honourable Lord, his tongue is the keie of his heart, and his heart the locke of his soule. Therefore what he speakes you may constantly beleeve; which is that in duetie and service to your Majestie he would be second to none: in praieing for your happinesse equall to anie.

"*Tuus, O Regina, quod optas explorare favor: huic jussa capescere fas est.*"

Wherewithall her Highnes tooke the keye, and said, she would swear for him there was none more faithfull: then being alighted, she embraced the Ladie Montecute and the Ladie Dormir her daughter. The Mistresse of the house (as it were weeping in her bosome) said, "O happie time! O joyfull daie!"

That night her Majestie tooke her rest, and so in like manner the next day, which was *Sunday*, being most Royallie feasted. The proportion of breakefast was three oxen, and one hundred and fourtie geese.

Mundaie, August 17.

On Munday, at eight of the clock in the morning, her Highnes took horse with all her traine, and rode into the parke: where was a delicate bowre prepared, under the which were her Highnesse musicians placed, and a crossebowe by a Nymph, with a sweet song, delivered to her hands to shoote at the deere, about some thirtie in number, put into a paddock, of which number she killed three or four, and the Countesse of Kildare one.

Then rode hir Grace to Cowdrey to dinner, and aboute six of the clocke in the evening, from a turret, sawe sixteene buckes (all having fayre lawe) pulled downe with greyhoundes in a laund.* All the huntinge ordered by Maister Henrie Browne, the Lord Montague's third sonne, Raunger of Windsore forest.

Tuesdaie, *August* 18.

On Tewsday hir Majestie wente to dinner to the Priory, where my Lorde himselfe kept house; and there was shee and hir Lordes most bountifully feasted. After dinner she came to view my Lorde's walkes, where shee was mette by a Pilgrime clad in a coat of russet velvet, fashioned to his calling: his hatte being of the same, with skallop-shelles of cloth of silver, who delivered hir a speach in this sort following:

PILGRIME.

"Fairest of all creatures, vouchsafe to hear a prayer of a Pilgrime, which shall be shorte, and the petition which is but reasonable. God graunt the worlde maie ende with your life, and your life more happie than anie in the world: that is my praier. I have travelled manie countries, and in all countries desire antiquities. In this Iland (but a spanne in respect of the World) and in this Shire (but a finger in regard of your realme) I have heard great cause of wonder, some of complaint. Harde by, and so neere as your Majesty shall almost passe by, I saw an Oke, whose stateliness nayled nine cies to the branches, and the ornamentes beguiled my thoughtes with astonishment. I thought it free, being in the fielde, but I found it not so. For at the verie entrie I mette I know not with what rough-hewed ruffian, whose armes were carved out of knotty box, for I could receive nothing of him but boxes; so hastie was he to strike, he had no leysure to speake. I thought there were more waies to the wood than one; and finding another passage, I found also a Ladie verie faire, but passing frowarde, whose wordes set mee in a greater heate then the blowes. I asked her name? she said it was Peace. I wondred that Peace could never holde her peace. I cannot perswade myselfe, since that time, but that there is a waspe's nest in mine eares. I returned discontent. But if it will please your Highnesse to view it, that rude champion at your faire feete will laie downe his foule head: and at your becke that Ladie will make her mouth her tongues mue. Happelie your Majestie shall finde some content; I more antiquities."

---

* Laund, a lawn.

Then did the Pilgrime conduct hir Highnes to an Oke not farre off, whereon hir Majestie's arms and all the armes of the Noblemen and Gentlemen of that Shire were hanged in escutcheons most beutifull. And a Wilde Man, cladde in ivie, at the sight of hir Highnesse, spake as followeth:

The Wilde Man's Speech at the Tree.

"Mightie Princesse, whose hapines is attended by the Heavens, and whose government is wondered at upon the earth, vouchsafe to heare why this passage is kept, and this Oke honoured. The whole World is drawen in a mappe: the Heavens in a globe; and this Shire shrunke in a tree; and what your Majestie hath often heard off with some comfort you may now beholde with full content. This Oke, from whose bodie so many armes doe spread, and out of whose armes so many fingers spring, resembles in parte your strength and hapinesse; strength in the number and the honour; happinesse, in the trueth and consent. All heartes of oke, than which nothing more constant, more naturall. The wall of this Shire is the sea, strong, but rampired with true hearts, invincible; where every private man's eie is a beacon to discover, everie noble man's power a bulwarke to defende. Here they are all differing somewhat in degrees, not duetie: the greatnes of the branches, not the greenesse. Your Majestie they account the Oke, the tree of Jupiter, whose root is so deeplie fastened, that Treacherie, though she undermine to the centre, cannot finde the windinges; and whose toppe is so highlie reared that Envie, though she shoote on copheigth,* cannot reach her, under whose armes they have both shade and shelter. Well wot they that your enemies lightnings are but flashes, and their thunder, which fills the whole world with a noise of conquest, shall ende with a soft shower of retreate. Be then as confident in your steppes as Cæsar was in his fortune: his proceedings but of conceit; yours of vertue. Abroad courage hath made you feared, at home honoured clemencie; clemencie which the owner of this grove hath tasted in such sort that his thoughts are become his heart's laberinth, surprized with joie and loialtie; joie without measure; loyaltie without end, living in no other ayer than that which breathes your Majestie's safetie.

"For himselfe, and all these honourable Lordes and Gentlemen, whose

---

* *Cop-head* was the word for a tuft of feathers or hair on the head of an animal. "Copheight" probably means a great height.

shieldes your Majestie doeth here beholde, I can say this, that as the veines are dispersed through all the bodie, yet when the heart feeleth any extreame passion, sende all their bloud to the heart for comfort: so they being in divers places, when your Majestie shall but stande in feare of any daunger will bring their bodies, their purses, their soules, to your Highnesse, being their Heart, their Head, and their Soveraigne. This passage is kept straight, and the Pilgrime, I feare, hath complained: but such a disguised worlde it is, that one can scarce know a Pilgrime from a Priest, a Tayler from a Gentleman, nor a Man from a Woman; everie man seeming to be that which they are not, onelie doe practise what they should not. The Heavens guyde you, your Majestie governes us: though our peace be envied by them, yet we hope it shall be eternall.—*Elizabetha Deus nobis haec otia fecit.*"

Then, upon the winding of a cornette, was a most excellent crie of hounds, and three buckes kilde by the bucke hounds; and so went all backe to Cowdrey to supper.

Wednesdaie, August 19.

On Wednesdaie the Lordes and Ladies dined in the walkes, feasted most sumptuously at a table foure and twentie yards long.

In the beginning, hir Majestie comming to take the pleasure of the walks was delighted with most delicate musicke, and brought to a goodlie fish-pond, where was an Angler, that, taking no notice of hir Majestie, spake as followeth:

The Angler's Speech.

"Next rowing in a westerne barge well fare angling. I have bin here this two houres, and cannot catch an oyster. It may be for lacke of a bait, and that were hard in this nibling world, where everie man laies bait for another. In the Citie, merchants bait their tongues with a lie and an oath, and so make simple men swallow deceitful wares: and fishing for commoditie is growen so farre that men are become fishes, for landlordes put such sweete baits on rackt rents that as good it were to be a perch in a pike's belly, as a tenant in theyr farmes. All our trade is grown to trecherie, for now fish are caught with medecines; which are as unwholsom as love procured by witchcraft unfortunate. We Anglers make our lines of divers colours according to the kindes of waters: so men do their loves, aiming at the complexion of the faces. Thus Merchandize, Love, and Lordships, sucke venom out of virtue. I think I shall fish all daie and catch a frog: the cause is neither in the line, the hooke, nor the bait, but some thing there is over beautifull which stayeth the veric minow (of all fish the most eager) from biting. For this we Anglers observe, that the shadow of a man turneth back the fish. What will then the sight of a Goddesse? 'Tis best angling in a lowring daie, but here the sunne so glisters that the fish see my hooke through my bait. But, soft, here be the Netters: these be they cannot content them with a dish of fish for their supper, but will drawe a whole pond for a market."

This saide, he espied a fisherman drawing his nettes towarde where hir Majestie was. And calling alowde to him,

"Hoe, Sirra" (quoth the *Angler*), "What shall I give thee for thy draughte?"

"If there be never a Whale in it, take it for a noble," quoth the *Netter*.

Ang. "Be there any * maydes there?"

Net. "Maydes, foole! they be sea-fish."

Ang. "Why?"

Net. "Venus was borne of the sea, and 'tis reason she should have maydes to attend hir."

Then turned he to the Queene: and after a small pawse, spake as followeth:

"Madam, it is an olde saying, There is no fishing to the sea, nor service to the king: but it holdes when the sea is calme and the king vertuous. Your vertue maketh Envie blush and stand amazed at your happines. I come not to tell the art of fishing, nor the natures of fish, nor their daintines; but with a poor fisherman's wish, that all the hollow hearts to your Majestie were in my net, and if there be more then it will holde, I woulde they were in the sea till I went thether a fishing. There be some so muddie minded that they cannot live in a cleere river, but a standing poole: as camells will not drinke tell they have troubled the water with their feet, so can they never stanch their thirst till they have disturbed the state with their trecheries. Soft, these are no fancies for fishermen. Yes, true hearts are as good as full purses, the one the sinues of warre, the other the armes. A dish of fish is an unworthy present for a Prince to accept: there be some carpes amongst them,

---

* *Maid*, the thorn-back ray, a salt-water fish.

no carpers of state ; if there be, I would they might bee handled lyke carpes, their tongues pulled out. Some pearches there are, I am sure ; and if anie pearch higher then in dutie they ought, I would they might sodenly picke over the pearch for me. Whatsoever there is, if it be good it is all yours, most vertuous Ladie, that are best worthie of all."

Then was the Net drawen.

The Netter having presented all the fishe of the ponde, and laying it at hir feete, departed.

That evening she hunted.

Thursday, August 20.

On Thursday she dined in the privie walkes in the garden, and the Lordes and Ladies at a table of fortie-eight yardes long. In the evening the countrie people presented themselves to hir Majestie in a pleasaunt daunce, with taber and pipe ; and the Lorde Montague and his Lady among them, to the great pleasure of all the beholders, and gentle applause of hir Majestie.

Fryday, August 21.

On Friday she departed towards *Chichester.*

Going through the arbour to take horse, stoode sixe gentlemen, whom hir Majestie knighted ; the Lorde Admirall laying the sworde on their shoulders.

The names of the six Knights then made were these ; *viz.:*—

    Sir George Browne, my Lordes second sonne.
    Sir Robert Dormer, his sonne in lawe.
    Sir Henry Goaring.
    Sir Henry Glemham.
    Sir John Carrell.
    Sir Nicholas Parker.

So departed hir Majestie to the dining-place, whether the Lord Montague and his sonnes, and the Sheriff of the Shire, attended with a goodly companie of gentlemen, brought hir Highnes.

The escutchions on the Oke remaine, and there shall hange till they can hang together one peece by another.

Valete.

CHAPTER VI.

Anthony Maria Browne, second Viscount Montague.

ANTHONY MARIA BROWNE, second Viscount Montague, the "young childe very comely," who had been taken to Tilbury Fort, succeeded his grandfather in the October of 1592. He was then only twenty, but he had been married since the February of 1591 to Lady Jane Sackville, daughter of Thomas first Earl of Dorset, Lord High Treasurer of England.

He it was who compiled the curious Book of Orders and Rules, for the direction of his household;* an abstract of which will be found in the next chapter. This book still exists; it is in the possession of Mr. Alexander Brown, and is beautifully written. On the title-page the shield of sixteen quarterings surmounted by the coronet is carefully drawn in ink. The preface, signed Anthony Mountague, follows: then the Table, or Index. This portion of the book occupies five pages, written on one side of the leaf. The rest of the book fills twenty-nine pages closely written on both sides of the leaf. The book is simply bound, in thin boards, and is in perfect preservation.

Horace Walpole mentions the second Lord Montague in his catalogue of royal and noble authors, but his remarks are anything but complimentary. In speaking of the Book of Household Rules he says, "It is a ridiculous piece of mimicry of royal grandeur; an instance of ancient pride,

---

* This book was printed in the *Sussex Archæological Collections*, vol. vii.

the more remarkable as the peer who drew it up was then barely twenty-four years of age. There are no fewer than thirty-six different ranks of servants whom he calls his officers; and yet it is observable though the whole line were rigid Catholics, that no mention is made of his chaplains or priests. His only ecclesiastic is his almoner, and his business, it seems, was to light the fires in his hall."

But Horace Walpole, and many others since his time, make a mistake in supposing that this almoner (who is the last but one on the list of the members of Lord Montague's household) was an ecclesiastic. He was called the almoner, as he assisted the porter at the gate in the distribution to the poor of alms, broken bread, and meat and beer; but in reality he was a servant under the orders of the usher of the Hall.

In spite of Horace Walpole's severe remarks, the second Lord Montague seems to have been looked upon as "a patron of literature." For in 1596 a copy of allegorical verses was dedicated to him by Anthony Copley. The poem was called, *A Fig for Fortune*. Four years before it was written, Copley was described as "the most desperate youth that liveth. He did shoot at a gentleman last summer, and did kill an ox with a musket, and in Horsham church he threw his dagger at the parish clerk, and stuck it in a seat of the church. There liveth not his like in England for sudden attempts." * In the poem dedicated to Lord Montague, Copley explains to his patron, that though he had been "disastred for virtue," he was "now winnowed by the fan of grace and Zionry." His improvement, however, was but of short duration, for in 1603 he was tried and convicted for his participation with Sir Walter Raleigh in the Arabella Stuart plot, and though eventually pardoned, he at the time narrowly escaped with his life.

Probably the most beautiful picture at Cowdray was that by Isaac Oliver (who died in 1617), of the second Lord Montague and his brothers. It was most fortunately saved from the fire. The original is now at Burghley. From Mrs. Poyntz, the last heiress of the Brownes of Cowdray, it passed to her daughter Isabella Poyntz, wife of the second Marquess of Exeter. A beautiful copy of the picture by Sherwin is now at Althorp.†

---

* Letter to Queen Elizabeth from Topclyffe. [*Records of the English Province of the Society of Jesus*, vol. i. p. 355. *Sussex Archæological Collections*, vol. xiv. p. 264.]

† This copy belonged to Frances Selina Poyntz, wife of the eighteenth Lord Clinton. Lady Clinton left it to her niece Lady Sarah Spencer, by whom it was given to her brother the present Earl Spencer.

Of this picture by Oliver, Horace Walpole says, "At the Lord Montacute's at Cowdray, is another invaluable work of Isaac. It represents three brothers, of that lord's family, whole lengths, in black: their ages twenty-one, twenty-four, and eighteen, with the painter's mark Φ. These young gentlemen resembled each other remarkably; a peculiarity observable in the picture, the motto on which is *Figuræ conformis affectus*, 1598. Another person is coming into the room, aged twenty-one. The picture is ten inches by seven."

The eldest of these youths was of course Lord Montague, the second was John, and the third William, who became a Jesuit lay brother. John married Anne, the daughter of —— Gifford, and from their eldest son, Stanislaus Browne, Mark Anthony, the ninth and last Viscount Montague, was descended.*

There was another picture of the second Lord Montague at Cowdray, a three-quarter length on panel, but this was burnt.

It is said that Lord Montague "very commendably followed the example of his grandfather." He certainly was greatly esteemed by his father-in-law the Earl of Dorset,† who thus mentions him in his will: "To my dearly beloved son-in-law, Anthony Browne Viscount Mountague, a great gilt cup with his arms therein to be graven, of the weight of 200 oz., desiring his lordship to keep it as a remembrance of his hearty love to him. . . . Considering as well the great incertitude of mortall comfortes, as the common ingratitude of this iniquitous world, where for the most parte mislikes and misconceipts, though never so unjustly apprehended, are graven in brasse, and good tournes and benefittes, thoughe never so kindlie bestowed, are written in the duste."

It was no doubt owing to the influence of Lord Dorset that Lord Montague suffered only fine and imprisonment for his complicity in the Gunpowder Plot. He, Lord Mordaunt, Lord Stourton, and the Earl of Northumberland were the four powerful Roman Catholic peers who were looked upon as the main support of the Catholic cause in England.

---

* Stanislaus Browne lived at Easebourne. He married Honor, the daughter of a merchant named Malbrank who had settled at Cadiz. She was heir to her brother in the manor of Methley in Warwickshire. Francis, the eldest son of Stanislaus and Honor Browne, preferred living at Cadiz, and gave up Methley to his brother Mark. Mark Browne of Easebourne, Lord of Methley, married twice. By his second wife Anastasia, the fourth daughter of Sir Richard Moore, Bart., of Fawley in Berkshire, he had several children. The eldest was Mark Anthony Browne, ninth Viscount Montague. Mark Browne died on the 7th of February 1755, when his son Mark Anthony was only ten years old, and was buried at Midhurst. [*Extinct Peerages*, by Sir Bernard Burke, Ulster.]

† Lord Dorset died suddenly in 1608, whilst seated at the council table at Whitehall.

In less than eight weeks after the capture of Guy Fawkes all these lords were prisoners in the Tower. Lord Montague's case was particularly serious, as Guy Fawkes had been a member of his great household at Cowdray. Besides this, he was known to have intended to be absent from his place in Parliament on the fifth of November in consequence of a hint from Sir Robert Catesby. Lord Montague was asked to explain these circumstances. He made a somewhat shuffling reply. Guy Fawkes had been placed in his household by his grandfather the first Viscount Montague, when he himself was only nineteen and newly married. But Guy Fawkes had only remained with him for four months. When Lord Montague was asked if he had ever seen Guy Fawkes since that time, he owned that after old Lord Montague's death Guy had served at his table and slept in his house. This, however, he endeavoured to explain by saying that his steward Spencer, a relative of Guy's, had allowed him to spend a few days in the house at Montague Close when Lord Montague was there, and had made use of him in the service of the table. But he added that this had occurred twelve years before the Gunpowder Plot, and that he had scarcely seen or thought of Guy Fawkes since. As to Catesby's hint, Lord Montague declared that when they met in the Strand on "the Tuesday fortnight before All Saints' Day," as Lord Montague was on his way to dine in the Savoy, their conversation had turned merely on general subjects. Lord Montague owned that he had meant to be absent in the country on the day of the opening of Parliament if he could, through Lord Dorset, obtain leave from the King. If he could not get leave he intended to have been in his place. His grandmother, the old Viscountess Montague, had urged him not to go unless he could get a sufficient leave of absence, as the hard riding would be too much for his health.

This was Lord Montague's explanation of the suspicious circumstances in which he found himself. He was forthwith brought before the Star Chamber, and condemned to pay a fine of four thousand pounds, and to be imprisoned during the King's pleasure.

Lord Montague escaped more easily than did his friends. He compounded for his fine, and was released after an imprisonment in the Tower of about forty weeks.*

---

* The State Papers giving an account of Lord Montague's connection with Guy Fawkes and the Gunpowder Plot were examined by Mr. Hepworth Dixon, and quoted by him in *Her Majesty's Tower*, vol. ii, chap. xxii. p. 229.

Lord Montague had only one son, Francis. Of his six daughters Anne and Lucy became nuns "beyond sea;"* Mary married, first, William Lord St. John of Basing, eldest son of the Marquess of Winchester (who died in his father's lifetime), and, secondly, William, the second son of Lord Arundel of Wardour; Catherine married William Tirwhitt of Kettleby in Lincolnshire; Frances married John Blomer of Hathorp in Gloucestershire; and the youngest daughter, another Mary, married Robert Petre, afterwards third Lord Petre.

From the Book of Household Rules it might be thought that Lord Montague did all in his power to avoid extravagance and waste. But in his later life he was greatly impoverished. The payment of part of his heavy fine, the maintenance of his large establishment, and the keeping up of his five houses, Battle, Cowdray, Byflete, West Horsley, and Montague Close, may in some degree account for his indebtedness.† But in other ways his expenditure was lavish; for, on the occasion of the marriage of the Princess Elizabeth to the Elector Palatine in 1612, he gave fifteen hundred pounds to his two daughters in order that they might be suitably dressed at the wedding. It is not therefore to be wondered at that among the half-burnt papers found at Cowdray by Sir Sibbald Scott in 1853 was a fragment of a petition to the King for pecuniary help. Only the beginning could be found; it ran thus:—

"The [humble petition of] Viscount Mount[ague tow]ards the Payment of his Debts and Charge of his Daughters' Portions.

"In most humble wise beseecheth your moste [excel]lent Majesty your humble and loyal subject Anthony Viscount Mountague, as well for himself as on the behalfe of the Lady Mary Ste. John, Frances Browne, Mary Peter, daughters of your said . . . " ‡

As Mary Browne married Robert Petre in 1620, this petition must have been prepared after that date; but it is not known if it was ever presented to the King.

---

* In 1651 the first stone of the convent of the Poor Clares at Rouen was laid there by seven young English ladies of rank. Two of these were the daughters of Lady Montague, and they afterwards became nuns there. [*Records of the English Province of the Society of Jesus*, vol. iv. p. 30.]

† The second Viscount Montague sold the estate of Waverley Abbey to the Coldham family. [Brayley's *History of Surrey*, vol. v.]

‡ *Sussex Archæological Collections*, vol. vii. p. 179.

Lord Montague died on the 23d of October 1629, and was buried under the great Browne monument in Midhurst Church.

His widow survived him for many years. She sent a petition to the House of Lords,* for help in repairing the damage sustained by her property during the occupation of Cowdray by the parliamentary army, and it may therefore be concluded that she resided at Cowdray and not at Battle.

---

* *Journal of the House of Lords*, vol. vii.

CHAPTER VII.

The Book of Household Rules.

HEN the second Viscount Montague compiled his Book of Household Rules he was only twenty-three years of age. But in the book he shows great forethought, carefully even providing for "tymes of extraordinary action," such as the marriage of his children. The title of the book is as follows:—

> A Booke of Orders and Rules established by me Anthony Viscount Mountague for the better direction and governmente of my householde and family, together with the severall dutyes and charges apperteynninge to myne officers and other servantts. Whereunto I have prefixed a preface declaringe my purpose and intendement in that behalf, with a brief view of the severall matters which are herein handeled annsweringe to the particular treatises as they are placed in the Booke. Anno Domini 1595.

THE BOOK OF HOUSEHOLD RULES.

Lord Montague explains in his preface the object of his Book of Rules:— "For as moche as neither publique weale nor private family can continue or long endure without lawes, ordinances, and statutes to guyde and direct ytt, nor without prudent and experienced ministers to execute the same: I, therefore, being desirous to live orderly and quietly within my lymytte, and to mayntayne the estate of myne honor and callinge, according to my degree, have esteemed ytt meete for the accomplishmente thereof, to sett downe and declare in this Book of Orders ensewinge, myne own opinion, judgement, and resolution touching the manner and order of the government of my private house and family; and what officers and other servantts I shalbe occasioned to use, what number of them, and what different authoritye and place every one of them shall have in their degrees; together with a distinction of their severall charge, office, or dutye whereunto they shall be particularly deputed and assigned. All whiche I have thoroughely considered of with the most mature and deliberate advice that either myself or others whom I have thoughte in theise affayres best experienced weare any wayes able to afforde. And I dare boldely affirme that they are both honourable and profitable to myselfe and very easye to alle my servantts; whiche be the especiall respectes that I did propose unto myself in the very beginninge when I first intended to sett downe orders, and whiche I have sythence carefully observed in the pennynge of them. The first whereof I have affected for myne owne behoofe and contentement: the other for the behoofe of my servants, uppon whome I would not wyllingly ympose that service whiche they shall notte be able even with greate facillitye and quictt to themselves to performe; whiche being soe done on my parte I am likewise to expecte, and soe doe vehemently both expecte and require of them that they doe carefully and dilligently ymploye themselves to performe their dutyes unto me in their service after suche manner as I have here prescribed: whiche, if they shall fayle to doe, they are in reason to conceave that according to the quallitye of their contempt they shall incurre my like discontentment with them; and that much more than if they had been tyed to more harde and unequall condicōns. But if I shall perceave that they shall dulye and cōmendably dispose themselves to the performance of their severall partes and dutyes they shall be well assured to have att my handes that countenance, creditt, and advancement whiche shalbe meete for them to receave and for me to yelde unto them."

The preface concludes thus:—"Ytt only nowe resteth that I exhorte, admonishe, and require all my people of what sorte soever that they studiously ymbrace unitye, peace, and goode agreemente amonge themselves as the only means whereby they shall procure quiett and commendacōn to themselves and much honor and comforte to me; and that they forbeare to be the revengers of their owne wrongs (if any be offered), referringe themselves and their cause to my stewarde or other officers appoynted in that behalfe, who, if they shall not yelde unto them suche satisfaccōn as shalbe in reason meete, they may boldely repayre to myselfe, who desire noe longer to be Governowe of a family than I shall use such justice and equitye that nott my best affected officer or dearest childe shalbe able to abuse the meanest in my house, but shalbe by me reproved for the same to the full contentement of the partye injuryed. Herein, althoughe I have sincerely delivered myne owne intendemente whereby my servantts may be the better incoraged to performe their dutyes and may stande in more securitye from sufferinge any wronge,—yett my mynde is not that any quarrelsome personne shall take more advantage of my woordes than they doe truly ymporte, which promise noe satisfaccōn but uppon an injurye first offered. And thus much may suffice for my preface.

"Given att Cowdrye the first of this present November, A.D. 1595."

"ANTHONY MOUNTAGUE."

The Table.

1. My Stewarde of Householde.
2. My Comptroller.
3. My highe Stewarde of Courtes.
4. My Auditor.
5. My Generall Receaver.
6. My Solliciter.
7. My other Principall Officers.
8. My Secretarye.
9. My Gentlemen Ushers.
10. My Carver.
11. My Sewer.*
12. The Gentlemen of my Chamber.
13. The Gentlemen of my Horse.

* The officer who set and removed the dishes, tasted them, &c. [*Halliwell.*]

14. The Gentlemen Wayters.
15. The Marshal of my Hall.
16. The Clarke of my Kitchen.
17. The Yeomen of my greate Chamber.
18. The Usher of my Hall.
19. The Chiefe Cooke.
20. The Yeomen of my Chamber.
21. The Clarke of myne Officers' Chamber.
22. The Yeoman of my Horse.
23. The Yeoman of my Seller.
24. The Yeoman of myne Ewrye.*
25. The Yeoman of my Pantrye.
26. The Yeoman of my Butterye.
27. The Yeoman of my Wardroppe.
28. The Yeomen Wayters.
29. The seconde Cooke and the Reste.
30. The Porter.
31. The Granator.†
32. The Bayliffe.
33. The Baker.
34. The Brewer.
35. The Groomes of the Great Chamber.
36. The Almoner.
37. The Scullery Man.

Long as is this list, it by no means embraced the whole of Lord Montague's establishment. Many of the officers named in *The Table* were at the head of departments, to each of which was attached a staff of servants; and, besides these, other persons are incidentally mentioned in the book, such as the Housekeeper, the Footmen, the Boyes of the Kytchen, and others.

Large establishments were very usual in the sixteenth century. Stowe says, in speaking of the Earl of Derby, that he had two hundred and forty servants; whilst Strype points out that Lord Burleigh, though frugal and having no paternal estate, "kept a family of one hundred servants." Amongst these he had twenty gentlemen retainers each worth a thousand

---
* "An office in the king's household where they take care of the linen for the king's own table, lay the cloth, and serve up water in silver ewers after dinner." [*Bailey*.]

† The officer in charge of the granary.

pounds a year, and many wealthy persons were among the number of his retainers. But it should be recollected that at the death of Queen Elizabeth there were only fifty-nine temporal peers in the House of Lords. Each of these was a great personage, the head of a noble family, and young gentlemen were glad to accept offices in the household of such magnates.*

It is almost impossible to imagine how all these persons could have found room at Cowdray, for Lord Montague gives express orders that no one should "lodge abroad." Cowdray was celebrated for its great hall, its large rooms, and its two long galleries, and we must therefore conclude that, as the tradition in Midhurst is that the house could afford sleeping accommodation for two hundred persons, many must have lain on the floor upon those "palletts" which Lord Montague is so particular in having removed every morning. Lord Montague's orders as to the constant supply for the rooms of "perfumes, flowers, herbes, and bowes † in their season," may have had some reference to this overcrowding of the house.

Lord Montague alludes to female attendants only once. This occurs when he speaks of the "Gentlewomen's service," which was immediately to follow his own dinner. These gentlewomen were probably attendants on Lady Montague, for except as "Lawnederers" women servants could hardly have been required at Cowdray. The Yeomen of the Chamber acted as housemaids, and mended Lord Montague's "lynnen and roabes;" others of the household attended to the sitting-rooms and the fires; and the boys of the kitchen had "to keepe it, with all things therein, cleane and sweete."

Lord and Lady Montague probably dined in the large dining-parlour, on the walls of which were the celebrated frescoes. "The place of my dyett" is the description always given of it by Lord Montague. In this apartment the "Gentlewomen's service" was probably laid on a separate table. The officers of the household who are mentioned in Lord Montague's list dined together in the Buck Hall, seated at four tables. After their meal there was

---

* The following notice (taken from a Louvain MS.) of one member of Lord Montague's household appears in the *Records of the English Province of the Society of Jesus*, vol. vi. p. 329 :—
"Richard Lambe, Esq., descended of a good house in the north country, where his ancestors lost their property in the civil wars of the houses of York and Lancaster. Some parts of the remnants of the estate fell by right to him upon his eldest brother's death, but failing to recover it in consequence of his being a Catholic, he lived with Lord Montague, his wife's uncle, being his gentleman for many years."

† Green boughs.

a "second service" also in the Hall, for the rest of the establishment. The dinner hour was ten o'clock. Supper was served at five o'clock, but after that hour "lyveryes" (or slight meals) could be had by any persons in their own rooms. Nothing is said about breakfast. Perhaps enough might remain of the evening "lyverye" to supply an early meal. Fires in the Great Hall were allowed "from All Hallows Eve att night" [October 31] "to Good Frydaye morninge."

Cards were provided in the hall for "such strangers as shall be willinge to playe and passe some tyme thereatt." Each player put a donation into the "play-box," the contents of which were afterwards divided among the Yeomen officers.

The first fourteen persons named in *The Table* were gentlemen by birth; the two next in order were gentlemen by office; and the rest were Yeomen officers.

The *Steward* was the head of the whole establishment, and his office was no sinecure. Lord Montague goes into many details with reference to the duties of this gentleman. He was to undertake all superintendence "as well in my forreyne affayres and outward provisions as in domesticall matters and civill government of my Family." "Forreyne affayres" included the provision of all necessaries for the household, such as "beeves, muttons, grayne, wynes, saltstore of sortes, hoppes, spyces, and fruytes of sortes, lyveryes, badges, woode and coals, necessaryes, carryeages, utensilles for every office, and wilde fowle." The Steward was to attend to all repairs of Lord Montague's houses, and of all fences and hedges in the grounds; and to "often ryde into my parkes, pastures, marshes, and other grounds, to see that they bee nott abused or disordered by my bayliffes or keepers of them." He had to provide "extraordinaryes, as nettes, sowes of Leade,* cases of glasse, &c.;" to "make sale of the hydes of oxen slaughtered, and of the felles† and woolle of the muttons; and order and dispose of the tallowe, some for lyghtes to serve my house, some for sale, and the like for kitchein stuffe." The Steward paid all wages, and overlooked the accounts of the other officers. He entered his receipts and payments in a book which was inspected monthly by Lord Montague, and by the auditor at the end of the year.

These were the principal duties of the Steward in "forrayne affayres,"

---

* A pig or sow of lead was an oblong mass of metal. [*Bailey.*]   † Skins.

but the "matters domesticall" were next explained. In these the Steward is told that "First my will is that he take uppon him the carriage and porte of my chiefe officer, and assiste me with sounde advice in matters of most ymportance and greatest deliberacōn, and therein faythfully keepe all my secrettes." The other officers and servants were strictly to obey the Steward even in things which seemed inconvenient to them, "excepte ytt be dishonest in ytt selfe or undutifull to the Prince* or State, or directly to the manifest hurte of me, my wiffe, &c." Complaints of the Steward's conduct might, however, be made to Lord Montague, who by his "masterly authoritye" would if necessary correct him. "But my forsight and care in my choyce of an officer in soe high authoritye shall be such that I will make small doubte of his cōmendable carryeage of himselfe in his place accordinge to the greate truste that I repose in him." The Steward was "in civill sorte to reprehende and correcte the negligent and disordered parsons,† and reforme them by his grave admonition and vigilant eye over them, the ryotous, the contentious, and quarrellous parsons of any degree, the revengers of their own injuryes, the privye mutiners, the frequenters of tablinge, cardinge, and dyceing in corners and att untymely houres and seasons, the conveighers of meate and other matter out of my howse, the haunters of alehowses or suspicious places by daye or by night, the absenters from their charge, and lodgeing abroade without leave, and they thatt have leave of absence that doe nott returne home at their tyme lymited without lawfull lett." These offenders, whether gentlemen or yeomen, were to be admonished and forbidden to attend upon Lord Montague until "readye to be reformed." "But the incorrigible personnes and wilful maynteyners of their outragious misgovernmente and unsufferable disorders (if any such be fownde) whom neither [the Steward's] perswasions, reason ytt selfe, nor authoritye can conteyne, within the lymytte of their dutie," were to be dealt with by Lord Montague himself.

---

* As Queen Elizabeth was on the throne when the Book of Rules was compiled, Lord Montague probably used the word Prince as equivalent to Sovereign.

† The words *parson* and *person* are both derived from the Latin *persona*. [Latham's *Dictionary*.] It has been thought that the "parsons" mentioned by Lord Montague were "the superior members of the household," but these officers are not likely to have been riotous, negligent, or disordered. *Person* and *parson* were often used indiscriminately at the time in which Lord Montague wrote. Holinshed says, "Jerom was vicar of Stepnie, and Garrard was *person* of Honielane." We may therefore conclude that Lord Montague meant "persons," in the modern sense of the word.

The Steward was to keep "and have allwayes in readiness a perfecte checkrolle both of all my parsons and nomber domesticall, and of all my reteyners* that are interteyned and allowed by me." The Steward himself was to take an inventory of all the "wardroppe stuffe whatsoever," and of all the plate and silver vessels, "with the weight and poyse of the same and note of the goldsmythes' marke and yeare." Three copies were to be made of these inventories, of which Lord Montague himself kept one. The Clerk of the Kitchen had to furnish the Steward with a "perfecte Inventorye of all the pewter vessells, brasse, and other ymplements, as well of the kitchin as of all the other inferiour offices, (to witt) seller, butterye, pantrye, bakehouse, laundrye, scullery, larders, porter's lodge, and brewehouse, bycause he is to renewe ytt beinge decayed."

Lord Montague adds "Remembrances and Instruccōns" for his Steward. In these the Steward is cautioned to buy "somer Beeves" and small oxen for "expence of householde" at fairs, or of the "farmers neare hand" in the "Springe and pryme of the yeare." But "the oxen for wynter expence, stalle, and sale (especiallye if I lye at Cowdrye), be provided of large boane, and well comeinge either att Coventrye Fayre on Corpus Christi daye,† or att Uxbrydge on Saint Margarrite's daye." ‡ The Steward is to provide "muttons needeful to be boughte for slaughter of my howse of reasonable boane, and out of harde, leare,§ and choyce pastures, either of the Scheppe Masters from the Downes, or att fayres holden neere hande in the Springe." Forty or fifty ewes were to supply Easter lamb.‖

The Steward had to see that "herringe and wynes are best provided in respecte of choyce, price, and carryeage for my expence (when I lye att Cowdrye), at Chichester, Southampton, or other portes uppon the sea costes." Lord Montague urges the Steward to see "that the woode and coale provided for expence of my howse att Cowdrye be carefully husbanded, for that woode is much wasted of late and waxeth scantt about Cowdrye:" . . . "that a lesse proportion of salt store, hoppes and spices be taken when they be scantt and deare, and a more large when they be plentifull, and better cheape." In

---

* These retainers were not members of the actual household.
† The Thursday after Trinity Sunday.
‡ St. Margaret's Day, Old Style, was on the 8th of July.
§ Stubble-land. In Cheshire such pasture for sheep is now called "leers".
‖ In many parts of England it was reckoned as important to eat lamb on Easter Sunday as to eat pancakes on Shrove Tuesday or plum pudding on Christmas Day.

conclusion the Steward is to recollect "that my reteyners be comanded nott to resorte to me without their lyveryes."

Lord Montague desired the Steward to "dispose and distribute in his discretion to the inferiour officers (yeomen and groomes of the Greate Chamber excepted) the rewardes given by Noblemen, Gentlemen, and others repayring to my howse." These presents appear to have been deposited in the play box, and if the condition of the box was "but meanely beneficiall" the Steward was desired to "consider the yeomen and groomes of the Great Chamber at his discretion."

The Steward and some of the chief officers of Lord Montague's household held from time to time an inquiry into the state of the household, its expenses, and the conduct of the various servants. This inquiry was to be held always "in the accustomed place (whiche att Cowdrye shalbe the lower baye windowe chamber on the right hande of the greate gate)."

When Lord Montague went on journeys the Steward with the rest of the principal officers was to ride immediately before him, unless Lord Montague's brothers, children, or uncles were present. The Steward was to dine and sup in the hall, taking the head of the chief officers' table, "and that allwayes in a gowne, unless he be booted." He is especially cautioned "nott to give place unto any." But "in tyme of state and extraordinarye action" the Steward and the Comptroller were to walk through the Great Hall preceding the first and second courses when Lord Montague's dinner was carried into the dining-parlour. The Steward was reminded by Lord Montague that it was his duty at all times "to use himselfe towardes me, my wiffe, and (in some sorte) to my children submissively and with all reverence," as an example to others; and he was "nott to presume to enter into myne, or my wiffe's bedchambers or private places untill he first knocke att the dures, or give some other signification by his voyce or message of his beinge there and desire to come in."

The Steward had, as has been said, many duties to perform. But in all these he was to be assisted by the rest of the principal officers of the household, so that his labours may not have been so great as might at first sight appear.

Lord Montague says of the second officer of his household, the *Comptroller,* "a Comptroller is a principal officer belongeinge unto me as I am a vizcounte." But the duties of this person appear to have consisted in giving his lord "faythfull and sounde advice," and in being present when the Steward "delyvered his mynde" to the servants. When the Steward had finished his remarks, the Comptroller was to "use some speeche to the like effecte ... in some modeste manner." Lord Montague evidently anticipated difficulties to arise between the Steward and the Comptroller, for he exhorts them to "agree the one with the other, affecte the one the other, and seeke the credit the one of the other, without jelousyes or suspicons, as if they weare brothers." The Comptroller was to dine at the Steward's table, and to "sytt on the forme syde right over agaynst him and not yelde that place to anye whosoever." He "must allwayes goe in a gowne (unles he be booted to ryde), for soe the gravitye of his place and person will require." When he accompanied the Steward, "in the attendaunce uppe of my dynner and supper, att tymes of speciall service," he was "nott to fayle to beare his white stafe in his hande."

The *High Steward of Courts* held all Lord Montague's "Leetes and Courte Barons," and undertook all business conneeted with them. His place at meals was at the Steward's table, next to the Comptroller.

The *Auditor* audited all accounts once a year, including those of the household, the ironworks, sales of wood, "rentes, revenwes, fynes, perquisites," &c. At dinner he sat next to the High Steward, but at audits he was to sit "att the borde's end," between the Steward and the Comptroller.

The *Receaver Generall* assisted the Steward of Courts, and also received all Lord Montague's "revenewes, perquisitts of Court, and other casualtyes;" he paid all "annuyties, tenthes, and other fees." He also took his meals at the Steward's table, sitting next the Auditor.

The *Solliciter* took charge of all law suits, either "moved by me agaynst others, or commenced by others agaynst me;" he instructed counsel, and he took care that "the secreeye of my letters patent, court rolles, and auntient evidences," were not "needelessly disclosed or discovered in open courte to my prejudice or ymparement of myne inheritance." At the end of every term, he was to give an account to Lord Montague of the progress of each suit that had been entered upon. The place of the Solicitor at meals was next to the General Receiver.

The rest of my principall officers were to assist those already named by Lord Montague, and at all times be ready to give "faythfull and sounde advice." They all dined at the Steward's table, taking their places according to their seniority in Lord Montague's service.

The *Secretary* was to be "a man of a good, grave discretion, and especially very secrett." He was always to be ready to attend Lord Montague, keeping "letters of weight fyled upp together in good order," answering such as Lord Montague had not time to reply to himself, and entering in a book an alphabetical table of all letters written. He was to consider all petitions to Lord Montague, and always with a "respecte of the ymportance and hast of the matter." Lord Montague adds, "He shall nott, butt att verye speciall tymes, weare his lyverye, and that att my speciall appoyntemente. His upper garment in the howse I wishe to be a comely blacke cloake." The Secretary also dined at the Steward's table, sitting below the principal officers unless he were one of them, in which case he was placed next to the Receiver.

The *Gentleman Usher* was an officer to whose share fell varied duties. Lord Montague begins his instructions to this officer as follows: "I will that my Gentleman Usher (I being a Vizcounte) shall usher me or my wiffe, in all places conveniente, (Videlt) through cyttyes, townes, &c., bareheaded, as well on horsebacke as on foote, saveinge that in the presence of an Erle or upwardes, he shall forbeare soe to doe : neither shall he ryde bare before us, within the precyncte of the Prince's palaice, but on foote he may goe bare to the greate chamber dure within the Courte, and noe further." The Gentleman Usher took charge of all the inventories "of the wardroppe stuffe of my several howses," receiving them from the Steward of the Household, and going over the items room by room, in the presence of three or four witnesses. He was "to oversee the contineweall furnishinge and cleanely keepinge of all lodgeinges, galleryes, great chambers, dyneing rooms, parlours, &c ;" but he was not to concern himself with the offices, nor was he to meddle with the arrangement of Lord Montague's "owne lodgeings" after once going through the inventory belonging to them upon Lord Montague's "removeall to any place." The Gentleman Usher selected the Carver and Sewer, and had authority over the officers beneath him in rank. Lord Montague proceeds: "He shall at his discretion appoynte all servantts' chambers and who shall lye in them ; alloweing thereto conveniente beddinge and such like furniture to ytt, soe as two goe to a bedd, allwayes provided that a gentleman be matcht with a gentleman and a yeoman with a yeoman, unless the contrarye by me be especially appoynted. . . . He shall in the morninge first give attendaunce to strangers (if there be any), associateinge unto himselfe for that purpose another gentleman or two, and then serve them breakfaste and afterwarde attend them as shall seeme most convenient." At ten o'clock he attended at Lord Montague's dinner, and was then at liberty till supper time. After supper the Gentleman Usher took strangers to their rooms, and saw that they had any "liveryes" that they might require. "And if there be divers (as ytt will often happen) att one tyme to goe to their severall chambers, he shall cause one gentleman to goe with every stranger, soe that the most sufficient be allotted to the stranger of most worthe. This done he maye for that night dispose of himself as him best lyketh till bedde time." On great occasions Lord Montague employed two Gentlemen Ushers, one being "for increase of state," and having no authority except in the absence of the senior of the two. One of these gentlemen dined at the Steward's table, sitting next to the Secretary; the other dined with the Gentlemen Waiters, sitting "the uppermoste on the benche side." Every week they changed their course.

The *Carver* carved the meat, and the *Sewer* handed it to every one "accordinge to their places." The Carver dined at the Waiters' table, sitting next to the Gentleman Usher, and the Sewer sat immediately below the Carver.

The *Gentlemen of the Chamber* were to remain in Lord Montague's "withdraweing chamber" throughout the day, so as to be ready to receive his orders and to tell him if anybody wished to see him. If he left his room, and if he walked out, they were to follow him. One of them waited on Lord Montague's "trencher and cuppe," and the next in rank waited on Lady Montague in like manner. Lord Montague explains their further duties as follows: "Att night if I be out of my lodgeings (ytt beinge dark) some one of them shall wayte for my comeinge in with a candle to light me to my chamber: where after I am, and woulde goe to bedd, they shall helpe me into ytt, and beinge layed to reste, they shall either by themselves or by some of the yeomen take care that the dures be all fast lockte." The "auntientest" of these Gentlemen, assisted by the Senior Yeoman of the Chamber, kept an inventory of all Lord Montague's clothes. The Gentlemen of the Chamber dined with the Gentlemen Waiters.

The *Gentleman of the Horse* attended to the management of the stable, and gave "expresse commandement to the groomes to attend their charge by daye and by nighte, and nott to frequente ale-howses, nor lodge abroad." He was to look carefully after the "growndes appoynted for the somer pasturinge" of the horses, and to see that "the haye layd into the barnes and loftes of the stable for wynter foode of them be nott wilfully wasted or spoyled." When Lord Montague rode, the Gentleman of the Horse was "to helpe me to my horse, appoynteinge the Yeoman of my Horse to holde my styrroppe, and my footeman to stande to his heade."

The *Gentlemen Wayters* assisted the Gentlemen of the Chamber in their personal attendance on Lord and Lady Montague and on their visitors. Some of them were "to hearken when I or my wiffe at any tyme doe walke abroade, that they may be readye to give their attendance upon us."

These officers completed the list of the Gentlemen by birth in Lord Montague's household. The next in rank were the two *Gentlemen by office*, who were the *Marshal of the Hall*, and the *Clarke of the Kytchin*. The Marshal of the Hall was only employed "att tymes of extraordinary action (as in repayre of the Prince, marriage of my children, or att Christmas, and the like) when I have occasion to use one." On these great occasions the Marshal undertook the duties of the Ushers of the Hall. He dined at a separate table, to which he was bidden to invite the Ushers "and such servitors or others as he shall thinke meete and convenient."

The *Clarke of the Kitchin* was the manager of the whole house under the direction of the Steward: combining the duties of the housekeeper, bailiff, and butler of modern days. He was to make inventories of "all the utensilles, ymplementts, and necessaryes," and to "indente the same tripertite," giving a copy to the Steward, another to "the officer of the plate," and keeping the third himself. Lord Montague details the duties of the Clerk at some length. He says: "I will that he keepe a whole and perfecte booke of the dayly expence of all kynde of victualls, . . . and that he shewe me beforehande the proportion of myne owne fare and dyett that I may add thereunto or dyminishe att my pleasure. I will that he suffer none to stande unseemely with his backe towarde my meat while itt is at the raunge." The Clerk had authority over all the cooks, and was to take care that every meal was "orderly dressed without spoyle, waste, or needlesse expence." He was "to keepe and order the spice and fruyttes, and see carefully that there be noe waste of them." He was to watch that the baker made proper use of the flour, and that the loaves when made of good wheat weighed sixteen ounces, and when of "course and hungrye" wheat "fifteen ounces one dram." He had to superintend the brewer also, and to see that he made "good and wholsom beare and eighteen gallons att the least of everye bushell." The Clerk was to "see the slaughter-man perform his dutye in slaughteringe and powderinge * of the Beife, and appoynte what messes shall be cutt out of the slaughtered oxe." He had to provide "apparell for the boyes of the kitchin," rabbit nets and fishing nets, "entralles of beastes and cheesecurdes for wyldefowle, oates and barlye for poultrye, and rye for bakeing of redd deare;" and to watch over the stock of salt provisions and of "lyve fishe." The Clerk was constantly to go into the offices to see that they were clean and neat, and "at some tyme as his leisure will permitt to oversee the Almoner and Porter in the distributeinge of almes to the poore." The Clerk kept a book in which he charged every week the "expenditure of wyne, beare, and breade," both for the household, and for "comers att the barre;" and in this book he entered "in the margent" the names and number of "strangers repayringe" to the house. The book was shown every fortnight to the Steward, who reported its contents to Lord Montague. The Clerk sat at the head of one of the tables in the hall.

The *Yeomen Officers* were a numerous body. At their head was the *Yeoman Usher of my Greate Chamber.* He was to see that the chairs, stools, and tables were placed ready before meals, and that they were afterwards put back in their proper places. Every morning he was to see that all the large rooms were neat and well swept, and "kept swete with perfumes, flowers, herbes, and bowes* in their season." He had to attend to strangers and see that they had all they might "wante or desire to have." He was to "have a vigilant eye to the meate, to the extente that ytt be nott ymbezeled or conveighed to corners." And he took a principal part in the serving of Lord Montague's own dinner.

The *Usher of the Hall* saw that the Steward's table was properly laid, and that no one sat down by it till the meat was placed upon it. He placed strangers at meals according to their rank, looked after the waiting at the Steward's table, and held "the towell whilest the Almoner doth give water and my chiefe officers and gentlemen strangers doe washe." He had to "commaund order, and silence in the hall: to remove unfitt and disordered parsons owte of ytt," and to see that the Almoner did his duty. The Usher dined at the table of the Clerk of the Kitchen, and sat next to him.

The *Chiefe Cooke* prepared Lord Montague's own dinner, assisted by the "inferioure Cookes." He is enjoined to "see everye thinge wholesomely

---

* Salting, sprinkling with salt. † Green boughs.

and cleanely handeled, and with as little expence of spyce as conveniently may be: and looke that all manner of poultrye or wilde fowle that comes to myne own table be well pulde that there remayne noe kynde of fethers or stumpes uppon them." The cook was to serve out Lord Montague's meat "in cleane vessels and well scowered." He sat at dinner next to the Usher of the Hall.

The *Yeomen of the Chamber* received from the chief Gentleman of the Chamber, "by inventorye indented between them," all Lord Montague's "lynnen, roabes, and jewells," kept them in presses, "clean, swete, and safe," and mended all that was torn. Every morning they were to rise early and "remove the palletts (if there be any) owte of my withdraweing chamber," to "make ytt cleane and swete with flowers and bowes in their seasons," to arrange Lord Montague's bedchamber, "brushe the carpetts, make the fyers, and prepare brushe and laye forthe my wearinge apparell for that day." Some of them were always to attend Lord Montague when he walked out, "one to carrye my cloake, the reste to doe myne errands, to take uppe and make cleane my bowles." They were to "serve a lyverye" in Lord Montague's bedroom every night, and he adds: "I will that they be verye carefull to extinguishe the fyre and lights after I amme in bedde, and that they locke faste and barre all the dores, and performe their business silently without clamour or noyse for fear of my disturbance." Some of the yeomen were to attend on Lady Montague.

The *Clarke of myne Officers' Chamber* kept the room in order in which the chief officers of the household held business meetings; he provided writing materials at Lord Montague's expense, wrote at the dictation of the officers, and kept a record of the business transacted, to be preserved "as a president for ever."

The *Yeoman of the Horse* discharged the duties of the Gentleman of the Horse during his absence, or when none had been appointed. He helped Lord Montague to mount if there was no Gentleman of the Horse in attendance; at other times he held his stirrup.

The *Yeoman of my Seller* took charge of the plate and of the wine, and sat at dinner next to the chief Cook.

The *Yeoman of myne Ewrye* received all "naperye and lynnen" from Lady Montague or "her assigne." He kept "a perfecte reckoninge of all torches, lynkes, and candles," and gave an account of them every month to the Clerk of the Kitchen. He laid the cloth at Lord Montague's dinner, placed the silver vessels on it, and after dinner he was desired to "coverre them with napkyns, and sett them uppon the Ewrye boorde." He also had the ordering of the daily " lyveryes."

The *Yeoman of my Butterye* was to receive of the Yeoman of the Cellar, " by billes indented interchangeably betweene them, all such plate (namely, pottes, bolles, cuppes, &c.) as doe apperteyne to his office, and be answerable to him for the same : and [to] receave of the Clarke of my Kytchin all such other thinges, (Videlt.) pewter pottes, tynne iugges, caskes, &c., as belonge to his office, and be likewise accomptant to him for the same." This Yeoman had charge of all ale and beer, receiving both from the brewer " by tale," and accounting for the same weekly, having been careful that there was " noe waste or spoyil made of ytt," to the Clerk of the Kitchen. He, as all others of Lord Montague's houschold, was charged to keep his office " cleanly and swetely."

The *Yeoman of my Warderoppe* had charge of all " howschold stuffe whatsoever" belonging to his office: he received linen for the use of his department from Lady Montague " or her assigne," and " as ytt shall weare oute or decaye he [must] deliver it upp and crave a new supplye." Lord Montague proceeds: " I will that he see the Galleryes and all lodgeinges reserved for strangers cleanely and sweetly kepte, with herbes, flowers, and bowes in their seasons, and the beddes of such as shall hither resorte att their first cominge to be mayde, and the better sortes of quiltes of beddes att any tyme to be used to be at nightes taken off, and Yrish Rugges layd in their places ; and in the morninge to be agayn layd on. . . . And that he see the chambers of such as doe departe to be well and handsomely dressed upp, and nothinge be missinge ; and that he have greate care of their fyres lefte (if any be), and after such care hadd the dores be lockte uppe. I will that he looke well to the keepinge cleane of all leades, gutters, and spowtes about my howse, except only those within the compasse of myne own lodgeinge." Every month he was to look over the servants' rooms, and " see if there be any defalt in there beddinge or furniture ; and if such be, that he cause it to be mended."

The *Yeomen Wayters*, of whom the number is not given, were to attend Lord Montague whenever he walked out ; during his dinner they were to " reverently redeliver their dishes" to the Sewer, and throughout the whole meal to " give watchfull and diligent attendance, . . . nott useinge any uncomelye gestures or actions (as laughcinge, hearkeninge to tales, and the like), whereby they may neglecte or hinder their dutyes." They were to wait at supper as well as at dinner: and not "by anie means to lodge out of the howse." When the Yeomen Wayters were in attendance on Lord Montague "in the streets att London," they were "to be allwayes in their lyveryes, with handsome swordes or rapiers by their sydes." This rule was to be followed "in the countrye att all solempne feastes as Christmas, Easter, Whitsontyde, and greate meetinges."

The *Seconde Cooke and the reste* dressed all the meat except that intended for Lord Montague's own table, and were to assist " the Mr. Cooke," at his request, with "a helpeing hande." They are warned not to let "any harte burninge or disdayne growe " between them, but to " concurre well together and seeke the mutuall credit either of other." They were to serve all meat in clean dishes, and if a dish was dirty they were to "returne ytt back to the Scullerye man to be amended." And they were to look after the boys of the kitchen, making them in all things neat and clean.

The *Porter* kept the great gate, and "in tyme of extraordinarye action or att solempne feastes " he was to " have his messe of meate into his office " there. This was to enable him " to give his dilligent attendance att the gate, as well for the repayre of strangers as for disordered parsons that would come in att no convenient tyme," and he is desired to "answere all comers of meaner sorte att the gate." He assisted the Almoner in the distribution of alms, and might "conveniently weare a gowne all wynter, and att solempne tymes." Lord Montague adds: "I will that att Cowdrye he keepe the conduyte cleane, and the ynner courte, with the helpe of the pore the longe alleyes without the gate, and the greene before ytt." When the Porter dined in the hall he sat next the Yeomen of the Chamber.

The *Granator* was to " keepe a perfect talle of all such corne as he shall receave of any manner of parson," and delivered it to the Baker and Brewer. Lord Montague proceeds : "And further, that he see the corne which he is to receave of my Farmers to be goode, swete, well wynnowed, and answerable to the covenantts of their leases."

My Bayliffe of Husbandrye fulfilled the duties of a modern farm bailiff. He looked after all the parks and the cattle in them, and was every year to lay up the meadows for hay, have them "rydde of all beastes (excepting att Cowdrye and Battell a brase or leashe of old Buckes) betweene the five and twentieth of Marche and the firstt of Aprille." The Bailiff engaged haymakers, and provided them and the "domesticall servantts " with "a competent nomber of forkes and rakes." He watched over the number of loads of hay that none might be wasted or spoiled : had charge of the fish-ponds, and kept " a perfect note of the daye, moneth, and yeare of storeinge of them, and what nomber of fishes of what sorte and scantling*" was placed in them. In long frosts he was to have the ice broken on the ponds, and in wet seasons he was to "have a speciall care to the tymlye draweinge of the slewces and fluddgates" of Lord Montague's ponds. In "extraordinary tempestes" the Bailiff was desired to warn the millers to attend to their floodgates in time. Lord Montague reminds the Bailiff at Cowdrye to " continewe [his] right and clayme of the auntient usuall carteway through the north street into the *Gall meade*," and to see that "the gates at the Mill and Pryorye be cheyned and locked, especially uppon the markett dayes, and att other tymes also needefull, the better to avoyde and keepe out strange beastes and hoggs." The Bailiff sat next the Granator at dinner in the hall.

The *Baker* and the *Brewer* sat next each other at the table of the Clerk of the Kitchen, below " the seconde Cooke and the rest of them." Both were accountable to the Clerk for the amount consumed in their several departments.

The *Grooms of the Great Chamber* provided cards at their own expense for the use of company. They were under the orders of the Yeoman Usher, and had to keep wood ready at all times in case a fire was wanted in the hall. When Lord Montague supped by candle-light, one of the grooms was to carry a lighted torch before his " meate."

The *Almoner* kept the hall " cleane and swete with bowes and flowers," made the fires in it, held the basin when the chief officers washed, fetched beer and bread for the inferior officers, and drove out of the hall all " raunters † and dogges." He was to " preserve the broaken meate, breade, and beare for the poore," and to " distribute the almes considerately with due regarde and respecte to the porest and most needye." The Almoner dined with the gentlemen's servants.

The *Scullerye man* occupied somewhat the same position as the odd-man, who does so much, of our own day. He, however, was to have " a speciall regarde and care to the safe keepeinge and preserveinge of the silver vessell ‡

---

* Size, from *eschantillon*. [*Bailey*.]   † Rioters.
‡ Probably from *vaisselle*, silver plate.

cominge under his handes that ytt be neither ymbezeled nor abused." Every night the *Scullerye man* re-delivered the plate " by talle " to the *Yeoman of the Seller*, " clean scowered and well ordered." He was answerable for all the pewter vessels, and had to keep them " and all other thinges brought into his office decently and cleanely." The *Scullerye man* is desired to " have a singuler regarde to the temperinge and makeinge of mustarde with good seede, and to the well keepeinge and servinge of ytt." He dined in " his office," which was probably the scullery, " and the boyes of the kytchin with him."

Lord Montague's Book of Household Rules concludes with the Order of Service to be used at his table, and with his Determinacion for Officers' Fees. He remarks that the offices he has already mentioned are not by any meanes all that were " conceaved, not unfitt to be used under me," but he adds, " these be the offices whereof I have thought fit most expedient to speake."

" *My Determinacion for Officers' Fees.*

" Forsoemuch as I have beine informed by others, and also have seene and noted myselfe, both in the tyme of my late lorde my grandfather as also since in myne owne, the sundrye inconveniences that have arisen by such as by reason of their place and office then before and now under myselfe doe challenge certayne fees to be allowed them as of right adheringe and belongeinge to their office, and perhappes thinke that nott without injurye they can be debarred from haveinge that which they soe challenge to be due : I have therefore thought good to laye downe that for soe much as all such offices are myne, the officers myne, and att myne appointement and the thinges accompted as fees yssueinge oute or beinge parte of that which cannott be denyed to be myne : there can be noe color of reason why any officer of myne can of dutye or otherwise challenge that as due to himselfe which is soe manifeste to be myne : and therefore without wronge to anye, itt is in my power and authoritye as my likeinge shall leade me either to tollerate the haveinge of such fees, or else to frustrate and disannull them. Wherefore I doe herebye publishe and declare for all officers as well within myne howse as withoutt, that they shall nott have any fees whatsoever allowed them saveinge only such as my Stewarde shall, by note under myne hande from tyme to tyme to him delivered, have authoritye to appoynte or allowe, and that to continewe only dureinge my pleasure. This only amongst many I have thought good perticulerly to note, that my woodewardes for many especiall causes (as well in respecte of the greate decaye that I doe alreadye fynde in my woodes, as also of a farre greater that myne heires may hereafter fynde if greate consideracōn be nott had to preserve them) be nott permitted to have anie wyndefalles, dotterell* trees, or such like whatsoever, besides their accustomed fees for the markeinge, in respecte that under the colour of them great domage may issue, whereof just proofe can hardely to be made."

Lord Montague's dinner was served with very great ceremony, and he gives most particular directions about it. The account forms a curious and interesting picture of the manners and customs in a nobleman's household of that period.

"Att ten of the clock, ytt being covereinge tyme," the Gentleman Usher commanded the Yeoman Usher to " call to the Yeoman of the Ewrye, Pantrye, Butterye, and Seller to make ready." The Yeoman of the Ewrye was then to " arme " himself " with an armynge towell layd uppon his righte shoulder and tyed lowe under his lefte arme," and " haveinge everye thinge readye within his office," he was to " carrye them uppe to the Ewrye boorde." Having arranged the plate on the sideboard, the Yeoman was instructed to " laye the table clothe fayre uppon both his armes, and goe together with the Yeoman Usher with due reverence to the table of my dyett, makeinge two curteseys thereto, the one about the middest of the chamber, the other when he cometh to ytt."† The Yeoman Usher then kissed his hand and laid it on the table " in the same place where the Yeoman of the Ewrye" was to lay his cloth. The Usher assisted the Yeoman to " spreade " the cloth, " casteinge the one end the one waye, the other ende the other waye," and the Yeoman kissed the tablecloth before placing it on the table. "This service ended, and due curtesie done," the Usher conducted the Yeoman to the sideboard to fetch the plate which was required. The Usher then went to fetch the Yeoman of the Pantry, who " shall followe him through the hall to my dyning chamber dore," and, after the usual two bows, " shall place the salte, and laye downe the knyves, and then lay myne owne trencher with a manchet‡ thereon and a knyfe and spoone on either syde ; and my wiffe's in like manner." The Yeoman of the Pantry made "a small obeisance" as he laid down each article ; and when he had finished, he, " together with the Yeoman Usher," was to make " a solempne curtesye

---

* Decayed trees. In Sussex rotten trees are now called "doted trees."
† The attendants on Queen Elizabeth's table kneeled at the times when Lord Montague orders his to bow.
‡ A small loaf of fine white bread.

and departe, soe conducted out as he came in." The spoons and knives were "hefted with silver."

The Yeoman of the Cellar brought up the plate and placed it on the cupboard, or buffet, remaining in attendance to "fill wyne with discretion to such as shall call for ytt." In the arrangement of the buffet he was assisted by the Yeoman of the Buttery.

When at length the table was prepared, the Gentleman Usher sent to the kitchen to ask if the dinner was ready, and then went to inquire Lord Montague's pleasure, knocking at the doors although they might be open. The Gentleman Usher saw that the Carver and Sewer washed at the Ewerye board, and were properly "armed," the Carver with a towel "cast about his necke and putt under his girdle at both sides, and one napkyn on his lefte shoulder and an other on the same arme." The Gentleman Usher then conducted the Carver with the usual two bows to the table, where he is told to "stande seemely and decently with due reverence and sylence," till Lord Montague's " dyett and fare" were brought up. The Sewer, commanded by the Gentleman Usher, went to fetch the dinner. As he passed through the hall the Usher of the Hall cried, "with an audible voyce, Gentlemen and Yeomen, wayte uppon the Sewer for my Lorde." The Sewer was attended to the Kitchen by " halfe a dosen Gentlemen and Yeomen atte the leaste," and receiving the dishes "all covered" from the chief Cook, he handed them to these gentlemen according to rank, calling out, " For my Lorde," as he approached the kitchen dresser. When the procession returned to the hall, the Usher stood ready at the screen, and said to those present, " By your leave, my Masters, causeinge them to stande uncovered" while the dinner was carried through the hall, and himself walking before it to the upper end of the room. Here the Yeoman Usher met the Sewer and preceded him to the " greate chamber dore," where he and the dinner were received by the Gentleman Usher. When all was prepared, the Gentleman Usher appointed " a comely yeoman to waight at the cuppborde," and then informed Lord Montague that his dinner was ready. The Gentleman Usher remained in the room during dinner, and when he saw it was time for the second course he sent the Sewer for it with the same ceremonies as before. When the meal was over, the Gentleman Usher approached the table with a towel, " gentlemen followeinge with basons and ewers," and Lord and Lady Montague washed their hands;—a necessary ceremony as they had had no forks. The attendants then, "after due reverence, retired to their own dinner, the

Gentleman Usher first looking that no meat had been carried to corners. Afterwards he returned, with the Carver and Sewer, and the Gentlemen Waiters, and waited till Lord Montague was "rysen and gone."

These tedious ceremonies were daily observed at Lord Montague's "ordinarye service." On great occasions, "in extraordinarye actions and festivall times," the Steward and Comptroller, dressed "in fayre gownes nott unlike, and haveinge white staves in their handes," preceded the Sewer through the hall, "and the Marshall before them and the two Ushers before him: and the Marshall, as the meate passeth the screene," was to say "with a comendable voyce, By your leave, my masters." When the procession reached the dining-room on these great days, the two Yeomen Ushers "after reverence done" went to either side of the room, and the two Gentleman Ushers went one to each side of the table, meeting "att the salte." The chief officers "after reverence done" were desired to "stande a little above the middest of the chamber by the carpett." On these occasions the Gentleman Usher was to spread two tablecloths on the table, so that when the time came for washing, the "uppermoste" cloth was removed, and the "seconde shall appeare." On this the towel was laid, which on days of "ordinary service" was spread on "the bare table." The Gentleman Usher was cautioned at no time "to suffer wayters to carrye a dishe or attende att [Lord Montague's] table in dublett and hose only, without either coate, cloake, or some upper garment." But "in greate repayre of strangers" he was to "appoynte a sufficient man to attende the silver vessells and meate," as well as additional Sewers, Gentlemen, and Yeomen to wait upon "strangers of accompte."

The conclusion of Lord Montague's Book of Household Rules is curious. He says: "Thus have I nowe breifely runne over all such orders as I have esteemed most convenient for the civill governemente of myne howscholde, howebeitt nott so largelye as the matters themselves might well require; neither soe that the strickte observeinge of noe more than is herein sett downe should be sufficient to be performed by them in whose offices matters of lesse momente, to avoyde tediousness, are lefte oute. And yett is ytt heere sufficiently enoughe (as I conceave) layde downe for the full instruction of everye one in that that belonges unto him. In the doeinge whereof I thought ytt nott unmeete to inserte such customeable ceremonys of service as are best fitteinge the degree of that place and calleinge wherein by her majestye's favour I nowe lyve, meaneinge thereby neither in presumption to

CHAPEL AT COWDRAY.

hazard the displeasure of the state nor in any sorte to incroache uppon the rightes of my superiours, neither yett intendeinge to yelde to any degree just cause of conceyte, that this my course hath proceeded either of vayne gloryc or any other light and ydle fancye, but only of a carefull regarde moved to see my people lyve under me in such civillitye and seemelye behaviour as may stande most with myne honour and the dutifull discharge of their service in their severall offices and places." Lord Montague adds, " in order that ignorance hereafter be no excuse for negligence," that the whole Book of Rules is to be read over publicly once a year, "and that about the audite tyme," in the presence of all his servants. If any one was doubtful as to the meaning of any part of the Book he could have access to it by the discretion of the Steward, and thus would be able " there to learne and be resolved in all poyntes and circumstances apperteyninge to his dutye."

It is strange that amongst the members of so large a household there should have been no chaplain. The Almoner, as will have been seen, was one of the inferior servants, and has been ranked as the chaplain only by persons who have looked at *The Table* without studying the Book of Rules.

But it is stranger still that, according to the account of Queen Elizabeth's visit to Cowdray, no religious service was provided for her on the Sunday. To quote the words of Mr. Freeman, " Long before that time all the doubtings and haltings and compromises of the earlier part of her reign had come to an end, and men were, as they are now, either distinctly Protestant or distinctly Roman Catholic." Mr. Freeman asks, " Did successive Viscounts Montague venture on anything so like public celebration of forbidden rites as to have mass said in this chapel? Was no worship of the kind enjoined by law provided for Queen Elizabeth on her visit?" It is probable, however, that no chapel existed at Cowdray at the time of Queen Elizabeth's visit, and that it was built by the second Viscount Montague only four years before his death. The following letter from Pope Urban VIII. to Lord Montague, with reference to the chapel, is still preserved among the Archives of the English College of Jesuits at Rome.*

---

* *Records of the English Province of the Society of Jesus*, vol. vi. p. 537. It is probable that P. Theatino who signed this letter was the Secretary for the Propaganda at the time, England having been considered a "mission country" since the secession from Rome. The Pope's seal must have been attached to the document.

K

"*Letter of His Holiness Urban VIII., Pope, to Viscount Montague,
April 17, 1625.*

URBAN VIII., POPE.

"Beloved Son, health and Apostolic blessing.

"The proofs of the sincere fidelity and devotedness you cherish towards Us and the Apostolic See deserves that We should, as far as in the Lord We may, comply with your desires. Having then been informed by you of late that you have erected in your own house, and fittingly adorned, a private chapel in honour of the Blessed Sacrament and of the Blessed Virgin Mary, for the which you crave of Us the following Indults. Of Our desire to show you especial favour, and absolving you hereby, and holding you to be absolved, from every bond of excommunication and suspension incurred, either by your own deed, or by judicial sentence, in case you should happen to have incurred any such censure, both solely with a view to the validity of these presents, We graciously assent to the humble petitions presented to Us in your behalf, and by the advice of Our venerable brethren, the Cardinals of the Holy Roman Church, who are set over the Sacred Rites, and of Our Apostolic authority, by the tenor of these presents, do decree and declare that the aforesaid chapel of the Blessed Sacrament and of the Conception and Assumption into Heaven of the Virgin Mother of God, shall hereafter and for evermore be held by all to be a sacred place, and be named as it ought to be named and known, by the title of the most Holy Sacrament and of the Immaculate Conception and glorious Assumption of the same Blessed Virgin Mary. And We further allow and grant by the tenor and authority of these presents, that in the aforesaid chapel may freely and lawfully be kept the Feast of the Conception of this Most Blessed Virgin Mary, in the month of December, with its Octave, according to the ordinary rubrics of the Roman Missal concerning Octaves, and that at Vespers and Lauds throughout the year a joint commemoration of the Conception and Assumption of the Blessed Virgin Mary may be made, and Masses both proper and votive, be celebrated. And this notwithstanding Apostolic Constitutions or aught else to the contrary.—Given at Rome, &c., April 17, 1625, the second year of Our Pontificate. P. THEATINO.

"To Our beloved Son Antony Mary Viscount Montague, English nobleman."

William Browne, the third brother of Anthony Maria second Viscount Montague, the youth of eighteen represented in Isaac Oliver's picture, is merely described in the Peerages as having died unmarried. But the Annual Letters of the Jesuit College of Liège (recently published in the *Records of the English Province*, vol. ii. p. 428) tell his curious and interesting story.

William Browne was born in 1576, and during his youth devoted himself entirely to his favourite pursuits of hunting and hawking. In the year 1613, he determined to make a pilgrimage to Loretto, and crossed over to Belgium for that purpose, leaving his servants, horses, hounds, and hawks, in the charge of his friends during his absence. On his way from Belgium to Loretto he visited the Jesuit Fathers at the College of St. Omer. To them he acknowledged that (as was natural in those troubled times) he had never been confirmed. He was confirmed at St. Omer, and at once resolved to belong to some one of the religious orders of the Roman Catholic Church. Pending his decision he returned to England, collected his rents, and disposed of his stable, kennel, and mew. After much deliberation William Browne, "though grandson, brother, and uncle of Viscounts Montague—his grandfather was Queen Mary's Ambassador to the Holy See—was himself content to spend his life in the humble duties of a Jesuit lay-brother." * He undertook the lowest and most disagreeable employments. " For fourteen years he spent almost two hours daily in the kitchen in washing the dishes, &c. He cleansed out the out-offices, lit the fires, and performed other like offices, with so great a sense of internal pleasure that showed itself outwardly in his countenance and was a sign of heavenly light whereby he penetrated into the hidden treasures of these employments which are not revealed except to such as are truly little." When the garden was being made at the College at Liège, William Browne worked as a common hodman. "With a sack or hodman's basket on his back, which he so fastened by a double cord over his breast as to leave his hands at liberty, in which he held his *Imitation of Christ* by Thomas à Kempis, he would carry rubbish backwards and forwards; and whilst they were filling his hod with earth or stones, &c., he would sit for a little upon the trunk of a tree and draw something from the book wherewith in the meantime to feed his soul; nor did any dilatoriness

---

* "Condition of Catholics under James I.,' Father Gerard's *Narrative of the Gunpowder Plot*, edited by John Norris, S.J., p. cxcix.

show itself in his countenance or gait." His mother and sisters, hearing by report of William's occupations, thought that his conduct was inconsistent with the honour of his family. He replied: "You have your delights, whilst I in the meantime, of the Divine bounty, overflow with heavenly joys. You are upon the stormy and perilous ocean; God grant that you may one day land safely in port." One day a youth belonging to the college met William carrying a bucket of pigs' wash, and said something as to "his title and family splendour. Upon which the brother in great confusion stopped for a moment, and laying down his load said, 'I had rather that the whole bucket should be poured down my neck than to have heard these words from you.' Then resuming his bucket he carried it to the pigs' trough." "When any one would see him perspiring in the performance of disgusting offices, and would put in a word upon the future glory of it, 'Believe me,' he would say, 'my brother, this it is I desire, this I aspire after, that I may please God and do His holy will. As to heaven, He will dispose of me as He sees fit.' . . . No one ever heard William complaining of food, clothing, or lodging,—no one saw him eager for recreation. After mid-day, being exhausted with labours, when rather overwhelmed with sleep than desirous of indulging in it, he would take a little repose, laying upon the ground with his head resting upon a brick. . . . If he saw any small bits of dry bread upon the table, he took them as quickly as he could, as so many delicacies. He could never be induced to take breakfast, unless indeed by way of antidote against the plague." Yet William "was not by nature formed for labour, nor did long habit ease the burthen, but the love of God alone, which never relaxed in his soul, made the burthen easy to him even to the very day in which he fell sick" of his last illness. Once when it was suggested to him that "our tepidity might be assisted by the hope of rewards and the fear of punishment," his answer was, "I do not remember for twenty years to have needed any other spur than the love of God alone."

William Browne materially assisted in the purchase of land at Liège when, in 1614, the Novitiate of the English Mission was removed thither from Louvain. He lived in the College at Liège until the year 1637. In that year he and two other lay-brothers "were victims of charity," nursing the people of Liège, during an outbreak of the plague. All three caught the plague and died. William Browne's death took place on the 20th of August 1637. In his later years he was occasionally confined to his bed owing to some injury to one of his legs. On these occasions he occupied himself in writing an ascetical book which is still preserved in the library at Stonyhurst. The volume, which is most beautifully written, contains thirty-four chapters (some 760 pages of very close manuscript). On the first page are the words, "This book, belonging to the English College at Liège, was written by Brother William Browne, my Lord Montague's brother, who lived and died a very holy man, in the quality of a lay-brother of the Society of Jesus at Liège."

Another Jesuit, Father Henry Lanman, was in early life one of the gentlemen in the household of the second Viscount Montague. Father Lanman entered the English College of Jesuits at Rome when he was twenty-seven years of age. In making the usual statement regarding his antecedents, he says that when he was about twenty he entered Lord Montague's household, and adds: "I was taken into the family of Viscount Montague, among the upper class of retainers; and spent six years in his service, with the interval of about a year, during which he was suffering an inhuman incarceration for his constant profession of the Catholic faith; nor was he allowed to have any Catholic attendant, not even myself, to assist him, until he obtained a little freer custody. In this interval I lived with my father. At length Lord Montague took me again, and retained me until, obtaining full liberty, or at least as much as he desired, he retired to his own house in the country, and through his great favour and liberality I have been enabled to make my journey hither."

Father Lanman continues: "Up to my twenty-third year I was a schismatic. My conversion came about as follows. Among the domestics of Lord Montague were many Catholics. One of them, with whom I was exceedingly intimate, often talked with me about religion; and his arguments raised within me doubts and an inclination towards the Catholic faith, to encourage which he furnished me with many books, which I read and reread with much satisfaction, especially those written by Rastall and Harding against Jewell. These, however, produced no other effect than in drawing me a little from attending the churches of the Protestants. At length, to free me from this state of doubt, I was taken by the same friend, whose name is William Coningsby, to Mr. Winckfield, a priest, and by his means, through the help of God, I was reconciled to the Catholic Church, on the Saturday within the octave of Corpus Christi, 1596." * From the latter part of his statement it would appear that there was no domestic chaplain at Cowdray at the time that Lanman was a member of Lord Montague's household.

---

* *Records of the English Province of the Society of Jesus*, vol. i. p. 174.

CHAPTER VIII.

Cowdray during the Civil War.

RANCIS, third Viscount Montague, succeeded his father in the autumn of 1629. He was at that time only twenty, but he was already married to Lady Elizabeth Somerset, the youngest daughter of the Marquess of Worcester; and his eldest son Anthony had been baptized at Battle Abbey in August 1629. This Anthony is said to have died unmarried, but Lord Montague had two other sons, Francis and Henry, who successively inherited the title. He had also one daughter, Elizabeth, who married Christopher Roper, fifth Lord Teynham.

The third Lord Montague was a great sufferer during the Civil War, being a Roman Catholic and a stout Royalist. He was most active in assisting Charles the First with money and arms. Evelyn, in his Memoirs, quotes letters from Sir Richard Browne, the ambassador at Paris, and Sir Edward Nicholas, the Secretary of State in London, as follows:—" 3 Sept. 1643. Much arms and ammunition sent. Lord Viscount Montague had fifty thousand livres Tournois to purchase arms,—thirty-five thousand only expended. Prays the other part may be ordered for him." In November of the same year Sir Richard writes: "Mr. Croft is gone to Rome joyntly with my Lord Viscount Montague and others, to treat with som merchants for furnishinge his ma'y with armes and ammunition."

Lord Montague's conduct in thus assisting the King was not unnoticed at home. In the Journals of the House of Commons are the following entries, showing that his punishment was both speedy and severe:—

"27 June 1643.—Resolved, that the estate of the Lord Viscount Montague, a papist, shall be forthwith sequestred."

"1 April 1644.—Ordered, that Captain Higgons do forthwith send up the plate, treasure, and other goods found in the Lord Montague's house."

"18 May 1644.—Ordered, that the goods brought up from Cowdray House in Sussex by order of this House be forthwith stored up in the stores of Cambden House." *

"6 June 1644.—Ordered, that the goods that are brought up which were seized at the Lord Montague's house in Sussex, and particularly those goods remaining at the Talbot in Southwark in Captain Higgons' custody, be carried into Cambden House, and that all the said goods be there sold at the best value."

These orders no doubt applied to Battle Abbey as well as to Cowdray, for the Battle estates were at that time valued at £1200 a year.

But Lord Montague had much to bear besides this spoliation.

When the Royalist general Sir Ralph Hopton surprised Arundel in the "exceeding hard frost" of December 1643, he left a garrison in Cowdray on his way. Lord Montague had no doubt given up his house to the soldiers, and he had wisely taken the precaution of covering the historical pictures painted in fresco on the walls with a thick coat of lime-wash. One of the officers, however, in exercising his partizan † against the wall, broke out from one picture the face of Henry the Eighth, and it had afterwards to be repainted. Some of the men, and many of the horses, were quartered at Easebourne Priory; and when, some two hundred years later, alterations were being made there by Mr. Alexander Brown, he found traces of this stable in a quantity of manure which had been covered over, and which lay where it had fallen, as fresh as if it had been there but a fortnight.

Sir William Waller, the Roundhead general (who was called by his friends William the Conqueror), marched hurriedly after Hopton. He wrote from Arundel to the House of Lords: "According to your commands I advanced the last Lord's Day from Farnham towards this place. I could not reach that night past Haslemere. The next day I marched to Cowdray,

---

* Cambden House was on Notting Hill.
† A kind of short pike. [*Halliwell.*]

where we, understanding there were four troopes of horse and one hundred foote, I resolved to give them the Good-night; and to that end I despatched away two regiments of horse to lay the passage round: but they were too nimble for me and escaped hither, where I overtook them on Tuesday night." The severe frost was no doubt of great service to Sir William Waller in his march through those roads which were described by Horace Walpole a century later as being "bad beyond all badness;" though letters from both armies complain of the "terrible coldness of the season."

In a paper by the Rev. H. D. Gordon, published in the *Sussex Archæological Collections*, vol. xxviii. p. 106, the following letter from an officer in Waller's army is given. It originally appeared in the *Mercurius Civicus* of December 21, 1643.

"Lord's Day, Dec. 10th, left Farnham about two of the clocke in the afternoon, marching towards Hazle*worth* [Hazlemere], our noble generall seeming to go another way to amaze the Papists and malignants, and the better to prevent intelligence; and about midnight came with his whole army to the said Towne where the Rendezvouz was that night. Monday, sunrising, his honour wheeled about towards Medhurst, where my Lord Mountacute's house is (Cowdray), which said Lord is a known and profest Papist: the house is now possest by the Parliament forces; where we staid that night and furnished the said castle (for indeed it may well be called so in regard of the strength thereof) with all necessaries for defence to awe the Papists and malignants, wherewith the s^d Towne is much infested and infected. Tuesday morning we marched from Medhurst, sending out a party of horse to Petworth, having thought to surprise the enemy there, but they fled before our successe, Hopton and the great ones to Winchester, and the rest to Arundel with bag and baggage: all that night we lay on a heath within a mile of Arundel."

The siege of Arundel began on Wednesday, December 13, 1643, and lasted till the 6th of the following January.

On Friday, the 29th of December, Waller recovered Chichester, and one of his soldiers says in his diary that for this "we brought our ammunition that was at Midhurst to Arundel." Mr. Gordon adds in a note that these stores were brought from Cowdray, which became from that time a Parliamentarian stronghold.

Some of Sir William Waller's troops were quartered in Midhurst church, where they amused themselves by firing bullets up into the roof. Many of these bullets were found during the recent restoration of the church, and it is remarkable that the Browne monument should have escaped injury at the hands of the Roundhead soldiers.

It is not to be wondered at that Lord Montague, after having been despoiled of his goods and plate, and after having had so large a body of troops quartered on him, was in great distress for money. One of his first attempts to improve his condition was by the sale of West Horsley. Evelyn writes in his Diary on September 14, 1665, "I went to Wotton, on 16 September to visite old Secretary Nicholas, being now at his new purchase of West Horsley, once mortgag'd to me by Lord Viscount Montague; a pretty drie seate on ye Downe."

But this sale represented but a small part of Lord Montague's pecuniary difficulties, and he determined to dispark the parks of Battle Abbey. In September and October 1659 he let the " Little Park of Battle " on lease to various persons; in February 1660 he let portions of " the Great Park of Battle lately disparked, containing by estimation three hundred acres more or less ;" and in December of the same year he let the dwelling-house called the " Almery or Almonry House, with the various parcels of land belonging thereto."

Lord Montague had thus every reason to avoid unnecessary expense ; but from the account-book of his steward from July 1657 to July 1658 he appears to have been most extravagant. In that one year he spent £1945, 10s. on the occasional items which were paid for by his steward. This sum appears large indeed when it is recollected that Lord Montague as a recusant had forfeited to the Commonwealth two-thirds of his estate. Among the papers at Battle Abbey were the following certificates:—" Certificate of the Value of the two-third parts of the Estates of Francis Viscount Montague of Battle, in the several Rapes of Lewes and Pevensey, sequestered for his recusancy. The whole Estate valued at 1,200*l.* per An. William Yalden of Blackdowne, Gent., offers to rent the two-thirds at 800*l.* per An. Exhibited to the Commissioners for Compounding of Sequestration, Dec. 16, 1650. Signed, Richard Sherwyn, Auditor, Oct. 15, 1651." " Certificate of the Value of the Estates of Francis Viscount Montague of Cowdry, in the several Rapes of Arundel and Chichester, the whole let at 1,575*l.* per An., two-thirds of which were sequestrated for his recusancy. William Yalden of Blackdowne, Gent., had agreed to rent the said two-thirds at 1,050*l.* per An. Exhibited before the Commissioners for Compounding, Nov.

22, 1650. Signed Richard Sherwyn, Auditor, Oct. 15, 1651." The curious account-book of Lord Montague's steward was preserved among the Battle Abbey muniments; and the following entries are interesting as showing the domestic expenses of a nobleman at that time.

Aug. 16, 1657. Paid the Bone-setter for setting Mrs. Hall's shoulder, 5s.
  ,, 19. Given to my Lady Gage's Coachman by my Lady's order, £1.
  ,, 23. Given to the Fidler for playing to my master, 1s. 6d.
Sept. 11. For two quarts of Acamarabilis,* which we had from London for my Lady, at 8s. the quart. For the bottle to put it in, 8d.
      For washing Will Stapler, 1s. 2d.
  ,, 23. Paid the fruiterer at Lewes for cherries and other things, £4, 1s.
Oct. 17. Accounts for the house here at London.†
      Crossing the water at Lambeth, 4d.
  ,, 20. Paid Mrs. Mary £3, 4s. which she laid out for two coats for my little Master and my little Mistress.
  ,, 29. Paid Mr. Staley the Goldsmith for the use of thirty-seven pound of Gold which my Lord had to Newmarket, at twopence a piece, £10, 6s.
      Paid‡ the Chairman for carrying my Lady to Whitehall, being three hours and a half, 3s.
Nov. 3. For a new Almanack, 2d.
      Paid the man of the Jackanapes £4, 0s. 6d. for things for my mistress.
      Paid Will Stapler 3d. which my Lord bid him give the chairmen for a link.
  ,, 15. Paid for two French caps laced with silver lace for my Master and Mistress, £1.
  ,, 22. Paid for a Torch, 8d.
      Given to Mr. Walsingham's keeper for a Doe, 10s.
      Paid Lewes Carrier for bringing a box of Puddings for my Mistress and my Master, and the Porters bringing them out of Southwark, 1s. 4d.
Dec. 10. Paid a Hackney-coachman for carrying my Lord, 3s.
      Given to the Minister of St. Giles by my Lord's order, 5s. §
1658. Jan. 17. Paid for sweeping four Chimnies, 2s.
      Paid Mr. Fiske the Dancing-master for teaching my Master to dance, being two months, £4.
Feb. 2. To a Link-boy for lighting my Lady, 2d.

---

* Aqua Mirabilis.   † The house at St. Mary Overy. See p. 19.
‡ From other payments in this book it appears that a sedan-chair could be hired for one shilling an hour.   § This was a half-yearly gift from Lord Montague.

Feb. 10. Paid the chairmen for carrying my Lord and my Lady to Sir John Thimblebe's supper, and waiting until 6 o'clock in the morning for my Lady.
„ 20. Paid the chairmen for carrying my Lady to the French Ambassador's supper, and fetching my Lord home, and waiting for my Lady until 7 o'clock in the morning.
Mar. 26. Paid Mr. Phillips for half a pound of Tobacco he bought for my Lord, 5s.
„ 30. Paid Mr. Houblon for a puncheon of Paris wine, £14.
April 5. For a bottle of Spruce-beer for my Mistress, 3d.
„ 17. Delivered to my Lord to give to the Nurse and Midwife at Mrs. Cornwallis' christening, £4.
„ 21. For a Tooth for my Lord, 7s.
May 13. Paid Hadlowe for scouring the hangings of the coach and the seats, 5s.
June 2. Given to one Mr. Huddleston * by my Lord's order, 10s.
July 2. Paid Rowland Rayler for two couples and a dog, £7, 14s.
For two bushels of Roses, 10d.

In 1666 a tax was levied which fell heavily upon Lord Montague. This was the subsidy by which the King took one pound in every hundred pounds of personal estate. Servants, both male and female, had to pay out of their wages one shilling in every pound; and for aliens these taxes were doubled. Extra payments were exacted from gentlemen of rank; a Duke being taxed £50, a Viscount £25, and the eldest son of a Viscount, if of age, £17, 10s. Among the old papers found at Cowdray was the assessment of the members of Lord Montague's family, and of his establishment, for these taxes.

In 1670, the hearth-money tax also pressed heavily upon Lord Montague. This was a tax of two shillings a year on each hearth in every house rated above twenty shillings a year; and the returns show that Lord Montague had seventy-seven hearths in Cowdray House.

The third Lord Montague died on the 2d of November 1682. His widow survived him only two years. She seems to have resided at Battle, for leases still exist which were granted there by her; and in 1683 George Packe was appointed "Receiver of the Rents, quit Rents, &c., of the

---

* This was Father Huddleston the Jesuit, who was brought by the Duke of York to Charles the Second on his death-bed, and who is said to have received the King's confession that he died a Roman Catholic.

Manors of Battle, Barneholme, Swinham, and Stone, in Sussex, by Elizabeth, Viscountess Dowager Montague."

Among the pictures which were burnt at Cowdray was one which represented this third Lord Montague and his wife, but it does not appear to have possessed any particular merit.

Anthony, the eldest son of Francis third Viscount Montague, is generally believed to have died unmarried during the lifetime of his father. But a different account is given in an article in *The Reliquary*, by Frederick Bradley [vol. v. No. 20, April 1865].

According to this account, Anthony quarrelled with his father and went abroad, reaching the Hague just at the time of the outbreak of the Civil War. He immediately returned to England, and joined the Royalist forces under the Earl of Newcastle. Anthony was wounded during the siege of York, in January 1644, just after his marriage to Bridget, daughter of James Maskew of York, "a devoted Royalist and the owner of large estates" in the county. Maskew and his two sons were killed at the battle of Marston Moor, 2d July 1644. Anthony Browne was made prisoner at the same time, but managed to escape into Derbyshire with a brother officer named Adlington of Adlington Hall in Cheshire. Anthony now assumed the name of John Hudson and placed himself under the protection of a Roman Catholic family, the Eyres of Newbold near Chesterfield. His wife, who had also been imprisoned, joined him at Newbold, his retreat having been made known to her by a faithful soldier who had fought under him at Marston Moor. They bought a house and a small piece of land at Newbold from the Eyres, and the place is still called Hudson's Yard. At the Restoration Anthony Browne petitioned the King for the restitution of his wife's estates, which had been seized by Cromwell on the death of her father and brothers. But Charles the Second had already granted them to Sir George Barlow, and refused to act further in the matter. From London, whither he had gone on this business, Anthony Browne proceeded to his old home at Cowdray. Here he found new servants, who did not know him, and was told that his father had left England for a time. Poor Anthony, sad and lame, returned slowly to his little home at Newbold, and died there very shortly afterwards.

Anthony Browne was buried in the ancient Roman Catholic chapel at Newbold. A tablet, surmounted by the Montague arms, was erected to his memory, and bore the following inscription :—

"To the memory of the Honourable Anthony Browne, eldest son of Francis Viscount Montague of Cowdray in Sussex, Major in the Volunteer Regiment at York, who was Wounded in the leg in a Sally from thence 1644. [He married Bridget Maskew, daughter of James Maskew of York Esquire, who, together with his two Sons, was killed at Marston Moor fighting for their King and Country.] He left two Sons and two Daughters, John, Gervase, Christian, and Martha. He departed this life May, 6, 1666, aged 46 years. Requiescat in Pace.

>'Tis very well known he had a great deal of trouble,
>He suffered with patience, 'cause God made him able :
>He liv'd a good Christian and hoped to get Heaven,
>And hoped that through Christ his sins would be forgiven."

This tablet does not now exist. The chapel was dismantled in the time of William the Third. It was afterwards used as a cowhouse, and all the monuments and tablets taken from it were made into mantelpieces, or lintels of doors and windows. A copy of the inscription was however preserved by Anthony's children ; and his widow (who survived him for thirty-four years) left a paper impressing on them the rightfulness of their claim to Cowdray and the Montague peerage. She seems to have been in some degree recognised by the Montague family, as she received constant presents from them.

John, the eldest son of Anthony, died unmarried. About 1689 Gervase, the second son, went to London to see his uncle, Francis fourth Viscount Montague. " He was duly acknowledged, and promised the next succession to the title, when, it was argued, he might have it without trouble or expense." (The fourth Lord Montague had no family.) Gervase registered his claim in the Heralds' Office, but in 1696 he died, twelve years before his uncle. In the meantime he had worked as a mason, and having bought a piece of "marble land" at Ashford, he supplied a quantity of the marble used in the building of Chatsworth. At his death his personal estate was valued at only £99, 5s. 2d.

The sons of Gervase Browne seem not to have put forward their claim to the Montague peerage. But his grandson, Joseph Browne, on the death by drowning of the young Viscount Montague in 1793, did endeavour to establish himself as the next heir. He was old at that time, and very poor, and was unable to incur the expense of collecting the necessary proofs for making out his claim. He however was not devoid of the pride of his family, for he refused an offer of ten thousand pounds, which was made to him on condition of his relinquishing all claim to the title and property.

Joseph Browne remained a small farmer, living at Lings, in the parish of North Wingfield, in Derbyshire, and there his descendants have continued. Their likeness to the pictures of the first Viscount Montague is said to be very remarkable.*

The author of the article in *The Reliquary* explained the quarrel between Anthony Browne and his father by saying that the third Viscount Montague joined the Parliamentary forces at the outbreak of the Civil Wars. But this is manifestly an error, for, as has been seen, the father was a sufferer for his adherence to the Royalist cause.

---

* I am indebted to the above-named article in *The Reliquary* for the whole of this information.

CHAPTER IX.

Cowdray in the Eighteenth Century.

RANCIS fourth Viscount Montague was probably educated abroad, as he always signed his name Montaigu. Before his time the spelling adopted had invariably been Mountague, but his successors signed themselves Montague until the title became extinct in 1797.

He married Lady Mary Herbert, daughter of William Marquess of Powys,* widow of Richard Molineux, eldest son of Carryl Viscount Molineux. Lady Mary was the sister of the courageous Countess of Nithisdale, who in February 1716 contrived her husband's escape from the Tower.

In 1687 Lord Montague was appointed Lord-Lieutenant of Sussex by James the Second, being probably chosen on account of his firm adherence to the Roman Catholic religion.

But he, too, was sadly in want of money, and he demolished the great kitchen at Battle Abbey in order to profit by the sale of the materials. This kitchen seems to have been in a fairly perfect condition until 1682, and was a large detached building roofed with lead. It was, in fact, so large that its destruction occupied four whole years. The materials were sold to the tenantry and neighbours; the stone fetched four and five shillings the cart-load, and the lead twelve shillings and sixpence the hundredweight. As "Goodman Griffin" in February 1686 paid ten pounds, and in the fol-

---

* Sir William Herbert, Baronet, created Earl of Powys 1674, Viscount Montgomery and Marquess of Powys 1687, outlawed 1689, died 1696. All these titles became extinct on the death of the third Marquess, unmarried, in 1748. [*Historic Peerage of England*, by Sir Harris Nicolas.]

lowing May twenty pounds "in part of money due for lead," and as the accounts for that year alone show that other persons took as much as two tons of lead (even more was sold in the two following years), the vast size of the building may be imagined.*

Lord Montague continued to let on lease any portions of the Parks of Battle which had not previously been disparked. He also let the Cherry Garden, of three acres, all planted with cherry trees, the "Barn called the Sacristy Barn, with ten closes of land," the Horse Race, the Two Butts, the "six closes of land known as the Deanery Land," and many other portions of the Abbey property. His father had in 1676 granted a lease of some land in Battle to a joiner named Hammond, "with permission to erect a Powder-Mill," and in 1690 he himself relet it to William Hammond, "Powder-Maker." This plot of four acres was called the Perperingeye Lands, and the powder-mills remained upon it until 1874.

It was in the time of this Lord Montague that so much damage was done all over England by the terrible storm, which, beginning on the 24th of November 1703, raged with undiminished violence for a whole week.† Defoe collected and published accounts of the ravages of this storm in different parts of the country, and among these descriptions is the following:—

"From Medhurst in Sussex the following Letter is a short account of the Lord Montacute in his Seat there, which is extraordinary great, tho' Abridg'd in the Letter:

"SIR,—I Receiv'd a Letter from you wherein you desire me to give you an Account of what Damage was done in and about our Town. I praise God we came off indifferent well; the greatest Damage we received was the untiling of Houses, and 3 Chimneys blown down. But 4 or 5 Stacks of Chimneys are blown down at my Lord Montacute's House, within a quarter of a mile of us; one of them fell on part of the Great Hall, which did Considerable Damage: and the Church Steeple of Osborn [Easebourne], half a mile from us, was blown down at the same time; and my Lord had above 500 Trees torn up by the Roots; and near us Several Barns blown down, one of Sir John Mills', a very large Tiled Barn. Your humble Servant, JOHN PRINKE.

"MEDHURST, *Jan.* 18, 170¾."

---

* In the *Beauties and Antiquities of Sussex*, by Rouse, published in 1825, with illustrations by the author, the view given of this kitchen represents only a crypt under the refectory of Battle Abbey. The original kitchen was razed to the ground in 1685. Browne Willis, writing in 1718, makes a somewhat similar mistake, imagining the refectory itself to have been the kitchen.

† "The Storm, or a Collection of the most Remarkable Casualties and Disasters which happened in the late Dreadful Tempest, both by Sea and Land." Published 1704.

Francis fourth Viscount Montague had no child. He died in 1708, and was buried at Midhurst under the great Browne monument.

His brother Henry succeeded him as fifth Viscount Montague.

Henry Lord Montague married Barbara, the daughter of James Walsingham of Chesterford in Essex, and grand-daughter of Theophilus second Earl of Suffolk. They had one son, Anthony, and five daughters. Mary, the eldest, died unmarried. Elizabeth became a nun at Pontoise in Normandy. Barbara married Ralph Salvin of Tudhow, in the county of Durham, and died in 1709, the year after her marriage, leaving one daughter, Dorothy Salvin, who died unmarried. Catharine married George Collingwood, a Northumberland gentleman, and had a daughter, who married Sir Robert Throgmorton. Anne married Anthony Kempe of Slindon, and had a daughter, who became the wife of Lord Kinard. Henrietta, the youngest, married Richard Harcourt, a merchant, who lived at Boulogne, and had one daughter. The fifth Lord Montague destroyed a further portion of Battle Abbey, and sold a great quantity of underwood there to " Farrett Holloway of Salehurst, Gun-founder, at the rate of five shillings for every coard,* after the custom of Sussex."

Henry Lord Montague survived his brother only nine years, and died at Epsom on the 25th of June 1717.

The curious traditions relating to the fifth Lord Montague will be found in the extracts from the *Story of a Curse* appended to this volume. It is impossible now to establish the accuracy of these stories, but they are firmly believed in Midhurst and in its neighbourhood, and appear to have been handed down from father to son with very little variation.

Another story is that a younger son of one of the Viscounts Montague was outlawed for some crime, and lived for many years concealed in a hiding-hole contrived in the small pavilion which stood in the centre of the Close Walks. The site of this pavilion may still be seen. It was close to the shores of the beautiful lake, now the wharf, and a little creek ran up to it, so that boats could be brought to the door of the building. This lake was the " verie goodlie fish-pond " on the banks of which the Angler and the Netter met Queen Elizabeth.

Anthony, the only son of Henry Lord Montague, succeeded his father as

---

* A Sussex coard of wood is 14 feet long, 3 feet wide, and 3 feet 2 inches high ; the extra two inches in height being allowed for shrinking or settling. [*Thorpe*, p. 143.]

sixth Viscount in the summer of 1717. Very soon after this he determined to sell Battle Abbey. Cowdray had now become the favourite residence of the family, and Battle in its dilapidated and forlorn condition had been abandoned to the smugglers, who found in its ruined vaults convenient hiding-places for their kegs of spirits and bales of silk.

In 1719 Lord Montague sold Battle Abbey and the whole of his property at Battle to Sir Thomas Webster, Bart. Sir Thomas Webster was an antiquary of some note, and was particularly anxious to purchase houses of archæological interest. He had already bought Copped Hall in Essex, and after he became the owner of Battle Abbey he bought Bodiham Castle and Robertsbridge Abbey, both in Sussex.*

Battle Abbey remained in the possession of the Webster family till 1857, in which year it was sold to Lord Harry Vane, now the fourth Duke of Cleveland.

The year after the sale of Battle Abbey the sixth Lord Montague married Barbara, third daughter of Sir John Webb, Bart., of Hathorp in Gloucestershire. They had two sons, the elder of whom died at Rouen when only a year old; the second was Anthony Joseph, who afterwards became seventh Viscount Montague. Their only daughter, Mary, was married in Cowdray House, September 30, 1761, to Sir Richard Bedingfield, Bart., of Oxburgh Hall in Norfolk.

In 1732 Lord Montague was chosen Grand Master of the Freemasons.†

In 1767 he died, at the age of eighty-two, and was buried "under a raised table-tomb of black marble in the cloister of Easebourne Priory, at the east end

---

* In 1834 Thomas Thorpe, bookseller, of 38 Bedford Street, Covent Garden, bought all the Battle Abbey muniments for less than £300 from Sir Godfrey Webster, the fourth Baronet. [This Sir Godfrey married Elizabeth Vassall, the rich Jamaica heiress, who afterwards became the celebrated Lady Holland of Holland House.]

Thorpe published in 1835 a Descriptive Catalogue "of the Original Charters, Royal Grants, and Donations, many with the seals, in fine preservation, the Monastic Chartulary, Official, Manorial, Court Baron, Court Leet, and Rent-Rolls, Registers, and other Documents, constituting the Muniments of Battle Abbey . . . . also a great mass of papers relating to the Family of Browne, ennobled as the Lords Viscount Montague, of such extent and importance as to render them a desideratum of much consequence in the Grand National Depositary . . . ." He adds, "It is presumed no collection of manuscripts of equal importance in a national point of view has ever been offered for sale. The whole bound in ninety-seven volumes, folio, uniform in Russia, Price Twelve Hundred Pounds." The collection was sold for the sum named to a well-known antiquary, Sir Thomas Phillips of Middle Hill, Broomsgrove.

† Dallaway's *History of Sussex*.

of the south aisle of the church."* Sir William Burrell, writing in 1778, says, "In a small ruined chancel, without roof or paving, the late Viscount Montague and many other Roman Catholics are buried without any inscription to commemorate them." † The names of these Roman Catholics are not to be found in the registers of Midhurst church, owing to the refusal of the then Incumbent, Serenus Barrett (1717 to 1758), to make any entry as to the baptism, marriage, or burial of a Romanist.

In 1749, during the life of the sixth Lord Montague, Horace Walpole visited Cowdray, and described it in the following letter to his friend George Montague : ‡—

"STRAWBERRY HILL, *August* 26, 1749.

"DEAR GEORGE, . . . Mr. Chute and I are returned from our expedition miraculously well, considering all our distresses. If you love good roads, conveniences, good inns, plenty of postillions and horses, be so kind as never to go into Sussex. We thought ourselves in the northest part of England ; the whole country has a Saxon air, and the inhabitants are savage, as if King George the Second was the first monarch of the East Angles. Coaches grow there no more than balm and spices ; we were forced to drop our post-chaise, that resembled nothing so much as Harlequin's calash, which was occasionally a chaise or a baker's cart. We journeyed over Alpine mountains drenched in clouds, and thought of Harlequin again when he was driving the chariot of the sun through the morning clouds, and so was glad to hear the aqua-vitæ man crying a dram. At last we got to Arundel Castle, which was visibly built for defence in an impracticable country. It is now only a heap of ruins, with a new indifferent apartment clapt up for the Norfolks when they reside there for a week or a fortnight. Their priest showed us about. There are the walls of a round tower, where a garrison held out against Cromwell : he planted a battery on the top of the church, and reduced them. There is a gloomy gateway and dungeons, in one of which, I conclude, is kept the old woman who, in the time of the late rebellion, offered to show Lord Robert Sutton where arms were hidden at Worksop (a seat of the Duke of Norfolk's in Nottinghamshire). The Duchess

---

* Dallaway's *History of Sussex*.
† Sir William Burrell may have been mistaken in this statement. The raised table-tomb of black marble still exists in Easebourne church. The inscription upon it states that it was erected in memory of the sixth Viscount Montague and his wife (who died in 1779) by their only surviving son, Anthony Joseph, seventh Viscount, in the year 1781. Underneath are the words "Requiescat in Pace." The tomb had not, therefore, been erected at the time of Sir William Burrell's visit to Easebourne.
‡ *Letters of Horace Walpole*, vol. ii, p. 299.

complimented him into dining before his search, and in the meantime the woman was spirited away, and adieu the arms. . . . We were charmed with the magnificence of the park at Petworth, which is Percy to the backbone, but the house and garden did not please our antiquarian spirit. The house is entirely new-fronted in the style of the Tuilleries, and furnished exactly like Hampton Court. There is one room gloriously flounced all round by whole-length pictures, with much the finest carving by Gibbons that ever my eyes beheld. There are birds absolutely feathered, and two antique vases with bas-relieves as perfect and beautiful as if they were carved by a Grecian master. There is a noble Claude Lorrain, a very curious picture of the haughty Anne Stanhope, the Protector's wife (second wife of Edward Duke of Somerset, Protector in reign of his nephew, Edward the VI.), pretty, but not giving one an idea of her character, and many old portraits; but the housekeeper was at London and we did not learn half. The chapel is grand and proper. . . . Our greatest pleasure was seeing Cowdry, which is repairing: Lord Montacute will at last live in it. We thought of old Margaret of Clarence, who lived there; one of her accusations was built on the bulls found there. It was the palace of her great-uncle, the Marquess Montacute. I was charmed with the front, and the court, and the fountain, but the room called Holbein's, except the curiosity of it, is wretchedly painted, and infinitely inferior to those delightful stories of Harry the VIII. in the private apartments at Windsor. I was much pleased with a whole-length picture of Sir Anthony Browne in the very dress in which he wedded Anne of Cleeves by proxy. He is in blue and white, only his right leg is entirely white, which was robed for the act of putting into bed to her. But when the king came to marry her, he only put his leg into bed to kick her out. I have set up my staff, and finished my pilgrimages for this year. Sussex is a great damper of curiosity. Adieu! My compliments to your sisters."

Anthony Joseph, seventh Viscount Montague, succeeded his father in 1767. He was the first of his family to forsake the Roman Catholic faith. This was probably owing to the influence of his wife, Frances Mackworth, widow of Alexander Lord Halkerton.* She was a devoted friend and follower of Selina Countess of Huntingdon. Lady Huntingdon was a very distant cousin of Lord Montague, and was much in Sussex after he succeeded to the title. She founded chapels at Petworth and at Emsworth,

---

* The wedding waistcoat of the seventh Viscount Montague is in the possession of Mr. Peter Aylwin of Haslemere. It is of silver brocade, beautifully embroidered in coloured silks. The deep flaps of the pockets are covered with embroidered flowers of different sorts, and there is a border of the same work all round the waistcoat.

FOUNTAIN FROM COWDRAY.

and spent some time at Chichester. She preached at Cowdray, standing under the great chestnut-trees, and encouraged Lady Montague to follow her example. There is a curious engraving from a picture of Lady Huntingdon (the picture itself has disappeared) in which she is represented in the act of trampling on her coronet and holding up a crown of thorns. It is easy to trace in her countenance that spirit which was the secret of her influence. No doubt she believed that she was in all things acting from the highest motives, and that the neglect of her own relations, her overbearing, masterful conduct towards others (so painfully apparent in her Memoirs), were but part of her duty. Many persons might, however, be tempted to apply to Lady Huntingdon herself the description given by Mr. Toplady of Mr. Parker in a letter to her dated 1776:—"I have known Mr. Parker well, and he is among that particular sort of good men whom I hope to meet in heaven, but with whom I must beg to be excused from having much personal intercourse on earth."

Lord Montague kept a pack of buck-hounds at Cowdray. He made many alterations both in the park and in the house; and, according to Horsfield, he "attempted to render the vicinity of the park, which is sterile and capable of little improvement, more agreeable by plantations of fir, which in some measure have the desired effect." In 1770 he put himself into the hands of "Capability Brown," the celebrated landscape-gardener; and though it is to be feared that Brown "improved" the Close Walks by destroying a considerable portion of the thickets and trees which had formed their chief beauty, there is no doubt that he showed great taste in the planting of trees, both singly and in groups, in the park. Cowdray Park is one of the most beautiful in England, and its trees are celebrated. The Spanish chestnuts are said to be the finest in England, and Brown fortunately spared the magnificent avenue of these trees (many of which are fifteen feet in girth at three feet from the ground), which stretches for a mile and a half along one side of the Park.

The alterations made by Lord Montague in Cowdray House were unfortunate. He attempted to modernise the rooms in what Dallaway wisely calls "the false taste of that day." He employed Italian artists to decorate the staircase and some of the rooms, and the effect thus produced was entirely out of character with the date and style of the building.

But the occupation in which Lord Montague chiefly delighted was turning. In one of the rooms there was a picture of him at his turning-wheel; and there was also a cabinet filled with "very neat pieces of ivory work, many of them consisting of small and delicate flowers," all turned by him.

In the autumn of 1782 Dr. Johnson visited Cowdray. He was spending some time at Brighton with Mr. Philip Metcalfe, "being pleased at once with his excellent table and animated conversation." Johnson made many expeditions with Mr. Metcalfe, who had placed his carriage at his disposal. "They went together to Chichester, and they visited Petworth and Cowdray, the venerable seat of the Lords Montacute. 'Sir,' said Johnson, 'I should like to stay here four-and-twenty hours. We see here how our ancestors lived.'"

In 1783 Lord and Lady Montague settled at Brussels, and there, on Easter Sunday, the 11th of April 1787, Lord Montague died.

A few days before his death Lord Montague sent for the Abbé Mann, "and declared his regret and remorse for having abandoned the Catholic religion in which he had been educated. He solemnly and repeatedly protested that it had been no conviction of the truth of the Protestant religion which had made him take that step, but, on the contrary, what his Lordship termed the vilest of motives, to wit, libertinism both in faith and morals, ambition, and interest." The Abbé satisfied himself that Lord Montague's desire to return to the faith of his ancestors was sincere, and "his reconciliation [to the Roman Catholic Church] was accordingly performed with all its circumstances, during which his Lordship behaved with a becoming piety and perfect presence of mind." He then desired the Abbé Mann "to make his dying sentiments and declarations as publickly known to the world as it should be possible for him to do." This the Abbé (who was "very able and full of knowledge," a Canon of Courtray and Secretary to the Imperial Academy of Sciences at Brussels) did by means of a long letter to the *Gentleman's Magazine*. In this letter he explained that the death of the late Lord Montague was accompanied with circumstances that gave rise to considerable dispute in Flanders, "a noble lord[*] in a distinguished situation having said that he was literally besieged and taken by assault by the Roman Catholic clergy." The Abbé, who had "set out in a military line of life," defended himself and his fellow-clergy from this accusation with much warmth and at great length. His letter provoked several replies;

---

[*] This appears to have been the fourth Viscount Torrington.

in one of them a correspondent of the *Gentleman's Magazine*, who signed himself "Christ-Cross in the Corner," thus disposed of two of Lord Montague's reasons for abandoning the Roman Catholic faith :—

"*Ambition*.—Lord Montague was not distinguished in the House of Lords, where his renunciation enabled him to take his seat, and where, if he had ambition, was the opportunity of putting himself in the way to gratify it. *Interest*.—It would be too ridiculous to suppose that his Lordship could mean a reduction of those taxes which our law subjects a Roman Catholic to, but which the mildness of those who execute the laws seldom exacts."

This curious correspondence will be found in the *Gentleman's Magazine* for 1787, vol. lvii. parts 1 and 2.

Another account of the reconciliation of Lord Montague to the Roman Catholic Church is preserved among the records of the Benedictine Abbey of St. Scholastica at Teignmouth. Father Peter Joseph Rivers, S.J., was confessor to the English Benedictine nuns at Brussels in 1787, and was sent for by Lord Montague during his last illness. "Father Rivers was sent for on Tuesday in Holy Week to visit him. The secular chapel attached to the convent church was constantly attended by a poor man, who on account of his rare piety was considered by the neighbours a saint, and who usually spent many hours there in prayer. Father Rivers, before starting on his visit, asked this good man to pray for the Viscount's conversion. 'I will pray for him,' he replied, 'and I will not leave the church until my prayer is granted.' And such was his fervour that he continued his supplications the whole of the day and the following night and part of the next day without quitting the chapel. Father Rivers meantime was with the dying peer, whose wife, being a bigoted Protestant, endeavoured by every possible means to prevent her husband from being alone with him, hoping thus to hinder the sick man from making his confession. But her vigilance was happily eluded. Lord Montague became truly contrite, received all the last sacraments, and gave up his soul to God, assisted by the zealous Father, who remained constantly by him until Easter Day, when he peaceably expired."—*Records of the English Province of the Society of Jesus*, vol. vii. p. 143.

Lord and Lady Montague had only two children, a son and a daughter. The daughter, Elizabeth Mary, was born on the 5th of February 1767, and the son, George Samuel, on the 26th of June 1769.

Lady Montague survived her husband for twenty-seven years, and died in 1814 at the age of eighty-three. She was buried at Easebourne. The body of Lord Montague had been brought from Brussels and buried at Easebourne on the 5th of May 1787.

Early in the eighteenth century the Lordship of the Borough of Midhurst became alienated from the Lordship of the Manor, and several persons acquired shares in it under marriage settlements by which it was transferred. The seventh Viscount Montague repurchased these different interests. But during the minority of his son, George Samuel, eighth Viscount, the Lordship of the Borough was again sold. The purchaser was the Earl of Egremont; but in a short time it was re-sold by him.

Several letters from the seventh Viscount Montague were found by Sir Sibbald Scott, by whose kindness I am enabled to publish some of them.

"QUEEN ANN STREET, 17*th April* 1782.

"MR. NEWMAN,—Send up by the Chichester Coach on Friday one of the young Guinea Fowls.

"I have some reason to think there will be an opposition in the County. I therefore wish my Friends had a hint given them (without making use of my Name) not to engage their Votes.—I am, yours, &c., MONTAGUE."

"BRUSSELS, 22*d December* 1784.

"MR. NEWMAN,—I have received your unsatisfactory Letter of the 16th instant, the only one I have had since the 8th November. I call it so as it really is, as I have had no answers to the different orders I gave you, and questions I asked in two or three Letters I wrote you Since the 8th November. If You have wrote me any Letter betwixt the 8th November and the 16th December, send me a Copy of it, as possibly the Original was lost. I have asked what Servants you have at present at Cowdray and to know the amount of their Board Wages. I have heard Nothing of Mr. Luff's Estimate of the Timber on the Farms intended to be exchanged with Lord E. Nor of the Timber I can cut this year. You have never told me if Mr. Sandham had or intended to hold all my Courts in the West before Christmas as I had desired. Has Iping pond been fished and what fish did it produce. Have you disposed of the Turkeys and Fowls as I directed. Have my mares been taken up. I Desired no Doe Venison might be given to any body, except half a Doe to Lady Catharine and the Do. to Mr. Atkins, in the Neighbourhood of Cowdray.

"3 or 4 Does to be divided betwixt Sir Richard Bedingfeld and Mrs. Mackworth, and a Couple at least sent over here if fat and the weather was favourable. I have not had a Doe nor a Word on the Subject. I wish to know Mr. Warden's Situation, whether alive or in danger or past recovery. I also should have been glad to have been informed of the amount of the monthly Bills. Let me know when you close the half year at Christmas what you have received and disbursed Since Midsummer, and the Balance [will] pay your half year's Salary and Mr. Luff's. When you return from the East let me know the neat Cash you bring home and what the whole disbursements amounted to without sending me particulars in your usual way. I shall be glad also soon after your return to know the whole balance of your book, the rents from the East included. Inform me whether you wrote to me betwixt the 8th November and 16th December, which will clear the matter up. I intend to write again soon.—I am, yours, &c., MONTAGUE.

"Has there been any fines paid for admissions at Cocking."

"BRUSSELS, 9*th September* 1785.

"MR. NEWMAN,—Mr. Astle of the Society of Antiquaries will write you a Letter by a Person I have given leave to take a Copy of the procession of Edward the Sixth in the parlour at Cowdray, and I desire you will let him have every Convenience for that purpose, but he is not to take any *other* Copies of paintings in the House without applying to me: in haste.—Yours, &c., MONTAGUE.

"To Mr. Newman,
    Cowdray, Midhurst, Sussex,
        Angleterre.
Par Ostende."

"BRUSSELS, 1*st February* 1786.

"MR. NEWMAN . . . . It was quite right of you to give me the information you did from the East. I take it Well and it was Your Duty. There are Several Executors to Mr. Warden's will, and some gentlemen of good fortune, family, and character, but unfortunately this Attorney is the only one that Acts, and I am very sorry he exposes my Debt So much and refuses the Court Books: they were Never intended to be a Security for the money, as great part was lent in my Father's time before Mr. Warden was in possession of the Books. I have always wrote word to the Attorney I would get the Money as fast as I could and pay it in as I could meet with it: and the interest has been punctually paid to Christmas last. I really have the whole principal at my Bankers, but I want it for other purposes and therefore cannot conveniently spare it. I will think of the business and write to you again upon it; in the mean time if you hear any thing more about it inform me. I have some thoughts of sending you over to Mr. Sargenson who lives at or near Cuckfield, one of the Executors. I will write to you about Croydon another time, but in the present Situation of things, I believe I shall let Wildgoose stay till Midsummer.

"Mr. Sandham is welcome to the pheasants and young trees you mention. I will not take any thing from Mr. Parsons for the use of the house.

"Send up directed to Israel Mauduit, Esq., two brace of large Tench and one brace of the largest Carp you have in the Ponds near the House. I want to know the Size of the largest Tench you have, and the number of large ones, as I have thoughts of having some put into the large Pond at Cocking.

"Why don't you send me the Estimates of the Timber. I am, yours, &c.,
"MONTAGUE."

The last letter from Lord Montague which was found is as follows:—

"BRUSSELS, 26th December 1786.

"MR. NEWMAN,—The last Letter I received from you was dated the 14th. No mail from England to-day. Desire Mr. Higinson to Pack up carefully my Silver Epergne with all the Baskets, &c., belonging to it. I think there is a leather case in which all the different Baskets fit; send it afterwards to Mr. Fogg, who will forward it to me. Desire Mr. Higinson to weigh the silver part of it, and let me know its exact weight. I have it already, but desire it may be weighed again. When you return from the East you will let me know what money you bring with you, and pay all you can to Messrs. Hoares. I suppose Mr. Bull's money will be ready without fail next month. Give the guineas and half guineas as Christmas Boxes to those I gave to last year.—I am, yours, &c., MONTAGUE."

The following letter from Lady Montague appears to have been written from London on the occasion of the rejoicings for the recovery of George the Third :—

"Ap. 22nd, 1789.

"MR. NEWMAN,—I'm afraid ye ribon came too late for ye rejoicing Day. I am very glad it went off so well. The address was presented yesterday I understood. The Cyder arrived safe. We are to have more Illuminations on Friday next, I hear. My Daughter was at ye Opera House last night, and there was ye Greatest Crowd ever known they say. Mr. Fogg furnished 5 thousand Dishes and 12 thousand plates . . . W^d you be so good to tell me If I had a loaf of bread up every week what it w^d come to wth ye carriage, perhaps not much more than ye bread here, w^h is very bad.—Your sincere Friend and Humble Servant, F. M.

"*P.S.*—Y^e Fowl is exceeding good."

One letter from Lord Montague's son was found : it seems to show that the relations between father and son were not very cordial :—

"WINCHESTER, *July 9th*, '86.

"MR. NEWMAN,—I write to inform you that I have just received a Letter from Brussells, and in which I am sorry to say my Father does not consent to my coming over to him this summer. I think by that it is his intention to return to England in the autumn. If you should hear anything about it, I should be obliged to you if you would write, as I am very anxious to know. Direct to me at Winchester till the 22nd of this month, and afterwards to Mr. Fogg.—I am,

"G. S. BROWNE."

Another letter, without date, appears by the handwriting to have been written by this young man after his succession to the title. It is as follows :—

"CAVENDISH STREET.

"MR. NEWMAN,—We shall all be at Cowdray on Thursday Night, but not to dinner, as we intend dining upon the Road : the Room that Miss Gage slept in last summer must be got ready. I have at length fix'd the first week in September for my going abroad, and have settled everything accordingly.

"MONTAGUE."

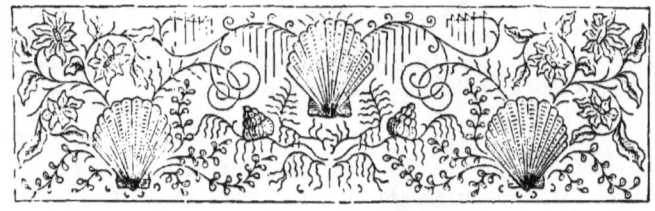

CHAPTER X.

George Samuel, eighth Viscount Montague.

HE eighth Viscount Montague was only eighteen at the time of his father's death. Both he and his sisters were brought up by their mother in the strictest school of Calvinistic Protestantism. Lord Montague, however, was sent to Winchester, and when at home he seems to have chafed and fretted against the severity of his mother's religious views.

In the summer of 1793, when the young Lord Montague was twenty-four, he determined to go abroad with his friend Charles Sedley Burdett, the grandson of Sir Robert Burdett, Bart., of Foremark in Derbyshire, and elder brother of the celebrated Sir Francis Burdett. According to the *Gentleman's Magazine*, Lord Montague on his return was to have married " the amiable and accomplished Miss Coutts, to whose sister Mr. Burdett was some time since united."

The two young men were bent on making an attempt to shoot the Falls of the Rhine at Laufenburg, a place about half-way between Basle and Schaffhausen. Both were first-rate boatmen, and they are said to have had a boat built expressly for this rash venture. The magistrates of the district endeavoured to prevent Lord Montague and his friend from risking their lives in so foolhardy an enterprise, and even placed soldiers on the banks of the river in order to stop them from launching their boat. But the infatuated young men contrived to elude the vigilance of these persons.

At the last moment, Dickenson, an old family servant, who had accompanied Lord Montague from Cowdray, tried to hold his young master back. He seized Lord Montague by the collar just as he was getting into the boat, but the foolish youth wrenched himself away, leaving part of his collar and neckcloth in poor Dickenson's hand, jumped into the boat, and immediately pushed off with his companion.* The following account of the accident was in 1867 taken down from the lips of an old man of eighty-five, who had, when a boy of eleven, been an eye-witness of the event :—

"Johannes Roller, a butcher here at Laufenburg, born in 1782, who is still in good health and vigorous, relates the story as follows :—Two Englishmen (he does not know their names) came with a servant, with travelling baggage, and a large black dog, in a small boat, round built before and behind, not pointed at the ends like our boats here. They were travelling along the Rhine, and stopped at the landing-place behind the inn called *Bear*, but they lodged at the *Eagle*, still the best inn at Laufenburg.

"These gentlemen made known that they intended to row and float through the cataract. All warning from the inhabitants representing that the attempt would certainly prove fatal was disregarded. They entered their small boat with their dog, the servant remaining behind, and passed the bridge down the Laufen.† At the first great surge the gentleman who was foremost in the boat fell or jumped into the Rhine; the boat was upset at the second wave of the Laufen, and the person who had remained in the boat swam with his companion, one after the other, through the Laufen, sometimes visible, sometimes concealed from view, and their dog with them.

"They were last seen swimming at the spot called Oelberg (Mount of Olives or Calvaire), and there, in the so-called strait, they disappeared in a vortex or eddy, and were never seen again, nor were their bodies recovered. At this strait of the channel of the Rhine the river has a great depth, more than 100 feet; indeed along the whole length of the rapids the depth is very great. The banks were crowded with spectators, but nobody could save the Englishmen, who swam together, endeavouring, as it appeared, to lay hold of the boat that was overset and floating along the current, but they could not reach it. They sank exhausted in the whirlpool into the depths, and their dog with them.

"Johannes Roller says that he stood on the bank behind the inn of the *Peacock*, and tried to get out with a long pole a small oar belonging to the boat. The servant remained at Laufenburg, and after a while departed with

---

* *Sussex Archæological Collections*, vol. xx. † Rapids.

the trunks. On two occasions afterward persons came from England and promised a large reward (1500 francs) for the discovery of the bodies, but they never reappeared."

The body of Lord Montague was, however, found. Mr. Wickham,[*] when acting as Chargé-d'Affaires at Berne, wrote to Lord Grenville on the 31st of May 1795 as follows:—

"MY LORD,—I have the honour to inform your Lordship that I have received, and in compliance with Lord Robert Fitzgerald's general directions, have opened a Letter addressed to his Lordship from the magistrates of Lauffenbourg, in which they state that the Body of the late Viscount Montague had been found in the Rhine very near the place where the melancholy accident happened that was the occasion of his Death; that as his remains were not in a situation to be embalmed they had caused them to be decently interred in the Churchyard of that place. I have not failed to return them all suitable thanks and acknowledgments for the attention they have shown on this occasion in paying the last honours to a Subject of his Majesty and a Peer of Great Britain. I have at the same time written to the Baron de Degelmann to request that he would give the necessary orders that a permission may be obtained for the remains to be removed to Bruck, the nearest Protestant town, in case the thing should be possible, and have applied to the Government here to give directions to the magistrates of that place that they may be interred there with the proper ceremonies. I have also taken care to communicate all these circumstances to his Lordship's Representatives."

At the time of Mr. Wickham's letter both Laufenburg and Brugg were under the dominion of the Canton of Berne, and he evidently addressed himself to the Bernese Government. Through the kindness of Mr. Adams, H.B.M.'s Minister at Berne, I am able to give a translation of an extract from the Archives of the Canton:—

"*Rath Manual of the Town of Berne*, 439, p. 369. *June* 5, 1795.

"*To the town of Brugg.*—The English Chargé-d'Affaires resident here has given us notice that Lord Montaigu, the last of his race, who was unfortunately drowned in the Falls of the Rhine by Schaffhausen, will be taken from Laufenburg to Bruck, in order that he may be buried there on Protestant ground. As we have no hesita-

---

[*] *Correspondence of Right Hon. William Wickham*, vol. i. p. 63. Mr. Wickham acted as Chargé-d'Affaires in Switzerland during the absence of the Minister, Lord Robert Fitz-Gerald. Almost immediately after the date of this letter Mr. Wickham was appointed Minister Plenipotentiary to the Swiss Cantons and the Grisons, in succession to Lord Robert Fitz-Gerald.

tion in giving our consent hereto, we desire to inform you thereof, and at the same time to charge you to make proper arrangements in order that the dead body of this unfortunate Englishman shall immediately after its arrival at Brugg be buried in God's Acre there in a respectable manner according to his position."

In the *Necrologium* or Register of Deaths at Laufenburg no mention is made of the death of Lord Montague or his friend. The Canton of Aargau, in which Laufenburg is situated, being strictly Roman Catholic, no entry appears to have been made in the registers with reference to Protestants.

At the time Schaffhausen, and not Laufenburg, was generally believed to have been the scene of the accident, Laufenburg having been almost unknown to English travellers. The *Annual Register* fell into this error in stating that Lord Montague and Mr. Burdett were drowned in an attempt to shoot the Falls of Schaffhausen. Such an attempt could not possibly have been made at those Falls. But at Laufenburg the rapids have been descended by boats with the help of ropes, although the enterprise is one of extreme danger. At this spot the Rhine makes a bend "and sweeps in a sort of torrent under a very picturesque and lofty bridge of one arch. Almost immediately below this bridge a large rock stands up in the middle of the stream, and this interruption to its rapid course seems to create a strong eddy, particularly on the left bank. It is altogether a very dangerous place, but still one that a daring boatman might attempt with some little chance of success." *

A letter from Lord Montague to his steward at Cowdray desiring him to make preparations for his return is now in the possession of Mr. Richard Fisher, of Hill Top near Midhurst, by whose kindness I am allowed to publish it : †—

"VENICE, *May* 19*th*.

"MR. NEWMAN,—I rec^d your letter in answer to mine of some late date in March, and also two others mentioning the money that you had pay'd into Sir

---

* *Sussex Archæological Collections*, vol. xx. In vol. xxvi. of the same *Collections* Mr. Greaves maintains that the attempt to shoot the Falls of Schaffhausen was possible, and he considers that the two young men were drowned in the pool at the bottom of the lower fall at Schaffhausen.

† It is not known whether Lord Montague returned to Cowdray for his birthday (June 26), and then set off to the Rhine, or whether he changed his plans and remained abroad till the preparations for his foolish adventure were completed. The former course appears from various circumstances to have been the most probable.

Robt Herries' hands; both of which I've answer'd, and hope by this time you have rec^d.

"I purpose by the latter end of this week to set out on my journey for England, where I fully intend to be either before or by the 20th of June, and shall certainly be at Cowdray on my birthday, therefore I beg you'll have everything in Readiness.

"I wish to have my Grey Mare taken up from grass, also the little Poney's and two or three others, those which you think the best. Sufficiency of Port Wine may be lay'd in immediately, and everything else which you think in the least necessary. The Port Wine may be had of Williams at Chichester, who I shou'd wish to employ.

"Direct your next letter to Calais Poste restante.—I remain, &c., &c., &c.,

"MONTAGUE."

The eighth Lord Montague was only twenty-four at the time of his death, the exact date of which has never been ascertained. "In October 1793" is the only date given in the contemporary notices of the event. By his will, dated the 13th of November 1792, Lord Montague left all his property to his sister, Elizabeth Mary Browne, who was then twenty-six.

There is in existence an engraving from a portrait of this Lord Montague. It belongs to Mr. Richard Fisher, and it appears to have been originally taken from a miniature.

The messenger sent back to England with the sad news of the young Lord Montague's death crossed another who was hastening from Cowdray with the tidings of the destruction of the house by fire. It is even said that the two couriers met at Calais.

Lord Montague, as has been said, left the whole of his property to his sister, but the title devolved on Mark Anthony Browne, who was descended from John, brother of Anthony Maria second Viscount Montague [p. 47].

Mark Anthony was born on the 2d of March 1744,* and had become a Friar at Fontainebleau. On the death of the young Lord Montague he received a Papal dispensation from his vows in order that he might marry and carry the title back to the Roman Catholic branch of the family. He did not, however, marry till 1797, four years after his succession to the title as ninth Viscount Montague.

In the list of marriages given in the *Annual Register* for 1797 the

---

* The following entry appears in the Register Book of the Parish of Easebourne :—

"1744. Mark Anthony Brown ye Son of Mark Brown Esquire (his Parents being of ye Romish Perswasion) was said to be baptized March 10th." (Signed) HENRY WOOD, Vicar. *November* 28, 1883.

following announcement appears: *—" Feb. 6.—Lord Viscount Montague to Miss Frances Manby, second daughter of the late Thomas Manby, Esq. of Beads-Hall, Essex." But in the following month of November the last Lord Montague died at Great Badow in Essex, without hope of an heir, and the title thereupon became extinct.

His body was brought to Midhurst in a gorgeous coffin, on which was a large crucifix of gold. It lay in state at the Angel Inn, and was buried under the Browne monument in Midhurst church.

In the list of deaths for 1797 recorded in the *Annual Register* an account of Lord Montague's claims is given as follows:—" Nov. 27th.—Lord Viscount Montague, who, though his connexion with the Sussex family does not appear in the peerages, had an undoubted right to the title which he assumed."

The three baronetcies which had been conferred upon members of the Browne family, the branches of which were settled at Betchworth in Surrey, and at Kiddington and Caversham in Oxfordshire, have all died out, though possibly collateral descendants exist. Dallaway says that "a branch, according to uncertain tradition, of this family was settled in Ireland in 1565; the ancestor having accompanied Sir H. Sydney, Lord-Deputy, from whom the present Marquess of Sligo is descended."

But in the death of the ninth Viscount Montague the family became extinct in the male line.

---

* The marriage took place at Little Bursted.

CHAPTER XI.

The Last of the Browne Family at Cowdray.

ELIZABETH MARY BROWNE, the only sister of the eighth Viscount Montague, a beautiful and an excellent woman, succeeded to the Cowdray estates on the death of her brother. On the 1st of September 1794 she married William Stephen Poyntz, Esq. of Midgham, near Newbury in Berkshire, who was three years younger than herself. Mr. Poyntz was a remarkably handsome man, very tall, and with a bright fresh complexion. His grandfather, the Right. Hon. Stephen Poyntz, Minister at Soissons in 1728, had had charge of the education of William, the "Butcher" Duke of Cumberland. Caroline, Princess of Wales, mother of the Duke, placed in the grounds at Midgham a very beautiful vase, ornamented with figures in high relief, representing the life of man, as a mark of her esteem for her son's governor.* (The Browne and Poyntz families were already connected, for about the year 1530 John Poyntz had married Catherine Browne of Betchworth, cousin of Sir Anthony Browne of Battle Abbey.) Mr. Poyntz sat in the House of Commons for many years; he represented Callington in Cornwall, Ashburton, Chichester, and Midhurst. In politics he was a Whig, being a follower of his friend Lord Althorp.

On the return of Mr. and Mrs. Poyntz from their honeymoon, they were met at the great gates of Cowdray Park by a crowd of the tenants on the estate, and were drawn to the entrance of the house by a number of boys dressed in white.

---

* This large vase is now in the possession of Mr. Alexander Brown.

But in spite of this kind welcome, Mrs. Poyntz must have felt that her return to Cowdray was a time of sorrow rather than of joy. Before her eyes was the blackened ruin of her beautiful old home, that magnificent seat of her ancestors, in which she felt so much interest and pride; and in her heart was the sad remembrance of the death of her only brother, to whom she had been devotedly attached. The accident to Lord Montague, and the fire at Cowdray, had both taken place only the year before Mrs. Poyntz's marriage.

Cowdray was no longer habitable, but in that year, 1794, the keeper's lodge in the park (about half-a-mile from the great house) was enlarged, and there Mr. and Mrs. Poyntz resided. They lived very quietly; and Mrs. Poyntz's mother, the Dowager Viscountess Montague, lived with them.

In 1801 a son was born to Mr. and Mrs. Poyntz, and was named William Montague Browne. In 1805 they had a second son, christened Courtenay John Browne.* They had also three daughters. The eldest, Frances Selina, married, 4th August 1814, Robert Cotton St. John, eighteenth Lord Clinton. After his death Lady Clinton married, in 1835, Sir Horace Seymour, K.C.B. She died in 1875. Elizabeth Georgina, the second daughter, married, 23d February 1830, the Hon. Frederick Spencer, R.N., afterwards fourth Earl Spencer, K.G.,† and was the mother of John Poyntz, the present Earl Spencer, K.G., and of Lady Sarah Spencer. Countess Spencer died in 1851. The youngest Miss Poyntz, Isabella, one of the greatest beauties of her time, married, 12th May 1824, Brownlow second Marquess of Exeter, K.G. She died in 1879, having survived both her sisters. Lady Exeter was the mother of the present Marquess of Exeter.

Poor old Lady Montague never recovered from the shock of her son's death, and was continually haunted by the fear that her two grandsons would be drowned.‡ "If they were out of her sight, she was always a prey to anxiety, especially if she knew they were near the river; and in her old age, when her powers were failing her, she would go to a large stone basin in the grounds and grope in it with her silver-handled stick, under the impression that her grandsons would be drowned there. 'Bessy,' she would say to the

---

* Two groves of oak-trees were planted in Cowdray Park by Mr. Poyntz, and called after his sons, who held the trees for the men as they planted them. These groves are close to the Easebourne gate of the park; the one on the east was called Montague after the eldest son, and that on the west Courtenay after the younger boy.

† Mr. Poyntz's aunt, Margaret Georgina Poyntz, had married John, first Earl Spencer.

‡ *Story of a Curse.*

house-steward's daughter, who often aided her failing steps, 'Bessy, I *know* it will come to them, as it came to my boy.' And then she would stand gazing at the weeds and floating water-lilies with a look of stony terror which had never left her since the Rhine had rolled its waters over the son of her love and pride."

But Lady Montague was spared the trial which was so soon to fall upon her daughter, Mrs. Poyntz. In the summer of 1814, shortly before the marriage of her eldest grand-daughter to Lord Clinton, she died at the age of eighty-three.

In June 1815 Mr. and Mrs. Poyntz, accompanied by their two sons (one aged fourteen and the other aged only ten) and their two unmarried daughters, went to Bognor, where they occupied the Pavilion House. The two Miss Parrys, daughters of Admiral Parry, who were connections of Mrs. Poyntz, came to pay them a visit.

On the 7th of July, as the weather was very warm and the sea quite calm, Mr. Poyntz proposed to take the whole party out in a boat. Mrs. Poyntz, who had a terror of the sea, strongly objected, but she was at last persuaded into giving a most reluctant consent to the expedition. Mr. Poyntz and his two sons set off accompanied by the two Miss Parrys: his daughter Isabella (afterwards Lady Exeter) was left behind, as she was not ready in time. She had been unpunctual before, and Mr. Poyntz said he would not wait for her. Her sister Elizabeth (afterwards Lady Spencer) remained with her to share her punishment. Both sisters ran down to the boat to see the party off, and the youngest boy gave to Lady Exeter a little locket which he always wore, begging her to keep it safe till he came back.

Mrs. Poyntz and her two daughters sat at the window in the Pavilion House watching the boat. All went well till towards the middle of the afternoon, when a sudden puff of wind struck the sail, and the boat was at once capsized.

The account of the accident was thus given in the *Gentleman's Magazine* (Part ii. vol. lxxxv. p. 79), July 7, 1815:—" In the afternoon, about four o'clock, as Colonel Poyntz, his two sons, and their tutor,* Miss Parry and Miss Emily Parry (daughters of the late Admiral Parry of Fareham), a fisherman and his son, were returning to land at Bognor in a pleasure yacht,

---

* The tutor was an Oxford man and a first-rate swimmer. He is said to have supported Mr. Poyntz for some time in the water. A more probable account is that Mr. Poyntz and the boatman clung to the mast of the capsized boat until they were saved by assistance from the shore.

a sudden gust of wind upset the boat, when the whole party, except Colonel Poyntz and the boatman, were drowned; the latter saved the Colonel by swimming with him on his back. Mrs. Poyntz was looking from the drawing-room window the moment the accident happened."

Mr. Poyntz managed to lay hold of the boat, and his two boys clung for some time to his coat, he supporting them as best he could. But all his efforts were in vain. Whether from fatigue or from cramp, their grasp relaxed, and their father had the misery of feeling one after the other slip from him and sink to rise no more.*

Just before the party started on their fatal expedition, one of the Miss Parrys completed a letter to a friend with these words, " I must conclude in haste as we are just going out boating with Mr Poyntz." Her friend received this letter by the same post that brought the news of the accident.

Mrs. Poyntz survived this dreadful calamity for fifteen years, but it seems never to have been absent from her thoughts. She died on the 30th December 1830, and according to her desire her coffin was made of one of the beautiful trees planted at Cowdray by her father. She was buried at Easebourne. A fine monument by Chantrey was erected in Easebourne church to her memory, and to that of "her two only sons, unhappily drowned in the flower of their youth under the eyes of their parents."

Mr. Poyntz did not live much at Cowdray after the death of his wife. His three daughters were married, and he spent his time partly with them and partly in London. In the winter of 1836 he was at Althorp, and whilst out hunting with his son-in-law, Lord Spencer, his horse put its foot into a rabbit-hole, fell, and threw him on his head with great violence. Mr. Poyntz lived for some years after this fall, suffering constant pain, which he bore with the greatest patience. On the 8th of April 1840 he died at Hampton Court, very suddenly. It had been long known that his end

---

* The bodies of the two boys were recovered, and were buried in a vault at Easebourne which was prepared by Mr. Poyntz. The funeral took place on the 13th of July 1815. The entry in the register at Easebourne (for a copy of which I am indebted to the Rev. Henry Wood) runs as follows:—

"*Extract from Easebourne Register of Burials in the year* 1815.

William Montague Brown Poyntz. Cowdray. July 13. 14 yrs. S. Arnott.
Courtney John Brown Poyntz. Cowdray. July 13. 10 yrs. S. Arnott.
The above is an accurate extract. H. Wood, Vicar of Easebourne. Oct. 2. 1883."

On the deaths of Mr. and Mrs. Poyntz, they were buried in the same vault.

would be sudden, and after his death the conjecture of his doctors was found to be correct. In his fall he had, as they had believed, injured a joint of the vertebræ at the upper part of his spine, and this injury had caused an excrescence to form on the spinal column.

Mr. Poyntz was buried at Easebourne, and a monument by Monti was erected to his memory by his three daughters.

The Cowdray estates were, on the death of Mr. Poyntz, divided among his daughters. Lady Clinton, the eldest of the co-heiresses, was even more strongly attached to Cowdray than were her sisters. The thought of selling the old family property was most painful to her, and she would willingly have bought out the shares of her sisters had she been able. But it was impossible.

In 1843 the estate was sold to the sixth Earl of Egmont, a naval officer who had distinguished himself at Navarino. The property was sold to him for £330,000, but a much larger sum could have been realised if the three ladies who owned it would have consented to sell separately a part of the estate. They refused, however, to dismember the property, and Lord Egmont purchased the whole.

Lord and Lady Egmont lived on in the keeper's lodge, and took but little heed of the ruins of the old house. Lady Egmont died in 1870, and her husband survived her only four years. On his death in 1874, his nephew, the present Earl of Egmont, inherited the property. The keeper's lodge was pulled down, and a new house has been lately built on its site.

THE QUADRANGLE, EASTERN SIDE.

THE QUADRANGLE, SHOWING THE GATEWAY & THE SOUTH GALLERY.

CHAPTER XII.

Cowdray in its Glory.

COWDRAY HOUSE, according to Mr. Freeman, "belonged to that happy moment of our national art when purely domestic architecture was at its height."

The house was approached from the highroad by a raised causeway four hundred yards in length, which was once shaded by an avenue of magnificent elm-trees. This road led from the entrance-gates of curiously wrought iron (still standing close to the northern end of the little town of Midhurst) to the small stone bridge of two arches which crosses the river Rother close to the west front of the house.

Cowdray was built in the form of a great quadrangle, enclosing a space of turf which measured a hundred feet from west to east and a hundred and forty feet from north to south. In the middle of this green court stood the exquisite fountain (now removed to Woolbeding) which was so much admired by Horace Walpole. It was surmounted by a bronze figure of Neptune (copied from that modelled by Giovanni di Bologna).

The western side of this quadrangle was occupied by the lofty turreted gateway with wings a hundred and eighty feet in length. The eastern side contained the main body of the house, including the great Buck Hall, the porch, the chapel, and the various sitting-rooms; and these were flanked on either side by a massive hexagonal tower. The west and east sides of the quadrangle were connected by two long galleries. The exterior of the north gallery was quite plain, but the façade of the south gallery was broken by two square towers.

The four octagonal turrets of the great gateway rose high above the rest of the house. They contained staircases, and have fine embattled parapets. These staircases were lighted by single and by cruciform loopholes, placed alternately on the faces of the octagons. The entrance to the quadrangle was under the outer archway, between the two outer turrets. It was closed by massive wooden doors, and above it was the achievement of the first Lord Montague. This achievement was carved in stone, and is similar in design to the fire-backs cast for Lord Montague. It shows the sixteen quarterings surmounted by his coronet, with lynxes as supporters; and underneath is the motto *Suivez Rayson*. High above is the clock, which has been for so long a sad remembrance of the fire, its hands having stopped for ever on that fatal night.

The eastern side of the quadrangle was rich in architectural beauties and full of variety. Its most important features were the magnificent mullioned window, reaching from the ground to the parapet of the roof, and lighting the Buck Hall; the beautiful stone porch built by Lord Southampton, and the great tower at each end of the body of the house. Besides these there were many other beautiful and singular features in the building: such as the groups of richly ornamented brick chimneys, and the buttresses of stone terminating in slender shafts which rose above the embattled parapet of the roof.

The house was entered through Lord Southampton's porch, which, as the builders of those days were not slaves to symmetry, was not placed opposite to the main gateway. It stood considerably towards the south side of the quadrangle. The porch was built of stone, and had octagonal turreted buttresses at its angles: outside it looked rather low, but inside the groined stone roof was very richly ornamented (p. 13). Lord Southampton's initials W. S. are repeated on the spandrils of the doorways. The porch is square and embattled, and over its door are the royal arms with Lord Southampton's motto, LOYAUTE SAPROVERA, beneath. Above the porch was a window which gave light to the gallery at the south end of the Buck Hall.

The porch opened directly into a wide passage running across the house. From this passage the Buck Hall was entered by two doorways fashioned in the carved screen beneath the gallery.

The Buck Hall was one of the noblest rooms in England, and was built somewhat in the style of the halls erected by Wolsey at Hampton Court and at Christ Church, Oxford. It was fifty-five feet in length, twenty-six feet in width, and sixty feet in height from the floor to the open louvre which formed so striking a feature in the middle of the roof. This louvre, "a beautiful combination of tracery and pinnacles," was constructed in the form of a slender cupola of three storeys in height, and was ornamented on the outside by nine vanes of gilded metal placed in rows on each side of the cupola and ranged one above another like a stepped gable. The magnificent open timber roof of the Buck Hall was made of the variety of oak called *Quercus pedunculata*. Gough imagined that this roof had been removed from Battle Abbey, and this error has been repeated by other writers on Cowdray. But Battle Abbey had been sold before the succession of the eighth Viscount Montague, to whom Gough attributes the removal; and the only unroofed building at Battle was so much larger than the Buck Hall, that the story of Gough is obviously inaccurate. The hall at Battle which in some degree corresponds in size with the Buck Hall retains its original roof, and appears, in a drawing made in Gough's time, as not only habitable, but furnished and in occupation.

The Buck Hall was paved with large squares of white marble nearly sixteen inches square. At the south end was a gallery, possibly intended as a music gallery, corresponding in width with the passage immediately below it, which communicated with the porch. The wooden screen covered with elaborate and delicate carving, in which the motto, cognizance, and initials of Lord Southampton were frequently repeated, stretched across the hall just below the gallery. The hall was surrounded on three sides with a very high wainscoting of cedar, corresponding in height with the screen, but panelled, not carved. Above the cornice of this wainscot and the cornice of the screen were brackets on which were placed the eleven bucks to which the Buck Hall owed its name. These bucks were carved in oak as large as life, and were represented in various attitudes.[*] At the end of the hall, just below the gallery, two were placed together. These "sat erect like supporters," and each held between his feet and supported against his shoulder the staff of a carved and painted banner. On one banner were the Royal Arms, and from the neck of the buck which bore this the bow and arrows used by Queen Elizabeth at Cowdray were suspended. There is a tradition that this buck was clothed in the skin and crowned with the antlers

---

[*] For a considerable period after the fire half-burnt fragments of these bucks were to be seen lying among the ruins.

of one of the deer killed by the Queen. His companion buck supported a banner on which the arms of Lord Montague were painted.

The windows of the Buck Hall were filled with stained glass showing the armorial bearings of the family. The great bay window looking west, with its five mullions, was filled with escutcheons of arms. In the centre were the arms of England and of France, with imperial crowns over them, each surrounded with a wreath of red and white roses. In another compartment of this window, which reaches almost from the floor to the lofty roof of the hall, were the arms of Henry the Eighth. The three other windows were also filled with painted glass: with the escutcheons of Fitzwilliam, Browne, and Sackville, and a number of other quarterings.

There were some large pictures in the Buck Hall, arranged with a singular disregard to the appropriateness of the selection. The story of Perseus and Andromeda was represented in four large compartments, "all adorned with architecture;" one of these was placed on either side of the fireplace, and two on the right of the hall,—the entrance being through the screen. Two other large pictures, one painted by Goupy* and the other by Roberti, representing Diana and her nymphs, and "The Fable of Actæon," were on the left side of the hall. Above the chimney-piece was a picture of Christ by Lanfranc; and pictures by the same artist of the twelve Apostles, larger than life, were arranged round the hall. On the wall at the back of the gallery was a portrait of Lord Belasyse † on horseback, also larger than life.

The great staircase was on the eastern side of the Buck Hall. It occupied an area thirty-six feet long by seventeen wide. The steps were very wide and extremely shallow, and the balustrade, though not in character with the house, was very handsome. Portions of the balustrade are still preserved in various houses near Cowdray. It was painted and profusely gilded on both sides, the design being of scrolls, foliage, and Tudor roses. The colour appears to have been reddish brown, and so much sand was mixed with the paint that it has the appearance of terra-cotta There was a dado along the walls of the staircase matching the balustrade.

---

* Joseph Goupy, 1729-1763, was a French artist who settled in England in early life. Hubert Robert (Roberti), 1733-1808, was a French painter of ancient buildings.

† John, first Baron Belasyse of Worlaby in Lincolnshire, was the second son of Thomas first Viscount Fauconberg. He died in 1689, and was succeeded by his grandson Henry. On the death of this second Baron Belasyse in 1692 the title became extinct.

The staircase was lighted by two windows, and its walls were painted with the story of Tancred and Clorinda, from Tasso, by Pellegrini.* Several "fancy pieces" by the same artist hung on the walls, and at the bottom of the stairs he had painted " Peace " and " Fame " in two large compartments. On the outside of the house (on the east or garden front), the "insulated angle of the staircase had a slender octagonal turret gradually diminishing from its base upwards, and terminating in a slender turret with a dome and a lofty vane." This ornament was employed in several places on the building at Cowdray.

From the foot of the staircase a door led into the dining-parlour. This room was thirty-six feet long and twenty feet broad: it had a large bay window looking into the quadrangle, and another window looking to the east. A handsome archway led from the dining-parlour to the high pace or dais at the north end of the Buck Hall.

In this dining-parlour were the great historical pictures, painted in oil on stucco, which were at one time attributed to Holbein. Sir Joseph Ayloffe, F.S.A., saw these pictures in 1772, when he speaks of them as being in fine preservation. His description was published by the Society of Antiquaries in the *Archæologia*, vol. iii.†

The pictures occupied the whole length of the sides of the room. On the left or south wall (for the dining-parlour was built at right angles to the Buck Hall) were three pictures.

The first represented the march of Henry the Eighth from Calais towards Boulogne. On a scroll introduced into this picture were the words "The Metinge of the Kinge by Sʳ Antoni Browne upon the Hill betwene Callis and Marquison."

The King is represented in armour, riding in the midst of a body of pikemen: his Majesty is received by Sir Anthony Browne ‡ at the head of a body of horse.

The second picture was called "The Camping of the King at Marquison." In this a terrible thunderstorm was represented: the tents were seen blown

---

* Antonio Pellegrini, 1674-1741, an Italian artist, resided in England for some time, and "executed several ornamental works for the mansions of the nobility." [Bryan's *Dictionary of Painters*.]

† These pictures were at a later period all engraved by Basire from careful drawings taken by Grimm for the Society of Antiquaries.

‡ Sir Anthony Browne was Master of the Horse to Henry the Eighth, and was encamped at Marquison with the English forces under command of the Duke of Suffolk.

down and torn by the tempest of wind which accompanied the storm; and in the background was the church and village of Marquison set on fire by the lightning.

The third picture was of the siege of Boulogne, and was called "The King's Camp." Henry the Eighth was shown commanding in person a battery of more than thirty guns; he was in a suit of complete armour inlaid with gold, and held a baton in his hand. This was the picture from which the King's face was knocked out by the partisan of the Royalist officer (p. 79), and it was very badly repainted. The "Siege of Boulogne" was a most complete representation of a siege of the period. Not only were the soldiers shown with their curious uniforms and arms, but their siege-train, with "the great ordnance, mortars, and military machines, with the method of working them, of carrying on approaches, and forming the attack; the fascines, camp colours, ensigns, banners, guidons, tents, and the singular ammunition waggons shaped like half-cones, and laid on their side." Several camps of the generals engaged in the siege appeared in this picture, and Sir Anthony Browne was represented riding into his.

On the right (or north) side of the dining-parlour were three other pictures on stucco.

The first represented "The Attempt made by the French to invade this Kingdome in the year 1545; and the Rendezvous of the English Army at Portsmouth." In this picture Henry the Eighth was seen riding from Portsmouth town to Southsea Castle on his way to the camp, attended by the Duke of Suffolk, Sir Anthony Browne, "three pages and two lacqueys on foot, bearing their bonnets in their hands. Two demi-lancemen, horsed and completely harnessed, followed all. . . . [The King] wears on his head a black bonnet ornamented with a white feather, and is dressed in a jacquet of cloth of gold, and a surcoat or gown of brown velvet, with breeches and hose of white silk. . . . The portrait hath by good judges been esteemed to be the greatest likeness we now have of that monarch. . . . Behind the King are two persons on horseback: that on the right hand is the Duke of Suffolk, the King's lieutenant in this expedition, mounted on a black horse: he is dressed in a scarlet habit, and hath a black bonnet on his head: his beard is remarkably white, curled, and parted in the middle. The other is Sir Anthony Browne, the King's Master of Horse, mounted on a white courser."

The second picture on the right side of the room (which was placed above the first, probably to allow room for the fireplace), represented the English and French fleets assembled at Portsmouth. In this picture was seen the sinking of the *Mary Rose*. This ship, the second in size in the English navy, sunk at Portsmouth with six hundred men on board. The cause of the accident was that she was overladen with guns, and had her ports (which were so placed as to be only sixteen inches above the water) open; in tacking, the sea rushed in and she sank at once. But the French believe that she was sunk by their fire. The *Great Harry* also appeared in this picture, the only ship with masts in the whole squadron. She was represented as bearing down on the French fleet, with the Royal Standard flying at her main, with all her sails set, and her bulwarks covered with targets charged with the cross of St. George; Spithead and the Isle of Wight were seen in the distance.

The last picture in the room was the bird's-eye "View of the Procession of King Edward the Sixth from the Tower of London before his Coronation" (p. 16).

The seventh Viscount Montague allowed this picture, and this only, to be engraved from among the collection at Cowdray.

Three other historical paintings hung in the great dining-room at the head of the grand staircase. These were painted on panels, and were doubtless the work of a contemporary of Holbein. One of them represented "two knights running a tilt" in one of the jousts of the Field of the Cloth of Gold. The English Knight, Sir Anthony Browne, acting for Henry the Eighth, was seen in the act of unhorsing his opponent, Francis the First. Another picture showed the "grand embassy" sent by Henry to Francis to betroth his daughter Mary to the Dauphin. The third picture represented an audience given by Francis the First to some ambassadors from England.

In Horace Walpole's account of the painters in the reign of Henry the Eighth he says: "It may be wondered that I have said nothing of a work much renowned and ascribed to this master [Holbein]. I mean the chamber at the lord Montacute's at Cowdray; but it is most certainly not executed by him. Though the histories represented there, the habits and customs of the times, make that room a singular curiosity, they are its only merit. There is nothing good either in the designs, disposition, or colouring.

"There are three other historic pieces in the same house, of much more merit, ascribed to Holbein, and undoubtedly of his time. The first represents

Francis the First on his throne, with his courtiers and the duke of Suffo (so it is written) and the earl of Southampton standing before him on an embassy. This is by much the worst of the three, and has been repainted. The next is smaller, and exhibits two knights running a tilt on the foreground; one wears the crown of France, another a coronet like that of an English prince, composed of crosses and fleurs de lys, and not closed at the top. An elderly man with a broad face, and an elderly lady in profile, with several other figures, boldly painted but not highly finished, are sitting to see the tilt. On the background is the French King's tent, and several figures dancing, rejoicing, and preparing entertainments. A person seems leading a queen to the tent. Under this is written 'The meeting of the Kings between Guines and Arden in the Vale of Gold.' This is an upright piece. The third is the largest, broad like the first. Francis on his throne at a distance with guards, &c., on each side in a line. Before him sit on stools, with their backs towards you, four persons in black, and one like a clergyman standing in the middle and haranguing the king. On each side sit noblemen, well drawn, coloured, and neatly finished. On this piece is written 'The great ambassade sent to the French king, of the Earl of Worcester, Lord Chamberlain, the bishop of Ely, Lord St. John, the Lord Vaux, and others.' These pictures I should not think of Holbein; the figures are more free than his, less finished, and the colouring fainter; and none of the English seem portraits. The spelling too of *Suffo* is French. Probably these faces were done by Janet, who was an able master, was contemporary with Holbein, and whose works are often confounded with our painters. . . . In the great drawing-room at Cowdray is a chimney-piece painted with grotesque figures in the good taste of Holbein, and probably all he executed at that curious old seat; the tradition in the family being that he staid there but a month."

Sir Joseph Ayloffe attributed the historical pictures in the dining-parlour to Theodore Bernardi. This artist, about the year 1519, painted for the south transept of Chichester Cathedral a series of pictures of the kings of England and of the bishops of Chichester; and he afterwards settled in Sussex.

The chapel at Cowdray was on the ground-floor. It was lighted by five lofty windows, which were placed close together, almost in the form of an apse, at its eastern end. The chapel was forty-eight feet in length. The sanctuary at its eastern extremity was probably divided from the body of the chapel by a carved wooden screen; and from the centre of the building the width was increased westwards (on the south side of the chapel only) in order to afford space for the congregation. The fine tracery of the windows and the embattled walls of the chapel made it to the eastern front of Cowdray "a feature as bold and ornamental as a transept to a cathedral." It projected considerably beyond the body of the house. The chapel was entered by two doorways: one at the south side formed one side of the porch, which, with an entrance towards each point of the compass, stood at the end of that wide passage which crossed the house from the quadrangle to the garden front. The other doorway communicated directly with the space at the foot of the great staircase. (The staircase immediately adjoined the northern side of the chapel: its eastern wall, however, did not project as far as the spot at which the apse of the chapel commenced.) The altarpiece in the chapel was finely painted, in Rome, by Amigoni; it represented the Resurrection.*

The chapel was much injured when Cowdray was occupied by the troops in 1643. It was repaired and redecorated by the fourth Viscount Montague in the time of William the Third, and according to the taste of that day, the style of ornament being totally out of harmony with the ancient building. The chapel was surrounded with a mahogany wainscoting nearly ten feet in height, formed of panels, of which the edges were gilt; the altar-rails were also of mahogany and enriched with gilding. Above the altar was a lofty canopy, reaching to the roof, and enclosing Arrigoni's picture. The walls of the chapel above the wainscot were painted white and decorated with gilt ornaments. On the walls were panels of plaster enclosing whole-length plaster figures, and the emblems of the Passion, also in plaster. These figures and emblems were in raised work, but very poorly and coarsely executed.

The chapel was paved with square tiles, arranged in bold and intricate patterns, of which each tile formed a necessary portion. These tiles were probably made in Sussex, and were of considerable antiquity. They were highly glazed and coloured red and yellow.† The size of the tiles varied

---

* This fine picture was saved from the fire, and placed in the small Roman Catholic mission chapel at Easebourne. Unfortunately, it was placed against a very damp wall, and as it became completely spoilt it was destroyed. Jacopo Amigoni, born at Venice 1675, died at Madrid 1758. He came to England in 1729, and remained in this country for many years. He was employed by several English noblemen, and his best pictures are in England. [Bryan's *Dictionary of Painters*, vol. i. p. 24.]

† Many of the tiles that were preserved have lost their colours owing to the action of the fire. The heat caused the yellow to turn grey, and the red to turn black. But a few were underneath a

from five and a half to seven and a half inches square. Some of these tiles still exist, belonging to various persons in the neighbourhood of Cowdray, but many were used to mend a path to a stable. Most of those that remain appear to have been coated with the plaster which fell on them from the roof of the chapel at the time of the fire, and as this coating was fused by the heat on the surface of the tiles, it can only be removed with considerable difficulty.

Beyond the dining-parlour was a small withdrawing-room, looking east. Above the dining-parlour were two large withdrawing-rooms, opening into each other, and having each a beautiful window of singular form looking into the quadrangle. One of these rooms communicated with the Velvet Bedchamber, which was occupied by Queen Elizabeth when at Cowdray. This bedchamber was at the northern angle of the house, and had a very large and fine window commanding a view of the park. Adjoining it were some smaller rooms, looking east, and approached by a staircase enclosed in a fine octagonal turret at the north-eastern angle of the house. The withdrawing-rooms and the Velvet Bedchamber were entered from the head of the great staircase. In the Velvet Bedchamber was a large historical picture of the same date as those in the dining-parlour, representing the sea-fight off Brest in 1513, in which Sir Edward Howard, the English admiral, was killed in an attempt to board the French galleys. At a later period this room was hung with tapestry, the subjects of which were taken from Raphael's Cartoons.

The other rooms in the main portion of Cowdray are said to have been "stately and well furnished," but they were not numerous. One great beauty of the house was that every angle of the external or western front had a bow-window, but some of the rooms looking into the quadrangle and gardens seem to have been rather small and dark. One room, which joined the northern hexagon tower to the North Gallery, had no window whatever.

The North Gallery, which connected the east and west sides of the quadrangle, was wainscoted with Norway oak, "very neat," and seems to have been used as a picture-gallery. In this gallery hung the celebrated picture of Sir Anthony Browne in his parti-coloured wedding suit.

---

black-and-white marble floor which had been laid down over part of the chapel, and the colours of these are still as bright as when they were first made. It has been thought that the tiles are of the time of Henry the Eighth. If this opinion is correct, it would seem that some building was erected by Lord Southampton on the site of what was afterwards the chapel.

COWDRAY IN ITS GLORY.

The South Gallery, corresponding to the North Gallery but on the other side of the court, was in 1784 divided into bedrooms, "some of which had anterooms." This gallery had, previous to this alteration, been called the Apostles' Gallery, from the copies of Lanfranc's large pictures in the Buck Hall which hung in it.

There were two sitting-rooms (one twenty-five feet in length) on the south side of the passage through the house. These were divided by a passage which led directly to the hall from the kitchen. There were probably bedrooms above these sitting-rooms, as another octagonal turret, similar in design to, but larger than, that adjoining the Velvet Bedchamber contained a staircase and was placed at the eastern angle of this part of the building.

A catalogue was made in 1777 of the pictures at Cowdray. They were very numerous, but many of them seem to have been uninteresting, and were probably of no great value. Sacred and mythological subjects were frequent among them, and the pictures were grouped together in strange fashion. In one room a "Horse Fair" hung next to a picture of Christ and the disciples at Emmaus; in another, "Troy on Fire" was placed between "Queen Esther" and a "Holy Family." The fine miniature by Oliver of the three brothers was next to "Lord Montague's arms cut in paper;" and the curious portrait of Sir Anthony Browne was placed with pictures of Lot and his daughters, and of Judith and Holofernes.

There was probably at Cowdray a complete series of portraits of the Browne, Nevill, and Fitzwilliam families. Many of these have been already mentioned in the earlier portion of this volume. But there were also seven portraits of members of the Nevill family, in surcoats and robes powdered with coats of arms; and a picture of "Twin brothers of the Browne family, accidentally meeting in the Church of Saint Peter, after an absence of fifty years, and recognising each other by the likeness only." Unluckily no record has been preserved of this singular meeting.

A full-length portrait of Charles the Fifth as a boy, attributed to Titian, and a portrait of Erasmus, attributed to Holbein, were also in the house. The latter hung above the Sussex marble chimney-piece in the dining-parlour.

The kitchen at Cowdray was in the great hexagonal tower at the southwestern corner of the quadrangle; an uncovered triangular courtyard dividing it from the house. The walls of the kitchen were, at the bottom, of great substance. But above this " the walls were reduced in thickness on every face by recesses between broad piers, which, meeting in the angles, are as solid as the basement, and so continue to the parapet, just below which they are formed into rather tall and very strong hexagonal turrets, as severely plain as the tower itself: these are, in fact, the chimneys." The kitchen was twenty-two feet in diameter; it had four great fireplaces, set in deeply recessed chimney arches, and its windows were at some distance from the ground. Near it was the buttery; around which were a number of little recesses, said to have been used for holding plate in iron safes. A huge beam of charred wood still remains over the doorway to the buttery, vividly recalling the fire. A doorway in the kitchen opened into the uncovered yard,* across which the dishes had to be carried to the passage communicating with the Buck Hall. In the middle of the kitchen was a large round basin of water, in the centre of which a fountain was continually playing.

There was a room above the kitchen, approached from a small staircase on the south of the tower. This room appears to have been used as a library, in which the rare black-letter books and curious manuscripts belonging to the Montague family were collected; " the more useful or more fashionable library having been situated in the south angle of the west front." To this room, as the fire raged with greatest fury on the opposite side of the quadrangle, the few pictures and pieces of furniture which could be snatched from the flames were conveyed for safety. The kitchen was thirty feet in height, lighted by four large mullioned windows. The library above was of the same diameter, twenty-two feet, as the kitchen, and lighted by separate windows.

The hexagonal tower at the opposite or north-eastern corner of Cowdray was exposed to the full fury of the flames. It is more lofty, more massive, and plainer in design than the other tower; but although its outer walls resisted the fire so thoroughly that the staircase and the floor and ceiling or the room within the tower remained intact, it became, partly from damp and partly from neglect, too insecure to be entered. The room within it was " about twenty-two feet six inches in diameter, and groined with plain and very strong ribs of the most compact masonry, springing from the angles and forming a low domical roof, with a sculptured keystone in the centre."

The site of Cowdray is said to have occupied an acre of ground.

Many unfortunate alterations were made at Cowdray, chiefly by the fourth Viscount Montague. To him is attributed the alteration of all the upper

---

* This open yard was afterwards covered with a roof.

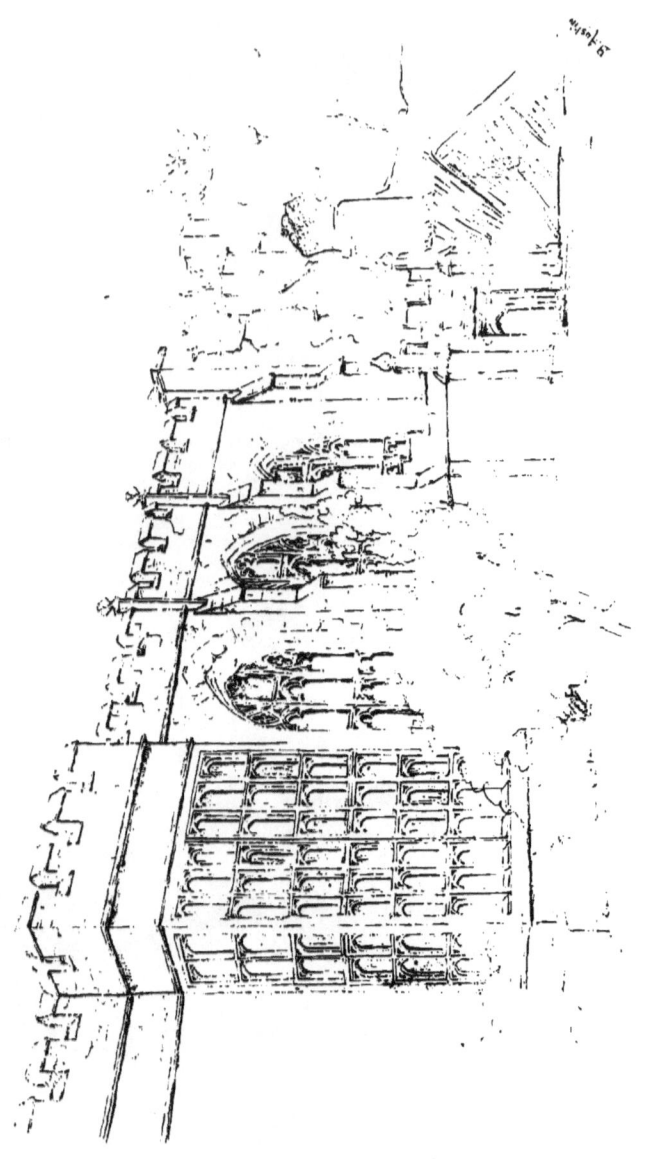
WINDOWS OF THE BUCK HALL, 1844.

windows on the eastern front; these were enlarged and heavy cornices added to them. The windows of the north hexagonal tower were altered at the same time and in the same style, and in this case the change much weakened the walls, and began the ruin which fire and neglect continued. The windows of the great gateway were spoiled at the same period. The fourth Viscount Montague demolished the fore [or external] court, through which those persons who were not of sufficient distinction to claim admittance at the great gateway could approach the house by way of the kitchen tower. Lord Montague built on this site (which was just behind the South Gallery) a narrow court joined at its eastern end to the kitchen tower, open towards the west, and surrounded on the east and south with buildings. These buildings comprised his stables, kennels, and other offices. They were built of brick, with low rooms and lofty red-tiled roofs, and though picturesque in themselves, were not in harmony with the embattled stone walls and towers of Cowdray. The approach to the ruins is now made through these buildings, most of which still exist.

About a hundred yards from the north side of Cowdray was a low octagonal stone building. It was twenty-four feet in diameter, with "a conical roof, a plain parapet, and several windows of different sizes." It was two storeys in height; the floor of the upper room was supported by a wooden pillar in the centre, with a base and a capital of stone; and this room was entered by two doors, each approached by flights of stone steps seven feet in width, and placed on either side of the chief entrance to the tower part of the building. The purpose for which this place was built has never been clearly ascertained. It has been called "the guard-room:" in it the firehose and buckets were locked up on the night of the fire at Cowdray: it was at one time used as a shelter for valuable plants during the winter, and more recently the upper part was made into a barn, and the lower portion served as a shelter for the cattle in the park. The building still exists, being now used as a lumber-room.

It is not known to whom the alteration of the Buck Hall, an alteration which almost amounted to a crime, is to be attributed. It is thus described by an Architectural Antiquary in the *Gentleman's Magazine:**—"The height of the hall was divided by a floor and its length by a partition. The lower part was a dark cellar, but the porch opening to a broad passage remained

---

* Vol. i., New Series, 1834, p. 38.

the chief entrance; and the principal upper room was furnished with a carved chimney-piece, the frame of which has not been entirely destroyed." * In all probability this alteration was made in the later years of the seventh Viscount Montague, or during the minority of his son.

Another alteration was made after the fire, during the time of Mr. and Mrs. Poyntz. It is mentioned by Sir Sibbald Scott,† who, in speaking of the south-east or kitchen tower, says, "An intermediate floor was introduced by taking off a portion of the height of the kitchen, and the space above was converted into an audit-room where the tenants for many years dined at the half-yearly audits, the dinner being cooked in the old kitchen below and then hoisted up through an aperture still existing in the modern floor; the room was externally lighted by the upper parts of the four great mullioned windows, which originally were in the great kitchen." The spiral staircase would not allow of the conveyance of the dinner. It led to the library above, which by means of shelves and cupboards was converted into a sort of office, in which all the muniments and papers were deposited.

The grounds of Cowdray were very extensive. Besides the park and the unique Close Walks, lawns extended eastwards from the house to a moat which was filled from the river Rother. Here probably was the bowling-green on which the second Viscount Montague played; but there are now no traces of it, nor of any of those fine hedges of yew, box, hornbeam, or holly which were the pride of so many houses of a similar date.

The Close Walks were formed by four narrow avenues of fine old yews planted at right angles so as to form a square. This square measured about one hundred and fifty yards each way. In the centre were circles, also of yews. From the size of the yew-trees and the arrangement of the Close Walks this portion of the grounds was most remarkable. It was here that Queen Elizabeth dined at the table four-and-twenty yards long.

Near the upper end of the great chestnut avenue in the park was the "Puzzle-walk" (as it is still called), or labyrinth, formed of large box-trees. The labyrinth was of very considerable size, and was intersected by numerous walks both wide and narrow. Near the labyrinth was a hollow in the shape of a horse-shoe which was called the Roundel.‡ It faced south-east at the

---

* The dividing floor and inserted chimney-piece may still be traced.

† *Sussex Archæological Collections*, vol. xv. p. 68.

‡ Roundel, or roundell, was a word used to express anything round, as a circle. Also a roundelay, or catch. [*Halliwell*.]

open part, and steps were cut round it to form seats like those in an amphi-theatre. It was completely surrounded by a wide drive, arched over by an avenue of large old yew-trees, and these again were surrounded by an outer ring of fir-trees of great height. There is a tradition that some of the enter-tainments provided for Queen Elizabeth took place in this spot.

Flower-gardens do not appear to have existed at Cowdray in its early days, and no gardeners are mentioned in the list of servants given by the second Lord Montague. The "fruytes of sortes" of which he speaks were probably furnished by orchards; and there is a tradition that the "Nanny" apple (one of the best apples in Sussex at the present day) was introduced from Nancy by one of the Lords Montague.

When the fourth Viscount Montague built his offices on the site of the demolished fore-court, he may have formed the large walled garden which still exists to the south of these low buildings. The appearance of the red-brick walls is consistent with the opinion, but there is no record of the fact.

There was a curious old sun-dial, apparently made of gun-metal, in the grounds, but this has been recently removed.

Among the papers found at Cowdray by Sir Sibbald Scott was a half-burnt fragment of an inventory of the furniture in the house. It begins: "An Inventory of the Goods Chattells and Household Stuffe Remaining and being in and about Cowdry House at the Decease of the Right Hon$^{ble.}$ Francis Lord Viscount Montaigu, taken the 7 day of May 1708.

" *In the Great Hall.*

"One long Shuffleboard Table wth Benches on either side fix'd to the wall and round the great Bay Window there: wainscoated, and hang'd about with printed Callico Hangings: wth Eleven Stags standing upon Pedistalls: allso Five Lamps."

In the Dining Parlour, or "Winter Parlor," there were "five and twenty Cane Chayres, Two of them being Armed, two needleworked Cushions, a pair of white Linen Damask Window Curtains, one Ovall Table, two Spanish Tables, fire shovel, Tongs, and a pair of Doggs, with one Steel Frame for warming of Plates." "A large Tea Table wth Furniture of Chinea" stood in "the Withdrawing Room nex the Parlor."

CHAPTER XIII.

The Fire at Cowdray.

ON the night of Tuesday, the 24th of September 1793, the fine old house at Cowdray was almost entirely destroyed by fire. About eleven o'clock on that night some men who were sitting up for brewing saw flames flashing out of the windows of the carpenter's shop at the top of the north-west tower of the house; and by seven o'clock on the following morning "that ancient and noble structure, with all the capital paintings, furniture, &c., a collection which no traveller of taste ever neglected to view or returned from ungratified," was a gutted and smouldering ruin.

According to the *Gentleman's Magazine* " the flames were so rapid that it was impossible to save any thing of value." But as the fire began at the top of the house, it is probable that even if modern fire-engines had been at hand little could have been done to arrest its course. As it was, the key of the detached stone building in which were kept the fire-hose and buckets was mislaid, and much time was lost in a vain endeavour to wrench the heavy door off its hinges. The steward endeavoured to get part of the house pulled down by the crowd of people who rushed to the spot from Midhurst, hoping in this way to stop the progress of the fire; but the great strength of the masonry rendered this impossible.

Lord Montague was abroad, but he was expected soon to return, and workmen were engaged in repairing and renovating the house. Lady Montague and her daughter had gone to Brighton with the intention of remaining there till the repairs at Cowdray were completed. The house was left in charge of a housekeeper and a very few servants, the establishment having been greatly reduced during Lord Montague's minority.

There was no doubt as to the cause of that disastrous fire, by means of which "the glory of Cowdray House, with the accumulations of years, all passed away as a tale that is told, being destroyed in one fatal night by the fury of an inextinguishable fire; and where festive preparations were in progress on the preceding evening, next morning there was nothing but blackened walls and dismay and ruin." For the workmen had not only been allowed to make their carpenter's shop in a room at the top of one of the towers, just above the North Gallery, but, with almost inconceivable recklessness, they had been burning charcoal there, in the midst of all the shavings and chips which strewed the floor.

During the repairs all the valuables in the house, the furniture, the relics from Battle Abbey, the books and curiosities, had been stored in the North Gallery. Every picture which could be taken from the walls had also been placed there.

The flames soon broke out in this North Gallery (immediately above which they had first been seen), and in it the fire raged with an all-devouring fury. The gallery was narrow and difficult of access, and scarcely a single piece of furniture was saved from among the quantity of articles with which it was crowded.

Three pictures only were saved. These were the group of portraits by Oliver, the copy of it by Sherwin, and the picture of the two brothers Fitzwilliam lying dead in armour.*

There is a picture at Woburn which is said to have been saved from the fire at Cowdray. It is a copy of the Van Dyck at Windsor of Charles the First, in which he is represented standing, the figure whole-length and life-size. This picture was in 1833 given by Mr. Poyntz to the sixth Duke of Bedford; but it is not mentioned in any catalogue of the pictures at Cowdray, and is more likely to have been among the collection of portraits at Midgham.

Many interesting relics from Battle Abbey were destroyed in the fire at Cowdray. Dallaway says that "against the parapet on the left side of the quadrangle were placed two ovals containing heads in baked clay, which were removed from Battle Abbey when it was sold." But the greatest loss

---

* This picture I have not been able to trace.

among these relics was that of the memorials of the Conquest. These consisted of the sword of William the Conqueror, his coronation robe,—"that royal pallium, beautifully ornamented with gold and very costly gems,"—and the Roll of Battle Abbey. The sword and the coronation robe are believed to have been presented by William the Conqueror to Battle Abbey, when he founded it in fulfilment of his vow made when his army was arrayed just before the battle of Hastings. "Upon this place of battle I will found a free monastery for the salvation of you all, and especially of those who fall. And this I will do in honour of God and His saints, to the end that the servants of God may be succoured; that even as I shall be enabled to acquire for myself a propitious asylum, so it may be freely offered to all my followers." The Roll of Battle Abbey was the list of the Barons who accompanied William the Conqueror to England; and though doubts have been thrown on its existence, the probability is that the Roll was made in some form, and kept in the church at Battle.

These relics of the Conquest undoubtedly ought to have remained at Battle Abbey; but, according to the tradition in the Montague family, they were removed to Cowdray when the seventh Viscount Montague sold Battle in 1717. They perished in the fire, together with several old "religious and military paintings from Battle Abbey."

Poor Lady Montague was overwhelmed with grief on hearing of the destruction of Cowdray. She was as yet ignorant of the far greater sorrow which was so soon to fall upon her in the death of her son;* but the loss of the beautiful house and of all the treasures it contained was a terrible trial to her.

A letter still exists which was written by Lady Montague from Brighton to her friend the Countess of Newburgh. The letter is only dated Friday, but it was evidently written immediately after the fire, possibly on the Friday of the week in which the fire took place: †—

---

* The tradition is that Lord Montague's death and the fire at Cowdray happened on the same day. But a few days at the least must have elapsed between the two events, although the exact date of Lord Montague's death has never been ascertained. The news of the accident reached England on the 1st of November 1793. [*Derby Mercury*, Nov. 7, 1793.]

† This letter, with another from Lady Newburgh to Lady Montague (in which an account is given of the festivities at Cowdray on Lord Montague's coming of age), are in the possession of a lady who was formerly companion to Lady Newburgh's daughter. Lord and Lady Newburgh resided at Slindon near Arundel.

"Brighton, *Friday*.

"O my dear Lady Newburgh, I am very little able to thank You as I wish and as You deserve for Your uncommon Kindness to me and my Daughter. I can't express what I feel, but must leave it to ye feelings of y^r own Heart, wch I'm sure will be Your best Reward for the Obligations You bestow. I hope to accept your very kind offer, but at present y^r House, wch I prefer to any other, is too near ye Scene of all my distress, and I do feel quite a Dislike to seeing any of ye people who are at Cowdray. I must blame Higgeson, for I hear it was his men who left ye Fire in ye Shavings in ye Work room. It seems a scene of Carelessness, or how could Such a House have been so destroy'd. O I ought not to look at Second Causes, the first had Doom'd it to Destruction; and I wish to submit to ye Decrees of Providence. However hard they seem they are not more than I am conscious I deserve. Bessy * is much affected, but she feels with me y^r great Kindness. Mr. Sergent † has just called, and put us in mind that if ye lead of ye House, wch must be worth fifteen hundred or two thousand pounds, is not saved it will be stole. So I am inclined to send a man over, as I'm sure ye Care of ye people there is not to be depended upon. A quantity of Water all round ye House, and yet it was not so employ'd as to save it.‡ But I shall feel angry and that is sinful, so I will only return to ye pleasing fact of your Kindness, and say that we hope to profit by it before we go to Town, and believe me with every sense of Gratitude, your much obliged, affectionate, &c., &c., F. M.

"*P.S.*—Best and grateful compts to Lord N. and ye L^{dy} Dowager."

Lady Montague's fears that the lead from Cowdray would be "stole" were not groundless. Numbers of articles were stolen from the house during the fortnight throughout which the ruins continued smouldering. There is many a house within a large circle round Midhurst which still contains some object once in Cowdray. Some articles have even been seen at Lewes which were saved from the fire. The extraordinary carelessness which allowed these thefts was no doubt due to the grief and despair which fell on the family in the contemporaneous death of Lord

---

* Miss Browne, afterwards Mrs. Poyntz.

† Mr. John Sargent, who built Lavington House. He represented Seaford and Queenborough in Parliament. He died in 1830.

‡ It is said that several of the servants in Cowdray were drunk on the night of the fire, and that the house-steward tried in vain to collect a sufficient number of men to hand buckets of water from the river to the house.

Montague. There seems to have been an entire absence of interest in saving what was left of the contents of the house, and the whole neighbourhood was allowed to roam through the ruins, carrying away anything that could be moved, either as a memento of the fire, or, more generally, as an article likely to be useful.

An interesting account of the condition of Cowdray a month after the fire was sent to the Society of Antiquaries by a gentleman who signed himself R. G. of Enfield. His letter is dated November the 7th, 1793, and is as follows :—

" *To the Rev. Mr. Wrighte, F.S.A.*

" DEAR SIR,—It is with real concern that I desire you to communicate to the Society any particulars of the loss which our national History has sustained by the destruction of Lord Montague's house at Cowdray. If they receive no account from any other person, you will be so good as to lay before them the result of a visit to the ruins on Tuesday, October 22, 1793, about a month after the catastrophe, in which, as far as could be done, I have endeavoured to ascertain how much of the valuable collection of paintings had been saved. A very inconsiderable portion indeed! an unfortunate concurrence of circumstances having occasioned the family portraits and all the historical paintings by Holbein or his contemporaries, which ornamented the four drawing-rooms and his Lordship's dressing-room, to be collected together during the repair of those several apartments previous to his Lordship's return from the Continent into the North Gallery, which was itself decorated with modern copies of the more curious whole-length portraits. At the west end of that gallery, by the strangest inadvertence, the carpenters and glaziers had been permitted to have their workshops, contrary to the established custom in houses of the same age and style. On the night of Tuesday, September 24, Mrs. Chambers the housekeeper, who, with the porter and one or two more servants, were the only inhabitants of the spacious mansion, had retired to bed at her usual hour of eleven, in the full confidence that all was safe, and not the smallest light was to be seen. She had scarcely slept an hour when she was alarmed by the watchman with the cry of ' Fire in the North Gallery !' and immediately saw it in flames with all its valuable contents without a possibility of saving a single article. The inhabitants of Midhurst, from which the house is not a mile distant, were soon ready to assist in great numbers, and no help was wanting to remove the furniture, pictures, and library from the three other sides of the quadrangle. But the firmness of the materials rendered it absolutely impossible to break down any part so as to stop the progress of the flames ; they quickly spread to the east side of the court, in which was the

COWDRAY TWO MONTHS AFTER THE FIRE

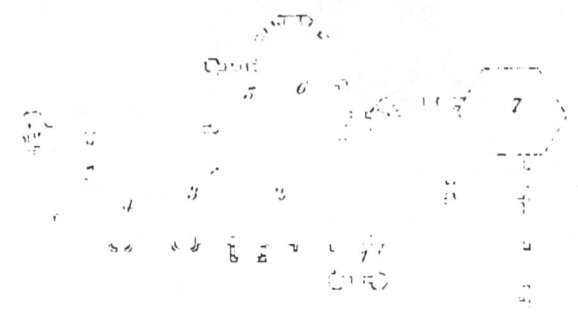

GROUND PLAN, 1844.

great hall, chapel, and dining-parlour. These there was opportunity to unfurnish, and to save the altar-piece by Arrigoni, but the historical paintings on the walls of the dining-parlour were involved in the destruction, and the stucco on which they were painted itself flaked off from the walls. A piece of it which I picked up from the north wall, whereon was painted the principal operations of sieges, will show the state to which they were reduced."

In the *Gentleman's Magazine* for 1794 (vol. lxiv. p. 13) an engraving is given of Cowdray from a sketch taken on the spot in November 1793. In this sketch the gateway is shown as but little injured by the fire, although the windows are burnt out: the west wing and the end of the South Gallery appear to have been almost untouched, but on the other side of the gateway the house even then was a ruin. The end of the North Gallery is marked by the remains of the wall on either side of the windows; in front are heaps of fallen stones, and the whole of the north wing is burnt down to the lower windows. Through these ruined walls are seen the remains of chimneys and windows at the north-east angle of the inner court; but these, even two months after the fire, seem to be tottering and about to fall. A paling has been erected across the great gateway, from which the doors have disappeared. From this sketch it is evident that no restoration of the northern side of Cowdray could have been possible, but the southern and western portions might probably have been habitable, and could apparently have been restored to their former condition without difficulty.

Mr. Quinton, writing to the *Gentleman's Magazine* in May 1798 (vol. lxviii. p. 371), gives some additional particulars as to the fire. He says:— "Lord Montague was engaged to the eldest daughter of Mr. Coutts (the present Countess of Guildford), and with a view to his marriage on his return to England the mansion-house had been for several months undergoing a complete repair and fitting-up. The whole was completed on the day preceding the night in which it was consumed, and the steward had been employed during the afternoon in writing the noble owner an account of its completion. This letter reached his hands. On the following day the steward wrote another letter announcing its destruction; but in his hurry of spirits he directed it to Lausanne instead of to Lucerne, by which accident it was two days longer in its passage to his Lordship's place of abode than it otherwise would have been. Had it not been for that fatal delay, in all human probability this noble family would not have had to deplore the double misfortune by which its name and honours have become extinguished; for the letter arrived at his Lordship's lodgings on the morning of his death, about an hour after he had left them, and, as nearly as can be computed, at the very moment in which he was overwhelmed by the torrent of the Rhine. Had it fortunately reached his hand, there cannot be a doubt but the deep impression its contents would have made on his mind would have instantly diverted it to far other thoughts and purposes than the youthful and dangerous frolick which cost him his life."

CHAPTER XIV.

Cowdray in Ruins.

O attempt seems to have been made to restore the ruin of Cowdray House after the fire, and but little care was taken to preserve it from decay. The wreck of the beautiful building was left as it appeared after the fire, and in a short time the walls were covered over with ivy. The ivy soon concealed the outlines of the structure which remained, and no doubt much contributed to the further decay of the stone.

In the beginning of November 1825 William Cobbett visited Cowdray in the course of one of his rural rides.* He came thither from Trotton, where he seems to have passed over the magnificent brasses in the church without notice, speaking only of "the good and commodious and capacious church." Cobbett remarks, "From Trotten we † came to Midhurst, and having baited our horses, went into Cowdry Park to see the ruins of that once noble mansion, from which the Countess of Salisbury (the last of the Plantagenets) was brought by the tyrant Henry the Eighth to be cruelly murdered, in revenge for the integrity and the other great virtues of her son, Cardinal Pole. . . . This noble estate, one of the finest in the whole kingdom, was seized on by the King after the possessor had been murdered

---

* *Rural Rides* by William Cobbett, p. 332.
† Cobbett was riding with his son Richard.

on his scaffold. She had committed no crime. No crime was proved against her. The miscreant Thomas Cromwell, finding that no form of trial would answer his purpose, invented a new mode of bringing people to their death, namely, a Bill brought into Parliament condemning her to death. The estate was then granted to a Sir Anthony Brown, who was physician to the King. By the descendants of this Brown, one of whom was afterwards created Lord Montague, the estate has been held to this day; and Mr. Poyntz, who married the sole remaining heiress of this family, a Miss Brown, is now the proprietor of the estate, comprising, I believe, *forty or fifty manors*, the greater part of which are in this neighbourhood, some of them, however, extending more than twenty miles from the mansion. We entered the park through a great iron gateway, part of which being wanting, the gap was stopped up by a hurdle. We rode down to the house and all round about and in amongst the ruins, now in part covered with ivy and inhabited by innumerable starlings and jackdaws. The last possessor was, I believe, that Lord Montague who was put an end to by the celebrated *nautical adventure* on the Rhine along with the brother of Sir Glory.* These two sensible worthies took it into their heads to go down a place something resembling the waterfall of an overshot mill. They were drowned just as two young kittens or two young puppies would have been. And as an instance of the truth that it is an ill wind that blows nobody good, had it not been for this sensible enterprise never would there have been a Westminster Rump to celebrate the talents and virtues of Westminster's Pride and England's Glory. It was this Lord Montague, I believe, who had this ancient and noble mansion completely repaired and fitted up as a place of residence; and a few days, or a very few weeks, at any rate, after the work was completed the house was set on fire (by accident I suppose), and left nearly in the state in which it now stands, except that the ivy has grown up about it and partly hidden the stones from our sight. You may see, however, the hour of the day or night at which the fire took place, for there still remains the brass of the face of the clock and the hand pointing to the hour. Close by this mansion there runs a little river which runs winding away through the vallies, and at last falls into the Arron. After viewing the ruins we had to return into the turnpike road, and enter another part of the park, which we crossed in order to go to Petworth. When you

---

* By this name was meant the celebrated Sir Francis Burdett.

are in a part of this road through the park you look down and see the house in the middle of a very fine valley, the distant boundary of which to the south and south-west is the South Down Hills. Some of the trees here are very fine, particularly some most magnificent rows of the Spanish chestnut. I asked the people at Midhurst where Mr. Poyntz himself lived, and they told me at the *lodge* in the park, which lodge was formerly the residence of the head-keeper. The land is very good about here. It is fine rich loam at top with clay further down. It is good for all sorts of trees, and they seem to grow here very fast."

This cruel composition shows that Cobbett as well as Horace Walpole imagined Margaret of Clarence to have been the owner of Cowdray. It is sad to think that, besides his brutal delight in the death of Lord Montague, Cobbett should have passed over unnoticed the loss of the two sons of Mr. and Mrs. Poyntz,—a loss which must have been fresh in the minds of all who visited Cowdray so soon after the catastrophe.

Mr. Poyntz apparently took no heed of the curious documents which had escaped the flames. In an account of Cowdray written in 1834 by Howard Dudley, a pupil at the Midhurst Grammar School,* the following description is given:—"At the south end is a massive tower of large dimensions braced with iron, which has escaped the fury of the flames: the kitchen occupies the ground-floor and is nearly filled with faggots and rubbish: by a winding staircase you reach another room of equal dimensions with the kitchen; the floor is covered with ancient deeds, valuable MSS., and private letters, which are suffered to lie about in wild confusion, submitted to the inspection of every visitor."

An "Architectural Antiquary" also visited Cowdray in 1834, and sent a long description of the house to the *Gentleman's Magazine*.†

He thus speaks of the ruin of the library:—"As if the calamity had palsied the surviving owners, the remnants spared by the fire were long neglected with the building‡ which contained them, and when at last either were remembered, the confused heaps of furniture in the kitchen and the library awaited a *selection* which was so slothfully performed that their value

---

* The account written by Howard Dudley, entitled *Juvenile Researches*, is still one of the best descriptions of Cowdray to be found. He wrote it when only thirteen years of age, printed it himself, and illustrated it with woodcuts, drawn, cut, and printed by his own hands. His early death cut short a career of great promise.

† Vol. i. new series, p. 33, and see p. 123 *ante*.   ‡ The kitchen (or south-west) tower.

was diminished or altogether lost. The last relics of old high-backed chairs, and one or two paintings, are of such a quality as to excite no regret that they are resigned to decay; but that the entire library should not have been removed with reverential care is an instance of cold neglect which excites the surprise and rouses the censure of all who are permitted to enter the room. These manuscripts lie in heedless heaps on the floor or are scattered on the shelves, and some more ancient, and known by their rightful owner to be more curious than the rest, are set apart for the vacant gaze and rude treatment of those who cannot read them—an idle ceremony, which, however, may not much longer exist for complaint, since their total destruction by fire has been urged, I am informed, from a quarter likely to prove influential."

The Architectural Antiquary adds:—"But the noble ruins of the house itself are fast hastening to extinction. In windy weather the public are not allowed to approach the walls lest the fall of some tall gable or lofty window should prove fatal to the visitors; and the owner, to avoid a calamity of this kind, caused a tower on the south side, and some other fragments, to be demolished. One of the handsome bay windows near the hall is on the eve of falling; indeed, several mullions have already given way, and a few wooden props once placed by a considerate labourer residing on the spot to sustain the tottering and delicate frame, are lying uselessly at its base. This is the system adhered to at Cowdray; a fragment that exhibits dangerous decay is pulled down to save its falling at an unlucky moment, and (what is of equal consideration) to save the few pounds which would secure it in its place: and let those who view with admiration, not unalloyed by painful sensations, these grand and still extensive ruins, remember that for their gratification they are indebted to the durability of the masonry, and (though to the liberality of free admission) not to the care of the owner." *

Mrs. Poyntz had died in 1830, and on the death of Mr. Poyntz in 1840 the curious practice of heriots was put in force. The owner of East Lavington (at that time Mrs. Sargent) seized Mr. Poyntz's best chattel, a team of four very fine home-bred Suffolk punch cart-horses, as heriots in respect of some land in the manor of Woolavington. This heriot was commuted for the sum of two hundred pounds.

---

* *Gentleman's Magazine*, new series, 1834, vol. i. p. 38.

KITCHEN TOWER AT COWDRAY, 1844.

GATEWAY AT COWDRAY, 1844.

On the sale of the estate to the sixth Earl of Egmont in 1843, "the vendors at the purchaser's cost enfranchised the heriots, quit-rents, and reversion, the lands in question being held on lease for ten thousand years, of which some three or four hundred only had expired."* To estimate the present value of this reversionary interest was an exceedingly difficult and complicated task.

At the meeting of the British Archæological Association in January 1845 a letter from Mr. Virtue to Mr. Charles Roach Smith was read, which gave an account of Cowdray. Mr. Virtue " stated that having heard that a number of interesting documents and papers had been stored away in a room in the ruined mansion of Cowdry near Midhurst in Sussex, the only portion of the building that escaped destruction by the fire, he took occasion to visit Cowdry House in November last. He ascertained that the room having become ruinous and unsafe, and many of the papers having been carried away by persons who chanced to visit the ruins, the remainder had been thrown into the closets which surrounded the room, which were then nailed up and the papers left to decay. The present state of this chamber is such that at no very distant time it must fall, and these old documents will probably perish." Mr. Thomas King of Chichester wrote next month " in reference to the collection of old papers at Cowdray House, that they had been deposited in a detached dovecot at the time of the fire, and that they related to the times of Elizabeth, James, and the Protectorate. Mr. King has some of these papers in his possession, one of which is a detailed account of expenses for liveries and tailor's work during Elizabeth's reign : he has also court rolls and other documents of the time of James the First. Part of these papers had been wantonly destroyed and used as wrappers or for kindling fires, but the Earl of Egmont has recently purchased the estate, and the ruins will no longer be accessible to mischievous idlers." †

Some eleven years later the remaining documents in this room were examined by Sir Sibbald Scott, Bart., F.S.A., and described by him in the *Sussex Archæological Collections* (vol. xv. p. 67). He says that when he visited the room, " the floor was strewn with parchments and papers; some had been thrust by handfuls into the cupboards, and many were gathered in little heaps in corners where gusts of wind had probably driven

---

* Mr. Alexander Brown supplied this information. He conducted the business.
† *Archæological Journal*, vol. ii.

them, and where the damp had caused them to adhere in masses, rendering many of them illegible; for small traces of glazing remained in the wide casements, consequently the rain could penetrate from any quarter; the ivy, moreover, had thrust its way to the ceiling, and jackdaws had evidently learned to look on this apartment as their own. . . . But more ruthless still than the rain, or damp, or jackdaws had been the spoiling hands of casual visitors before the door had been closed to the public. The collectors of autographs and seals had in frequent cases torn off these appendages; doubtless many documents had been carried away wholly, but generally they were thus mutilated, and then flung down on the floor as valueless." Important papers were, it is to be hoped, not dealt with after this fashion. But Sir Sibbald Scott mentions some that were extremely curious and interesting (*Sussex Archæological Collections*, vol. xv. p. 69). He adds, " There were piles of letters to and from different members of the family down to the last young Lord who was drowned." It is greatly to be regretted that these papers should never have been collected, or even preserved.

The beautiful fountain in the centre of the court at Cowdray seems to have excited no admiration. Lord Robert Spencer, an intimate friend of Mr. Poyntz, remarked to him one day that it was very fine. The fountain was then scattered in bits about the court at Cowdray. Mr. Poyntz replied that he might have it if he liked to take the trouble of moving and restoring it. Lord Robert, who was at that time the owner of Woolbeding,* at once removed it to his garden, where it still remains. I am enabled by the kindness of Lady Lanerton to give a sketch of this fountain.

The ivy, which was so long allowed to grow thickly over the ruins of Cowdray, has of late years been cut, but the damage it has done in forcing its way between the stones can never be repaired.

Above the great gateway the face of the clock still remains, with its hands still pointing to the hour at which it stopped; by the door is the old bell, and the original staples which held the doors of the gateway. The kitchen still contains the enormous dripping-pan, five feet long and four feet wide, and the great meat-screen and meat-block. Among these relics of old Cowdray are lying a fine mirror-frame, a chandelier, and Lady Montague's harp, on which are the words *H. Naderman à Paris.*

---

* Lord Robert Spencer purchased Woolbeding from Sir Charles Mills.

Unfortunately the sheltering trees inside and around the Close Walks have lately been cut down. The ancient yews, so long standing in those cloister-like avenues which were unique in England, are exposed to the winds; many are already broken and injured, some even have fallen to the ground.

A great portion of the Puzzle-walk or Labyrinth still exists, and some of the box-trees are of considerable size; but when, during the Peninsular War, no hard wood for turnery could be obtained from abroad, great numbers of the large box-trees which formed the Puzzle-walk were unfortunately cut down, and the wood sold for a large sum to London turners.

The seats in the Roundel or amphitheatre can still be traced; and above it the spot may now be seen on which a bonfire was always lit on the coming of age or marriage of one of the Viscounts Montague, or on the occasion of the birth of an heir to Cowdray. These bonfires were laid on a high mound with no trees near the spot, and could be seen for miles around.

Some of the large old oaks still remain in the Park, but a very large number of them were cut down in 1793 and the two following years, and sold to the Government. They were sent to Portsmouth and Plymouth,* no doubt to be used in the dockyards.

---

* *Glimpses of our Sussex Ancestors*, part ii. p. 228.

CHAPTER XV.

The Curse of Cowdray.

THE so-called curse of fire and water connected with the house of Montague will be found fully described in the Appendix to this volume.

Sir Anthony Browne's great possessions were chiefly derived from the spoils of the Church, and to him the words of the terrible curse pronounced in the church of every ruined monastery were supposed to apply. This curse was read by the priest, standing in front of the altar, and is given by Sir Henry Spelman in his *History of Sacrilege*.

"By the authority of Almighty God and blessed Peter, Prince of the Apostles, to whom is committed by God the power to bind and loose on earth, let vengeance be declared on the malefactors, robbers, and spoliators of the goods and possessions, rights and liberties, of the monastery of Saint——, and of the whole congregation of that monastery, unless they do effectually repent of their malignity. If the said malefactors should repent of what they have done, may the blessing of God Almighty come upon them and reward them for their good works. But if in truth their hearts are hardened in their iniquity, and they refuse to render up their possessions in the state in which they are bound to restore them, and to make amends by due penitence, may there light upon them every curse with which God Almighty has cursed those who have said to the Lord God, Depart from us, we desire not the knowledge of thy ways; and who have said, Let us possess by inheritance the sanctuary of God. May the torment of perpetual fire be their portion and inheritance with Korah, Dathan, and Abiram, who went down living into hell-fire, with Judas and Pilate, Caiaphas and Annas, Simon Magus and Nero, who are tormented for ever in torments without end. May they not dwell with Christ, neither with his saints, nor have communion with him in celestial peace, but dwell with the devil amid infernal torments, and perish for evermore. Cursed be they in the city, cursed be they in the field, cursed in the castle, cursed in the island. Cursed be the fruit of their womb, cursed their dwelling-place, cursed their going-out and entering-in, cursed be they wherever they may abide. May God send them hunger and thirst, chiding and reproof, and crush them in all their doings until he finally root them out of the earth. May the heavens above their head be as brass and the earth beneath their feet as iron. May God strike them with imbecility, blindness, and madness, and may they grope at mid-day as in the darkness of the night, and know not whither to direct their steps. May they suffer from calumny and cruel and violent oppression, and find no deliverer. May their carcases be devoured by the birds of the air and the beasts of the field, and may no man give them sepulture. May a wicked man be set over them, and Satan stand at their right hand. May all these curses come upon them, following in their track till they overtake and seize them and they perish utterly. Fiat. Fiat."

Such were the fearful words in which Sir Anthony Browne, in common with all those who despoiled the Church, was publicly cursed.

Two accounts are given of the manner in which the curse of fire and water was pronounced directly on him and on his descendants. One of these will be found in the *Story of a Curse*, p. 163, in which the speaker is the Sub-Prioress of Easebourne. But the more generally received tradition is that, when Sir Anthony was holding his first great feast in the Abbot's Hall at Battle, a monk made his way through the crowd of guests, and striding up to the dais on which Sir Anthony sat, cursed him to his face. He foretold the doom that would befall the posterity of Sir Anthony, and prophesied that the curse would cleave to his family until it should cease to exist. He concluded with the words, "By fire and water thy line shall come to an end, and it shall perish out of the land."

The following letter from a curate of Easebourne (published in *Notes and Queries*, first series, vol. iii.) refers to this tradition:—

"When curate of Easebourne, in which parish are situated the ruins of their ancestral hall of Cowdray, I frequently heard the village dames recite the tales of the rude forefathers of the hamlet respecting the family [of Montague]. They relate that when the great Sir Anthony (temp. Henry VIII.) was holding a revel, a monk presented himself before the guests and pronounced the curse of fire and water against the male descendants of the family till none should be left, because the knight had received and was retaining the church lands of Battle Abbey and those which belonged to the Priory of Easebourne. . . . The old villagers, the servants, and the descendants of servants of the family point to the ruins of the hall, and religiously cling to the belief that its destruction and that of its lord resulted from the curse. It certainly seems an illustration of Archbishop Whitgift's words to Queen Elizabeth, 'Church land added to an ancient inheritance hath proved like a moth fretting a garment, and secretly consumed both; or like the eagle that stole a coal from the altar, and thereby set her nest on fire, which consumed both her young eagles and herself that stole it.'—E. Rds.,* *Queen's College, Birmingham, Feb. 20, 1851.*"

The sorrows and misfortunes which befell the Montague family in their later days were very great, and it is remarkable that these should have been caused by fire and water. But, on the other hand, Sir Anthony Browne himself and most of his descendants lived in the full enjoyment of honour and prosperity for above two hundred years. It requires a stretch of faith to believe that a curse, so long deferred, should at last have been allowed to fall on the young heads of those who were so remotely descended from the original possessor of the Abbey lands.

* Richards.

CHAPTER XVI.

The Domain of Cowdray.

EASEBOURNE CHURCH, on the outskirts of Cowdray Park, is a very ancient building, and till its recent restoration it retained many of its characteristic features. In this church are the monuments already referred to of Sir Anthony Browne and of Sir Davy Owen. The font is massive, of dark Sussex marble; the basin is formed in the centre of a square block of marble, carved round the sides, and supported on one short massive pillar. The pillar rested on two square blocks of marble, the upper one being carved with four trefoils springing from a circle surrounding the base of the pillar. Sir William Burrell in 1778 made a careful drawing of this font. At the recent restoration of Easebourne church four small white stone pillars were added to this ancient font, one being inserted at each corner, connecting the base with the upper portion. Easebourne is the mother church of Midhurst, Farnhurst, and Lodsworth. In the churchyard is a curious tombstone erected to the memory of John Shotter, who died in 1776. He was believed to have caused the death of his wife by throwing her downstairs. On the tombstone is a representation of John Shotter's house, in front of which he is seen dragging his wife by the hair and trampling on her arm. Close to him is a skeleton, bending towards the murderer in a threatening attitude from the top of an adjacent tomb. John Shotter, however, married a second wife, who survived him. The tombstone is now much defaced by the weather, but drawings of it in its original state have fortunately been preserved.

Easebourne Priory stands close to Easebourne church, the south wall of which formed one side of the cloisters. The Priory was founded by John de Bohun about the middle of the thirteenth century for a Prioress and five nuns of the Benedictine Order. It appears that the Prioress of Easebourne in 1441 was severely rebuked by the Bishop of Chichester * for her extravagance. The Bishop sent his Commissary, Master Walter Eston, to hold a visitation in the chapter-house at Easebourne, and he made the following report:—" In the first place it has been proved and discovered . . . that the house was in debt to the amount of £40, and this principally from the costly expenses of the Prioress, because she frequently rides abroad, and pretends that she does so on the common business of the house, although it is not so, with a train of attendants much too large, and tarries long abroad, and she feasts sumptuously both when abroad and at home, and is very choice in her dress, so much so that the fur trimmings of her mantle are worth 100 shillings. Also the Prioress compels her sisters to work continually like hired workwomen, and they receive nothing whatever for their own use from their work, but the Prioress takes the whole profit." † The name of this Prioress has not been preserved. She was suspended by the Bishop from "all administration of the temporal goods" of the Priory; she was " by no means to compel her sisters to continual work of their hands, and if they should wish of their own accord to work, they shall be free to do so," reserving for themselves half of their earnings, and applying the rest to " the advantage of the house and unburdening it from debts." The Prioress was "with all possible speed [to] diminish her excessive household," and to retain only such persons as appeared to the Episcopal administrators to be absolutely necessary. If she had occasion to ride abroad she was not to make a lengthened stay, and "she must and ought rightly to content herself with four horses only." No guests were to be received without the consent of the administrators; and, hardest to bear of all, "the Prioress shall convert the fur trimmings, superfluous to her condition and very costly, to the discharge of the debts of the house."

Two other visitations were held in the chapter-house of Easebourne

---

* Richard Praty, Bishop of Chichester from 1438 till his death in 1445.
† *Episcopal Registry*, quoted in *Sussex Archæological Collections*, vol. ix. p. 7.

Priory, the one by Bishop Story in July 1478, and the other by a Commissary sent by the aged Bishop Sherburn in August 1521. Agnes Tawke was Prioress in 1478, and Margaret Sackfield in 1521. At both of these visitations bitter complaints were made by the nuns of the extravagance and unfair rule of their superiors. In 1521 all the nuns declared that their allowance of one mark (13s. 4d.) every year for their clothing was not paid to them by the Prioress, nor were they provided by her with apparel. Complaints were also made of irregularities in the conduct of the inmates of the Priory. The nuns there have been described as " wild females, scions of high family, put there to keep them quiet." Want of occupation may have been the cause of much evil.

In 1535 Easebourne Priory was suppressed. Margaret Sackfield, the last Prioress, surrendered the property to the King's Commissioners, and the few inmates of the Priory returned to their own homes.

The house and lands were in the following year granted to Lord Southampton; Baldwyn Hammet, chaplain to the nuns, receiving a yearly pension of one hundred shillings. In the Survey of the year 1568 the "house called Easebourne Priory" is mentioned, "wherein be granaries, and a brewhouse, all inclosed within the park of Cowdray, and subject to the deer coming in."

A very curious chest, once in Easebourne Priory, is now in the possession of Mr. Alexander Brown. The chest is of iron, possibly of Spanish origin. The lid, which is of very great weight, contains on its inner surface a medley of iron springs, bolts, and hinges, all in connection with the secret spring of the lock. After long examination and many trials by an expert, the final bolt had to be forced, for the spring could not be discovered. Inside the chest were household bills of the Lords Montague for wax candles at thirty-six shillings the pound, and for tea at three guineas the pound. There is a tradition about this chest to the following effect. It is said to have contained the deeds of Easebourne Priory, and that it was secured by two large padlocks (still in existence), the small keys of which were kept by the Bishop of Chichester and the Abbot of Waverley. The Prioress of Easebourne kept the great key which opened the central lock and another lock which was hidden under one of the large iron studs on the top of the chest. But this key was of no use unless the padlocks were unlocked, and unless a small skewer was applied to two springs, reached through tiny holes in the elaborate ornamentation of the lid. Tradition says that the Prioress contrived to let a smith named Gosden, living in Midhurst, take impressions of the keys kept by the Bishop and Abbot during one of their visits to Easebourne. Gosden thereupon made additional keys; the Prioress opened the chest, and pawned the Priory deeds which were in it.

In Easebourne Priory there was a curious strong room or safe. It was six feet square, built of stone and brick, banded about and laced across with Swedish iron bars, of such quality that when it was, with difficulty, demolished, these bars were "kept like gold" for future use.

Easebourne Priory has been considerably modernised, but the great oaken beams, fifteen inches square, and the steps of Sussex marble still remain. The plaster ceiling of what is called the "Abbess's Parlour" is probably the work of the Italian artists who were employed to decorate the chapel at Cowdray in the time of William the Third.

Dallaway considered that the windows in Easebourne church were of the date of Henry the Sixth. The lancet windows in the refectory or chapter-house* of the Priory are of the date of Henry the Third. These windows have been walled up. Dallaway believed that this was done when Lord Southampton converted the Priory into a dwelling-house. The windows can still be traced, and the fine buttress on the outer side of the refectory remains untouched. The building has long been used as a granary, and a portion of it was made by Mr. Poyntz into a pigeon-house, with nests formed in the wall to accommodate above a thousand pigeons.

The south aisle of Easebourne Church was the chapel of the nuns of Easebourne Priory, and it was also their burial-place.

Easebourne has always been considered to be a particularly healthy village. Sir William Burrell, writing in 1768, says that the ages of six persons buried at Easebourne amounted to five hundred and four years. In 1776 two brothers and a sister were living in Easebourne parish whose united ages amounted to two hundred and forty years.

The wall of the churchyard at Easebourne belongs to four parishes—Easebourne itself, Midhurst, Farnhurst, and Lodsworth. Sir William Burrell adds that in the tenth year of the reign of Queen Elizabeth the churches of Easebourne and Farnhurst were still considered to belong to Easebourne Priory. No Vicar was endowed, but the duties of the parishes were

---

* The number of inmates was too small to require a large refectory. The room was probably used as the chapter-house.

discharged by two stipendiary priests, " of whose wages the fermors are bound to discharge the lord."

The manor of Cowdray, situate in the parishes of Easebourne, Fernhurst, and Midlavant, is one of the hundred and forty manors in Sussex in which the custom of Borough-English prevails. This custom prevails to some extent, according to Mr. Corner, F.S.A. [*Sussex Archæological Collections*, vol. vi. p. 174], in many parts of England, but chiefly in Sussex, Suffolk, and Surrey.

Borough-English is the opposite of primogeniture, and it means the descent of lands to the youngest, instead of to the eldest son of the owner. In some cases women have been allowed to benefit by the custom. If the owner of the property died without issue, the estate passed to his youngest brother. The custom varied considerably in different manors. In some, women were not recognised at all; in others, " if the custom does not extend to prefer the youngest daughter, or youngest brother, or collateral heir, all the daughters would be entitled to the inheritance." [*Sussex Archæological Collections.*]

Another peculiarity of the borough of Midhurst was the issue of town tokens.* Rye and Midhurst were the only places in Sussex which issued town pieces, *i.e.*, one token struck for the use of the whole town. These town pieces are thus described in W. Boyne's *Tokens of the 17th Century*, p. 464:—

Obverse.—*A Midhurst Farthing in Sussex.* [In one circle]—*For ye Use of ye Poor.* [In an inner circle]—A Shuttle. 1670. *Reverse.*—Two Saints near a palm-tree.

The Tradesmen's tokens of Midhurst were four in number.†

Obverse. — Thomas : Aylwin : in : T. R. A.   *Reverse.* — Midhurst : in : Sussex. 1667.

Obverse.—Henery : Cortney : in :   *Reverse.*—Midhorst in Sosex. H. C. *Device.*—A double-headed eagle displayed in centre of token.

---

* Tokens were small coins struck by private tradesmen, and in a few cases by towns, of the value of farthings and halfpennies, and sometimes of pennies. The necessity for small change throughout the country caused this innovation. It was begun by private tradesmen, but afterwards their example was followed by cities, towns, and villages. But the custom only lasted from the year 1648 till the end of the year 1672. In Somersetshire thirteen towns issued town pieces ; in Dorsetshire, eight ; in Devonshire, five ; in Kent, one ; in Sussex, two. But not one town piece was issued in the whole of Yorkshire.

† The second initial is probably that of the wife of the tradesman, inserted as in the marking of household linen of the present time.

Obverse.—John Pepson 1669. *Reverse.*—In Midherst in Susex. I.E.P. *Device.*—A stick of candles.

Obverse.—Iohn Shotter. *Reverse.*—in Medhurst. I. S. *Device.*—The Grocers' Arms.*

A street in Midhurst is still called the Mint.

The selection of the weaver's shuttle as the device on the town pieces of Midhurst may have been made in consequence of the manufacture of coarse quilts, which was of some importance at Midhurst during the seventeenth century. The Grammar school of Midhurst (at which Richard Cobden, Sir Charles Lyell, and Charles St. John the naturalist were educated) was founded in 1672 by Gilbert Hannam, quilt-maker. He established the school during his lifetime "for twelve boys, to be instructed in Lattin and Greek, and in writing and arithmatick, if they be capable to learne." Owing to the inadequacy of the endowment of twenty pounds a year, the Grammar School at one time fell into decay, but it is now restored to its original and flourishing condition. The manufacture of quilts, however, has long ceased in Midhurst.

Midhurst church has recently been restored. The original building is thought by Mr. Durrant Cooper† to have been rebuilt at the end of the reign of Henry the Fifth, or very early in the reign of Henry the Sixth. But the lower part of the tower was then left untouched, and was late Norman or very early English. The church no doubt existed in the time of Henry the Sixth, for in 1428 there was a dispute between Sir John de Bohun and the Prioress of Easebourne on the one side, and the burgesses of Midhurst on the other, as to their respective rights. The quarrel was referred to John Rickinghale, Bishop of Chichester, who decided it in favour of the burgesses. They were to enjoy the right of burial at Easebourne, in consideration of their repairing the nave and cloister of the church there, and of keeping in order seventy-two feet of the churchyard wall. On the other hand, the Prioress of Easebourne was no longer to pay for the bell-ropes and belfry-wheels required for Midhurst church.

Michael Bageley of Midhurst, in the year 1422, founded a chantry in Midhurst church, and gave the endowment for a priest, afterwards called

---

* The Grocers' Arms were three cloves, or three sugar-loaves, or a chevron in the midst of nine cloves arranged in threes.

† *Sussex Archæological Collections,* vol. xx. p. 24.

the Morrow priest,* to sing matins there. Michael had succeeded his brother Thomas Bageley, who "being a valiant disciple and adherent of Wickcliffe," was martyred, "being brent in the place of Smythfield." The Chantry lands also maintained a lamp, which was always kept burning in Midhurst church.

The high-mass priest at Midhurst was, until the Reformation, provided by the Prioress at Easebourne, and he and the Morrow-priest served the church.

One Browne monument still remains on the east wall of Midhurst church, close to the spot on which stood Lord Montague's great tomb. This represents two figures, a man and a woman, kneeling on either side of an altar. On each side is a Corinthian pillar painted blue, and the monument bears a coat of arms. It was erected in memory of Joan, the wife of Francis Browne. The inscription runs as follows:—

Dyed 11 of March año : domini 1554.

Lo, here a Dame interred lies, a Courtney by descent,
A courteous, chaste and humble Wife whilst God here Life her lent.
To Francis Browne in Lyfe she was a worthy godly Mate,
Whose Patience, Myldness, Constancy, renowned her Estate.
Unto the Poor (each where) that lackt there wants she did supply
And wrought all Deeds of Charity with Zeal aboundantlye.
The World she did more loathe than love and most set her delight
In doing good and serving him devoutly Day and Night.
When Sickness did oppress her sore with Torments hard to byde
Christ's Death she thought on evermore, to him she only cried.
She lived to dye, she dyed to live; she longed there to be
Where are such Joys no Tongue can tell nor Mortal Eyes can see.
Thus living well and leaving Toil and dying virtuously
Let All that Virtuous Woman love in Heart say secretly
Farewell O Joan, set free by Death from worldly woes and Sinne
Our Lord grant that thy Soul in Heaven may endless Rest there Win.

In 1311, during the reign of Edward the Second, Midhurst for the first time returned members to Parliament. Two members were returned from

---

* Probably from Morwe, morning, morrow. [*Halliwell.*]

that period until 1832, from which time Midhurst has returned only one member.

The two first members for Midhurst were Henry Boteler (or Butler) and Henry le Puffere. They were elected by the free burgesses, that is, the owners of messuages or tenements in the borough from which free rents were derived, as distinguished from the villeins, cottars, and customary tenants of the Lords of Cowdray. Of these free burgesses the number in 1311 was thirty-six, but two of them, the Bishop of Durham and a widow lady named Joan de Bohun, were disqualified. Henry Boteler was not rich, for in the tax which was levied in 1341 on the ninth part of a burgess's goods he paid only for one horse worth 6s. 8d., two oxen worth 8s., and two pigs worth 3s. 4d.

William Yalden of Blackdown, the friend of Oliver Cromwell, was member for Midhurst during the Protectorate of Richard Cromwell.

The most distinguished man who has represented Midhurst was Charles James Fox, who was returned for the borough on the 10th of May 1768, when he was only nineteen years of age.* During the year and eight months which elapsed before Fox attained his majority he spoke frequently and with great ability in the House of Commons, particularly distinguishing himself in two encounters with Burke. The first of these occasions was soon after his election, when he spoke against the return of Colonel Luttrell for Middlesex in the great Wilkes controversy. Horace Walpole remarks that Fox then "answered Burke with great ability but with confidence equally premature." The second encounter between Burke and Fox took place on the 9th of January 1770. Fox spoke at the end of the debate on the Address, and his pungent comments on some passages in Burke's speech set the Treasury Bench in a roar of laughter. On one of these occasions, Burke, much nettled, turned on Fox and exclaimed, "You may speak if you like, but being a minor, you have no right to vote." †

Lower, in the *History of Sussex*, vol. ii. p. 52, remarks that in Midhurst "there were formerly about 120 burgage tenements, which entitled their respective owners to vote. One of the Lords Montague pulled some of them down that he might enlarge Cowdray Park, but had stones inscribed

---

* Fox was born on the 24th of January 1749.

† The debates in the House of Commons were at that time reported too slightly for this retort to appear. I am indebted for the anecdote to the Right Hon. Spencer Walpole, to whom it was told by his father.

A Burgage put into the wall to indicate their sites, whereupon a noble Duke remarked that 'So low had the elective franchise fallen, that at Midhurst the very stones appeared as voters for members of Parliament.'"

The Knights Hospitallers of St. John of Jerusalem built a Commandery at Midhurst, and had jurisdiction over a large district, still called the Liberty of St. John. The persons resident in this district were independent both of the manor of Cowdray and of the borough of Midhurst. The Liberty comprised a district reaching to Easebourne, to Milland Marsh (in the parish of Iping, five miles north-west of Midhurst), to Moses Hill (in the parish of Farnhurst, six miles to the north), and to Hoyle Farm (in the parish of Heyshott, three miles south-east of Midhurst). The exemptions of the inhabitants of the Liberty of St. John are very similar to those of the Liberty of Lodsworth. The Liberty of St. John was in 1542, after the suppression of the Order of the Knights of St. John in England, granted to the Earl of Southampton.

The beautiful Commandery House (a drawing of which still exists in the Burrell Collections in the British Museum) was pulled down in the present century, and a mansion, described by Horsfield [*History and Antiquities of the County of Sussex*, vol. ii. p. 94] as "a modern and commodious dwelling," was erected in its stead.

Midhurst used to be governed by a Queen's bailiff and a Lord's bailiff. The former still acts as returning officer at the Parliamentary elections, and presides at the Courts Leet. The duty of the Lord's bailiff is now obsolete. Before the establishment of County Courts the Lord of the borough had a court for the recovery of small debts. It was held once in every three weeks, and the Lord's bailiff, in connection with this court, distrained for moneys recovered.

Lodsworth, a small village east of Midhurst, enjoyed a Liberty of its own which was co-extensive with the parish. This Liberty was under the jurisdiction of the Bishops of London. The exemptions of the residents within this Liberty were *—" 1. Exemption from all suit and service to any Hundred Court. 2. No tolls to be paid to the King at any market or fair throughout England and Wales. 3. No money to be paid to the sheriff's turn nor to be subject to his jurisdiction, but the bailiff of the Bishop of London to return all writs. 4. A three-weeks' court to be held to recover

---

* Dallaway's *History of Sussex*, vol. i. p. 277.

debts by a jury of free suitors, with imprisonment for debt in the gaol belonging to the Liberty. 5. No inquisition *post-mortem* to be held for lands."

This Liberty was granted to Sir Anthony Browne with the manor of Lodsworth by Henry the Eighth.

The "gaol belonging to the Liberty" was underneath the manor-house called River House. The dungeon was entered from the outside, and was immediately below the great chamber in which the courts of the bishops of London were held. It is said that the rings in the wall of this dungeon, to which the unfortunate debtors were chained, were still existing when the place was demolished. The Bishops of London exercised the right of "pit and gallows" within their Liberty. Galley Hill, on the South Heath near Lodsworth, marks the site of their gallows. The River House has been much modernised; the fine chimney-piece (which no doubt in old days reached to the ceiling) can still be seen, but the house has been subdivided, and it is difficult to trace the outlines of the ancient rooms. The fine old fire-back, with Lord Montague's arms, is irreparably cracked.

North Heath, situated due north of Midhurst, and on the main road to Farnhurst, had once its gallows. On this spot the mail was robbed in the early spring of 1799. Two brothers named Drewitt were found guilty of the robbery. They were tried at the Spring Assizes, and executed at Horsham on the 13th of April 1799. The younger brother asserted his innocence throughout, and maintained with his last breath that he had had no hand in the robbery. But both brothers were hanged at Horsham, and according to the barbarous practice (instituted by George the Second in 1752 *) their bodies were brought to the North Heath, and hung in chains there. These chains or irons still exist. An iron collar and waistband were placed round the body of the criminal, iron bands extended on each side of his legs; these bands were connected at the knees, and meeting under his feet, were fixed to the waistband. It hardly admits of a doubt that the younger Drewitt was not guilty, but that he died to save the guilty person, his own father. After the execution the miserable father spent the remainder of his days in sitting at the foot of the gibbet on which swung the bodies of his two sons.

There is a curious tradition in Sussex to the effect that "the stroke of a

---

* The practice of hanging in chains was abandoned in 1833-34. [See *History of Criminal Law in England*, by Sir James FitzJames Stephen, vol. i. p. 477.]

dead man's hand" will cure any affection of the throat. Persons will walk long distances to have the benefit of this cure. Whilst the body of the younger Drewitt, who, as the tradition goes, "hung a many months, he not being guilty, and having on the new pair of deerskin breeches in which he was taken," remained on the gallows, children were held up and the dead man's hand was swung by their friends across their throats in order to cure their complaints. The gibbet remained on the North Heath for many years. At last it was cut down. The gibbet itself was made into a prop to support the roof of a neighbouring cottage, and the irons were sold. The gibbet is not now in existence. The man who placed it in his house as a support married a relative of the Drewitt brothers; she could not bear to look at it, and it was burnt.

Verdley Castle, in the midst of Verdley Wood, south of Midhurst and close to the North Heath, was once a building of some importance. It was, according to Grose's *Supplement to the Antiquities of England and Wales*, vol. ii., "a quadrangular building, nearly twice as long as broad, measuring on the outside thirty-three feet four inches by sixty-eight feet. The parts standing (in 1784) are the westernmost end, with small returns on the north and south sides; the first containing eight feet two inches, and the second eleven feet six; the thickness of the walls about five feet four inches. Near the door are some slight traces of a narrow winding staircase."

For what purpose Verdley Castle was built must be left to conjecture. The wet ditch around it seems to indicate a moat. It may have been a hunting-tower of the Lords de Bohun, or a place in which the Prioress of Easebourne kept her tithes of wheat and other produce. In the first year of the reign of Edward the Sixth, Verdley was held by Sir Anthony Browne by military service.

Verdley Castle was built in a spot which was well concealed from the eye of passers-by. A few ancient yew-trees only marked the hollow in which it lay.*

The castle was (according to Horsfield's *History of Sussex*, vol. ii. p. 104) "destroyed . . . some years ago for the purpose of applying the materials to the repair of the roads." This process has lately (1883) been continued; the foundations of the castle have been dug up, and the ancient

---

* Grimm, who took the sketch of Verdley Castle on the 31st of May 1782, says that the place was "only known to such as hunt the martin cat."

stones broken for repairs of roads. In the course of this recent demolition an ancient key was dug up, also a knife with ivory handle and silver blade.

Verdley Castle was built in the midst of a very extensive oak wood, which extends from Bexley Hill on the east to Holder Hill on the west, a distance of about two miles. Midway between these two hills lies the little village of Henley, through which ran the old coach-road to Chichester. This narrow and steep road is paved with large slabs of stone; and extra horses were kept at the King's Arms Inn at the bottom of the hill to help the heavy coaches and road-waggons up the ascent. In 1825 the new road was constructed. On Holder Hill still stands the semaphore, which, with its companions on Portsmouth Hill, Black-down, and other heights, transmitted the news of the battles of the Peninsular War to London. Below Holder Hill, in the midst of the oak wood, is the spot still known as Cavalry's Quarters. A troop of Royalist horse was concealed in these woods during the occupation of Cowdray by the Parliamentary forces. These horsemen contrived to capture the outposts of the Roundheads. Tradition says that their commander was a lady; but, although the story is well known, her name has been forgotten.

Verdley Castle and its neighbouring woods supplied many a hiding-place for the kegs of spirits and bales of silk conveyed by smugglers from the sea-coast. Persons now alive recollect seeing the long files of loaded horses crossing the hills on their way from the sea-coast.

Farnhurst, a little village, once in the midst of oak and beech woods, was originally looked upon as a "pannage of hogs."* Later its iron-works brought the parish into notice; and here were the last ironworks of West Sussex. The very large iron-foundry at Farnhurst remained for several generations in the family of Butler, and it was employed by Government for casting cannon in 1770. The foundry was situated close to a large wood which is still called the Mine Pits, and this wood is full of holes out of which the iron was dug. Many other woods in the neighbourhood bear similar traces. One of the Butler family brought skilled workmen from the North of England to be employed in the foundry at Farnhurst; and the descendants of these persons are now known in the neighbourhood by the surname of Far-miner. The ancient church of Farnhurst, dedicated to St. Margaret, and mother-church of Linchmere, has been thrice restored.

---

* Pannage, the acorns and beechmast on which pigs feed in woods.

The massive oak beams and the old font of Sussex marble still remain, also a few traces of painting in fresco on the north wall of the chancel. In 1520 Thomas Trybe of Farnhurst left "to St. Margaret's light of Farnhurst a shepe; and in 1535 William Byggenolde* left to St. Margaret's light of Farnhurst two shepe; to Saynt Sounday's light, a shepe;† to St. Anthony's light, a shepe." [*Sussex Archæological Collections*, vol. xii. p. 71.]

Shulbred Abbey, or Shelbred Priory, near Farnhurst, was founded by Sir Ralph de Arderne, during the reign of King John, as a Priory of five Black (secular) Canons of the Order of St. Augustine. Sir Ralph richly endowed the Priory, and dedicated it to the Virgin Mary. The heirs of Sir Ralph in 1240 sold the patronage of the Priory, with the third part of a knight's fee, to William de Percy, lord of Petworth. The Percy family were generous to the Black Canons of Shulbred, giving them a mill to grind their corn, and endowing them with the patronage of several Sussex livings. The Priory was, however, suppressed in 1535. The last Prior, who surrendered the property to the King's Commissioners, was George Waldene. In 1543 Shulbred and its lands were granted to Sir William Fitzwilliam, Earl of Southampton, and descended with his other property to his half-brother, Sir Anthony Browne.

Soon after the suppression of the Black Canons of Shulbred, the Priory was converted into a farm-house. The monks' room, thirty-four feet five inches long and twenty feet four inches in width, has a groined roof supported by octagonal pillars, from which the arches spring. This room is now a dairy, and the roof is only nine feet from the present floor. The original floor, formed of large square stones three inches thick, is about two feet below the present level. This portion of the building was probably a crypt. It was lighted by three small "parallelogram windows" on its southern side. Grose (*Supplement to the Antiquities of England and Wales*, vol. ii.) seems to have thought that the Priory was once very large, and modern research has proved the correctness of this view. Grose adds that there was once a large porch on the southern side of the Priory, "lately taken down" at the time of his visit. The best description of Shulbred Priory is given in the *Gentleman's Magazine* for 1799, part ii. p. 641. "The entrance is through a large doorway, which opens into a passage leading

---

* This name is still common in Farnhurst. † Saint Sunday is Easter Day.

to the common hall. On each side of the passage are several gloomy cells, the ceiling arched, with intersecting angles of ancient workmanship. Hence a flight of several massive stone steps, worn through age, leads the inquirer through a dark vaulted passage to the rooms above." The largest of these rooms is the Prior's chamber, with a small lancet window high up on its eastern wall, and a massive oak beam reaching across the whole width of the room. There is another window on the southern side. On the other walls are rude paintings in fresco, most of which are still in fair preservation. The paintings are with one exception executed on a plaster partition which divides the room. These paintings are of the date of James the First. The centre one represents the Royal Arms, and underneath is James's well-known motto, *Beati pacifici.* Some of the paintings represent hunting scenes. On one are seen two cocks fighting with broad-sword and shield; a view of the Priory is in the background. A third picture represents three ladies in dresses of the date of the sixteenth century. But the most curious paintings are those which represent the announcement by various birds and animals of the birth of Christ. The words they are supposed to speak are written on labels attached to their tongues, and have evidently been intended to resemble the sounds uttered by each. Above is the sentence "Ecce, virgo concipiet, et pariet filium, et vocabitur nomen Jesus."

The Cock says, "Christus natus est."
The Duck: "Quando, quando."
The Magpie or Raven: "In hac nocte."
The Bull: "Ubi, ubi."
The Lamb: "In Bethlem."

Underneath are the words "Gloria sit tibi, Domine, qui natus est de Virgine, cum Patre, et Sancto Spiritu, in sempiterna sæcula."

"Om'is spi' laudet Dom^m. Amen."

The Prior's chamber is thirty-five feet four inches in length and twenty-two feet in width. The floor is covered with tiles, some of which are richly ornamented.

Shulbred Priory is no longer used as a farm-house. The present tenant carefully preserves the ancient building and its surroundings.

The old bridge between Shulbred Priory and Farnhurst was probably built by the Canons; but the Priory was difficult of access, as it was buried in a wood through which there was no road. Even in 1835 Horsfield says that it was "not to be approached even in summer but with difficulty."

William Yalden, who represented Midhurst in 1659, is said to have entertained Cromwell at his house on Blackdown Hill, near Farnhurst. The Ealdwins and the Entingenappes (now Yaldwin and Enticknap) are among the most ancient of the families in West Sussex. The Entingenappes have now sunk to the level of the poorest cottagers, but they are said to possess a deed dated before the Conquest respecting an estate at Chiddingfold, near Blackdown. A William Yalden was living in 1330, and the family still possess deeds of the time of Edward the Third. Another William Yalden lived at Blackdown in 1590; but the present house bears the date 1640, and the initials W. Y. It was doubtless built by the Yalden who was the friend of Cromwell. Blackdown was sold in 1844, and the bed in which Cromwell was reported to have slept was, with other relics of his time, destroyed.

APPENDIX.

THE STORY OF A CURSE.

T was when I was young—now a long time ago—that I heard the story I am about to relate,—one of the most potent and forcible illustrations of the theory of Sir Henry Spelman in his *History of Sacrilege*, that the curse attending the spoliation of religious houses follows the successive races which have profited by it with a relentless and unerring retribution.

Do any of my readers know the little rural town of Midhurst in West Sussex? It was in my time far from the line of railways, and only once a day was its solitude and silence broken by the arrival of the London and Chichester coach, which changed horses at the Angel Inn. During the Goodwood week, however, it assumed an unwonted appearance of bustle and movement, for all the road was crowded by post-chaises, drags, breaks, and extra stage-coaches, conveying passengers to the great meeting across the Downs, whose green swelling sides rose a couple of miles south of the town.

On this occasion the North Street was filled with lookers-on; it was a privilege to possess or be invited to a window overlooking the stream of carriages. The Grammar School boys got a half-holiday, and cheered the more aristocratic equipages as they passed, and especially the great stage-coach, which on Monday evening took down the supernumeraries of the Goodwood household—an army of cooks and waiters, besides three large live turtles slung behind the dickey. Lord Chesterfield, Admiral Rous, the Duke of Beaufort, and Lord Milltown all passed yearly through the town in their own carriages, some with four horses,—and to witness the stream of life and brilliant company on its way to Goodwood Downs was the annual Saturnalia of the dull little borough.

After the last carriage had returned townwards on Saturday, Midhurst resumed its quiet ways, only varied at long intervals by the election, or it would be fairer to say the nomination, of its member by the neighbouring House of Cowdray, its local dynasty.

Well, in those early days, I was a school-girl of sixteen, who had scarcely ever seen a town, and to whom the carriages passing through to Goodwood had all the attraction of a Roman Carnival. As it was not considered proper by the local authorities on etiquette to witness this magnificent pageant save from a window, I was sent with my governess to the house of an old lady who possessed a curious little tenement crowned by a large bow-windowed room overlooking the street,* and there I was installed behind the muslin curtains, with a table spread with tea and strawberries and seedcake, such as I have never tasted since, to fill up the breaks of time and amusement caused by the occasional want of continuity in the stream of carriages.

It was thus I first made the acquaintance of Mrs. Barlow, then in her eighty-fourth year, and on taking leave of her and offering my thanks for her kindness, she said, "I hope you will come back some time, my dear, and see my curiosities. They are much better worth looking at than the carriages, and Anna and I are always glad to see you."

Anna, her niece and companion, was a quiet, kind, commonplace old maid, with nothing remarkable about her but her talent for making seedcake, and for cultivating the finest carnations in the neighbourhood. Her aunt, on the contrary, was one of the most intelligent women I have ever met, though nearly self-educated; and though born in an inferior position—she had been the daughter of the last house-steward of Cowdray—she was visited and universally respected by the neighbouring county families for her sterling worth, her exhaustless fund of old-world Sussex traditions and anecdotes, and her instinctive appreciation of all that was singular and beautiful in curiosities and works of art. Never having been further than Chichester from her native town, it was astonishing how she had collected a museum of bric-à-brac, which would have sent a modern hunter of china and old carvings wild with envy.

---

* This interesting old house was pulled down in 1880 to make room for a new Town-Hall. [J. R.]

How well I remember them all! The old Japan cabinets, fragrant with otto of roses and musk, and holding countless precious odds and ends wrapped in silver paper; the Venice-glass bottles formed like harps and ships and spiral cylinders; the quaint mourning-rings of a dozen half-forgotten friends or extinct families; the enamelled patch-boxes that Belinda might have envied for her toilette table; the snuff-boxes that Chesterfield and Walpole might have exchanged; the paste buckles and buttons that would have graced the court-suit of Sir Charles Grandison; lockets with initials and faded locks of hair, saddest of all memorials, whose very identity only lived in the memory of one ancient lady; letters tied up with ribbon whose colour had died out with the vitality of the writer. These, and hundreds of trinkets, painted fans, and pieces of old lace, filled those wonderful and apparently inexhaustible drawers.

There were shelves and cupboards, too, filled with priceless china, parrots and monsters in Bow and Chelsea, services of Crown, Derby, and Wedgwood, drinking-cups in pink and blue, and pale Chinese egg-shell sets, fragile and delicate as flowers.

Then came the ugly and tasteless rarities of the late Georgian period; the work-boxes and jewellery with portraits of Queen Charlotte and her court; the memorials of British victories, Waterloo and Peninsular souvenirs, medals of Sir John Moore, and of Nelson and of Wellington; bits of wood taken from the deck of the *Victory*, or from the famous tree of Quatre Bras; straw and ivory toys made by the French prisoners in England; bone models of the guillotine; portrait-rings of Marie Antoinette, silhouettes of Napoleon, and willow leaves from St. Helena.

Like the conjuror's bottle, the quaint old lacquer drawers appeared to be inexhaustible,—at least to a girl's imagination;—and half the summer passed and a bi-weekly visit left fresh treasures still untouched and unexplored.*

There were, however, two objects which I never tired of looking at again and again. One was a beautiful ivory triptych, evidently of Spanish or Italian workmanship, representing the Holy Trinity, the Apostles, and the three states of the soul after death—paradise, purgatory, and hell; the other was a very striking portrait in oil of a lady in a nun's dress, telling her beads. Both of these had come from the old Hall of Cowdray, where my venerable friend's youth had been passed. In the ruins of Cowdray I spent many an hour, dreaming over the fate that had pursued the owners, and gazing on that beautiful Tudor quadrangle, rich in mullioned windows, broken escutcheons, and crumbling battlements, which was, and is, even in its decay, the glory of the neighbourhood. The picture was

---

* Mrs. Barlow died in 1852 at the age of ninety-four. After her death her possessions were sold for a trifling sum, and were all dispersed. [J. R.]

that of Elizabeth Browne, a Benedictine nun of Pontoise, a noble convent much affected by the daughters of the great English Catholic houses, whom the penal laws forbade to follow a religious vocation at home. It appeared to have been painted about the end of the seventeenth century, and by a master-hand. The clear-cut noble features, the dark thoughtful eyes, the blue-veined hand, and the brown olive-wood rosary that lay in those slender fingers, were all rendered with the living touch of the best French or Flemish school, instinct with transparent though sombre colouring, and the mellow light that so well befitted the subject.

It was this portrait that one day introduced the subject of the old Lords of Cowdray, and the terrible fate that pursued their race like the avenging furies of a Greek tragedy. There is scarcely a more striking instance of the doom of sacrilege than in the story of the confiscator of Easebourne Priory as it lives in the memory and traditions of the neighbourhood, and as I then learned it from one who had in her childhood witnessed its literal accomplishment. As she told it to me I relate it now. The Protestant local guide-books have omitted all mention of its most salient incidents, and the later members of the family were extremely jealous of their becoming known.

Cowdray has twice changed hands since then, and all reason for silence is over. The last Browne of the old stock has long slept in the vaults of Easebourne Priory, and none live who can be pained by the revival of the oral tradition of Midhurst on the subject.

I repeat it from the narrative I heard from the lips of one whose position in the household of Cowdray gave her the most intimate knowledge of the family legend. It will carry greater weight from the fact of her being a strong Protestant, and an unwilling witness to the accomplishment of the curse known to have been pronounced on the confiscators or inheritors of Easebourne Priory.

EASEBOURNE PRIORY.

The little house of Benedictine Canonesses which bore the name of Easebourne Priory still exists, an ancient and picturesque mass of mullions and gables, at the upper end of Cowdray Park, adjoining the beautiful old parish church of Easebourne.

The convent garden still remains, divided by grey stone walls and arches: the convent parlour, part of the cloisters, and the refectory were turned into domestic offices, and the once stately Gothic chapter-house is now a barn and wood-house. The habitable part of the house has been for many years the dwelling of the agent for the Cowdray estates, and is still so occupied. Opposite to it on the other side of the road is the magnificent avenue of Spanish chestnuts, unrivalled in English "Sylva," and which stretches for more than a mile along the western boundary of the beautiful park. Behind the Priory is the parish church, which contains the memorials of some of the former Lords of Midhurst, and the mausoleum of the Viscounts Montague. The beautiful marble statue of the last of the line,—Mary, the wife of William Poyntz,—is one of the noblest works Chantrey ever executed: the lovely, sad, uplifted face, the mournful attitude, the eyes raised to heaven for strength and consolation, well befit the effigy of one in whose terrible bereavement the family curse received its crowning fulfilment, and whose piety and charity are still a living memory in Midhurst.

The Priory of Easebourne was founded by John de Bohun for a Prioress and five nuns. It seems to have been a quiet though rather a relaxed community; for we find a complaint was made of the Prioress for negligence, fondness of dress, and for unnecessary journeys to the Episcopal Court of Chichester before the Reformation. An ordinance of the Bishop applied a severe reform to the laxity of the house, and the rule was observed (not without some grumbling on the part of the inmates) till the final suppression of the monasteries by Henry the Eighth.

It is here that local tradition steps in and relates what took place. The Prioress had virtually resigned the government of the house and had been succeeded by her Sub-Prioress, Dame Alicia Hill, an austere and holy religious, whose efforts to restore monastic discipline had been crowned with partial success, although they had rendered her unpopular with the unzealous part of the community.

When the King's Commissioners called on the Prioress to resign the keys of the house, the valiant Sub-Prioress was called on to countersign the act of surrender.

"Heed ye well, my masters," she said, "what ye do. The pious founders of this house left a heavy and terrible malison on all who should molest and harry us, poor and unworthy servants though we be of Christ and St. Benedict, and on all who in after time should aid or profit by a deed of sacrilege. As the traditions of our house and of the faithful people of Easebourne attest, *a curse of fire and water* on the male children and heirs of the spoilers is invoked by those who gave lands and protection to the spouses of Christ dwelling in Easebourne Priory, for the rest of their souls, and in perpetual remembrance of their charity. That curse ye are about to incur. He who takes these lands it shall come upon him, and his name shall die out. It shall follow as the heritage of the race that comes after him, and it shall continue even until the end."

The community dispersed, and the fair cloisters and lands of Easebourne

Priory were given by the sacrilegious Tudor to the Earl of Southampton, with the lands of Shulbred Abbey, four miles distant in the parish of Lynchmere. Shulbred was an Augustine Canonry dedicated to Our Lady. The Earl, then Sir William Fitzwilliam, enriched with the spoil of the religious houses, and being a man of equal ambition and cultivated taste, applied his wealth to the erection of the magnificent mansion of Cowdray, once the rival of Audley End and Hatfield in architectural grandeur and beauty, and even now one of the noblest ruins in existence of the Tudor period.

On the death of Lord Southampton without heirs, the Cowdray property, including the confiscated priory lands, passed to his half-brother, Sir Anthony Browne, whose Catholic profession by no means prevented his being one of the most favoured courtiers of Henry VIII. and Edward VI.

Sir Anthony Browne's son and namesake was employed by Mary Tudor for the negotiations on the Spanish marriage and the renewal of relations with the Holy See, and was by her created Viscount Montague. He remained a faithful Catholic on the accession of Elizabeth, but an incurable courtier. Like other Catholic possessors of Priory lands, he wrung an unwilling act of renunciation from the Church. At any rate, he made no restitution during the brief return of England to the faith, and let the golden occasion of reparation pass from him, if he ever thought of it. In every country the "doom of sacrilege" has seemed to be the peculiar task of Divine justice. Even in cases where the Church has been coerced into a reluctant assent, the intentions of pious founders have been terribly vindicated, and Sir Henry Spelman's impartial and learned work on the judgments of Heaven on spoliation contains no more remarkable instance than that of the possessors of Cowdray and its sacrilegiously acquired dependencies.

But for a time in their case the curse slumbered. With all their shortcomings and omissions, the Lords Montague were true in the main to the proscribed faith, and used their favour with Elizabeth for the protection of its ministers. Their known loyalty—one might say courtiership—ensured Cowdray complete immunity from search or violation, and the visit of the Queen set the seal on their favour.

ELIZABETH AT COWDRAY.

". . . . On Tuesday the Queen feasted at Easebourne Priory." In this brief sentence we see how lightly the memories of his ancestor's spoliations sat on the owner of Cowdray. We can picture the scene—the old convent parlour decked in bravery borrowed from the great Hall—the improvised banquet, probably of a rural character, junket and cream and fruit, venison and poultry, covering the board where the Prioress and her nuns had kept austere fast or simple feast as the seasons of the holy rule bade them, and whence the ample crumbs had gone to feed the poor of Christ. Now the daughter of Henry VIII. revelled and banqueted in the despoiled and desecrated nunnery, amid her court of time-servers and flatterers; her host the receiver of the lands and wealth which were God's heritage, and which no law of man could give him. Did any there remember the awful words of the curse coupled with that possession? Or was there then a pious intention in the mind of the holder of restoring them in better times, such as all Catholics were then looking for through the accession of James of Scotland, or of some Catholic Prince, when Elizabeth should have been gathered to her unwept and childless grave?

We know not, but we know that at that very time hiding-holes and trap-doors were being cunningly fashioned, not only in Cowdray itself, but in the adjacent keeper's lodge, to hide the seminarist priests and Jesuit fathers who came from Rheims and Douay, and that perhaps at the very hour of the royal visit—certainly very shortly after, and for years following—the Montagues were giving shelter to the apostles of the faith, and keeping alight in their halls the lamp of the sanctuary. And it is easy to understand that the hand of God was stayed and the curse averted whilst the work of reparation went on.

Before the early dinner at the Priory the royal party adjourned to the beautiful old pleasaunce called the Close Walks, where a circle of ancient yews still marks the site of the Queen's visit. Narrow avenues of the same trees planted at right angles give the wood almost the appearance of a Gothic cloister, and the centre is occupied by a tangle of underwood, and carpeted in spring with wood-anemones and the large blue periwinkle with its wreaths of dark glossy leaves.

No fairer sylvan scene graces even the South Saxon land, so rich in woodland glories; and none could be fitter for the pageants of pilgrims and wild men, decked with scallop-shells or wreathed with ivy and armed with clubs, which the taste of the day arranged before the court. The pilgrim met Elizabeth at the entrance of the Close Walks, and made an allegorical description of peace, which seems to have had reference to the lately concluded Irish wars. Carew's *Pacata Hibernia* and Spenser's own letters tell us how that deadly peace was accomplished; and the Countess of Kildare, who had lost the royal favour the day before by proving too true a markswoman, could have told, from close personal knowledge, how the "Lady Peace" had been won in the valleys of Desmond by the swords of Essex and Mountjoy.

At an old gnarled oak in the middle of the Close Walks, a wild man, girt with ivy, addressed Elizabeth in the fulsome strain of almost Oriental slavishness to which the Tudor reigns had brought the once free but courteous speech of free Englishmen. He praised the clemency of the Queen. Clemency! while the soil of Ulster was reeking with blood; while the valleys of Craven and Richmondshire, the hills of Durham, and the wolds of Holderness were yet strewed with the bleaching bones of the brave Northern Catholics, who had sworn to restore the faith or die in arms round the standard of the Nortons! Clemency! while the Tower vaults echoed with the shrieks of tortured victims, and while the pavement of Fotheringay was yet freshly red with the blood of Mary Stuart,—while the gibbet of Tyburn claimed its daily procession of martyrs, priests, and faithful laymen! Truly the iron must have entered into the souls of those Sussex Catholic lords and gentlemen,—the Brownes, the Gorings, the Carylls, the Glenhams, the Parkers,—when they could tamely hear and favour such words in order to receive knighthood at the sword of the murderess of their brethren!

PENAL DAYS.

All hopes of court favour and patronage were soon dashed by the accession of James the First, and the advent to power of Cecil and the bitterest enemies of the Catholic faith.

The *priest's hole* in the keeper's lodge was soon needed, and Blackwell the archpriest is said to have died there.

During the tenure of Francis the third Viscount Montague, Cowdray seems to have been a frequent refuge of the persecuted priests. The wife of the third Viscount Montague was a daughter of the loyal house of Somerset (as zealous for God as it was true to the cause of Charles the First), and she seems to have been a devout and courageous woman. We find her daughters as nuns in the Low Countries, her sons in the army of the King at Hopton Heath and other south-country battlefields; and though Cowdray, from its position on the low meadows beside the Rother, escaped the fate of the fortified houses of Catholics and Cavaliers, the family were included in the black list of fine and persecution as " Papists and malignants."

The fourth Viscount Montague married Lady Mary Herbert, the daughter of the Marquess of Powys: under her pious auspices the better traditions of the house were fostered, the Church harboured, the poor fed and instructed, and the faith kept alive. To her is attributed the renovation of the beautiful chapel in the house at Cowdray,—a work evidently of that date. A statue of Our Lady still exists on the left-hand wall, garlanded now with growing ivy;—last witness to the faith of the owners, and to the hopes of a Catholic restoration that preceded the Revolution of 1688, and that encouraged the more powerful families at least to give some care to the beauty of the house of God and to all that marked the distinctive faith of Catholics.

MURDER AND APOSTASY.

It is at this point that I am obliged to have recourse to the verbal narrative of the aged lady whom I have mentioned for an event which still lives in Midhurst local tradition, but which no written work seems to have preserved. The Montague family had every interest in not recalling it, and the "troublous times" in which it occurred gave facilities for suppression and partial oblivion which would be sought in vain now.

The fifth Viscount Montague was, according to tradition, a violent and wicked man. That he preserved the outward form of his religion is certain, but his life was a standing negation of its precepts. He seems to have given great cause of scandal by persistent immorality, and to have been more than once refused absolution by his chaplain and confessor on this ground. The courageous priest had required the removal of the cause of sin before granting the pardon of the Church, and Lord Montague's pride revolted at such an act on the part of one whom he evidently considered as a mere officer of his household.

There is some discrepancy in the accounts of the crime I am about to relate. My aged informant always declared that the dispute arose in the confessional, and that Lord Montague killed the priest of God as he sat in the seat of pardon and judgment. The present local tradition is that the dispute on the absolution preceded another as to whether the chaplain should begin mass before the entry of Lord Montague. He refused to keep the congregation waiting—in those days a rapid celebration was almost a matter of necessity—and on the following Sunday he commenced mass without waiting. Lord Montague entered when mass was half over, and, furious at the slight which he conceived to be offered him, he drew forth a pistol and shot the priest at the altar.

The probability is that both stories are partially true, and that ill-blood had arisen gradually. To change a chaplain in those days of flight and proscription was no easy matter, and the perpetual presence of an authorised reprover of vice and ill-doing seems to have intensified Lord Montague's anger to the verge of madness.

Whether he fled from the fear of legal pursuit, or owing to the more terrible remorse of his own conscience is not clear, but he left Cowdray and was said to have gone abroad,—no unlikely assertion in the days when the presence of the exiled Court of St. Germains drew so many Catholic noblemen and gentlemen to the Continent.

Mrs. Barlow, however, stated that this was a mere pretence. Lady Montague, she said, kept up full state at Cowdray; the unhappy Lord Montague, by a just and striking retribution, living concealed for nearly fifteen years in the priest's hiding-hole in the keeper's lodge. This lodge was afterwards the residence of the descendants of the Montague family. The hiding-hole I frequently saw in my youth; it was about six feet square and very high, reaching through two low storeys, and opening with a sliding panel into a cupboard in one of the upper bed-rooms, behind a fireplace. When it was first opened in renovating the house it is said to have contained an iron chair, a table, a brass lamp, and a manuscript book.

In this dungeon, lighted from an aperture above and nearly airless, many a priest had sheltered from pursuivant and sheriff; and here, and probably in the adjoining rooms, the fifth Lord Montague expiated his crime, going out, it is said, at night into the Close Walks, and especially into a beautiful avenue of sweeping limes in Cowdray Park, to meet and converse with his devoted wife. These frequent meetings, and Lady Montague's habit, probably intentional, of wearing a long white dress and mantle, gave the spot the reputation of ghostly visitors, and when I was a girl it still bore the name of the *Lady's Walk*. The room where Lord Montague lived, and in which he died in 1717, was also said to be haunted, and was never given to visitors if it could be avoided. The *Extinct Peerage* of Collins gives his death as taking place at Epsom and his burial at Bath. It is a proof that some mystery attended both, as had he died at Epsom he would have been far nearer the family vault at Cowdray than Bath.

[The *Lady's Walk* is at the upper part of Cowdray Park, near the Lodsworth gate and the Steward's Pond. It runs from west to east. The priest's hole in the keeper's lodge at Cowdray communicated with the roof, and had also a secret staircase leading up to it. There was only just room in it for one person to sit down on a stone recess hollowed out in one of the walls: the opposite wall was so shaped as to admit the knees of the seated occupant. This hiding-hole, now pulled down, is fresh in the recollection of many living persons.

Most of the hiding-holes in English country-houses were contrived by the Jesuit Brother Owen, nicknamed Little John. "A great servant of God in a diminutive body. With incomparable skill he knew how to conduct priests to a place of safety along subterranean passages, to hide them between walls, and bury them in impenetrable recesses, which entangle them in labyrinths and a thousand windings. But, what was much more difficult of accomplishment, he so disguised the entrances to these, as to make them most unlike what they really were. Moreover, he kept these places so close a secret with himself, that he would never disclose to another the place of concealment of any Catholic. He alone was both their architect and builder, working at them with inexhaustible industry and labour, for generally the thickest walls had to be broken into and large stones excavated, requiring stronger arms than were attached to a body so diminutive as to give him the nickname of Little John. And by this his skill many priests were preserved from the fury of the persecutors, nor is it easy to find any one who had not often been indebted for his life to Owen's hiding-places. When he was about to design one, he commenced the work by receiving the Most Holy Eucharist, sought to aid its progress by continual prayer, and offered the completion of it to God alone, accepting of no other reward for his toil than the merit of charity and the consolation of labouring for the good of Catholics." Hinlip Castle, near Worcester, was full of Little John's hiding-holes. It belonged to the Abington family, but has been pulled down. The castle was frequently searched for the hidden priests.* The searcher, Sir Henry Bromley, had "Argus' eyes, and many watchful and subtle companions that would spy out the least advantage or cause of suspicion, and yet they searched and sounded every corner in that great house till they were all weary, and found no likelihood of discovering what they came for, though they continued the daily search, and that with double diligence, all the whole week following." Little John was there. He had hidden the two priests at Hinlip in a secure (though a very small) hiding-hole,† in which he had stored provisions to supply their need. He himself and his companion Ashley "had but one apple between them all those six or seven days. Whereupon they thought it best to come out; and yet, not so much to save themselves from death by famine, as for that they perceived the resolution of the searchers to be of staying in the house till they had either found

---

* Garnett and Oldcorne, supposed to have been concerned in the Gunpowder Plot. Owen and Ashley were also charged with complicity in that Plot.

† Garnett thus describes the situation of himself and Oldcorne :—"After we had been in the hoale seven dayes and seven nights and some odd hours, every man may well think we were well wearyed; and indeed so it was, for we generally satte save that some times we could half stretch ourselves, the place not being high eno', and we had our legges so straitened that we could not sitting find place for them, so that we both were in continuall paine of our legges, and both our legges, especially mine, were much swollen. . . . We were very merry and content within, and heard the searchers every day most curious over us, which made me indeed think the place would be found. . . . When we came forth we appeared like two ghostes."

or famished those whom they knew to be within." Little John and his friend gave themselves up, vainly hoping to save the hidden priests from discovery. But Little John's appearance showed the searchers that the supposed hiding-holes existed. "At the top of the mansion was a gallery running round the whole interior, and whose walls were covered with beautifully carved wainscoting. Behind these were the celebrated hiding-places, having their secret entrances so cleverly made as to appear a part only of the rest of the wall." Little John voluntarily came out of his hiding-hole, well knowing the fate that awaited him. He hoped, but in vain, to save his friends. He was, with his companion Ashley, immediately arrested. Cecil wrote on the occasion :—"It is incredible how great was the joy caused by this arrest throughout the kingdom, knowing the great skill of Owen in constructing hiding-places, and the innumerable quantity of these dark holes which he had schemed for hiding priests all through England." Cecil hoped by "coaxing, if he is willing thus to contract for his life," to get from Little John "an excellent booty of priests." If he would not confess, the secret was to be wrung from him. The story of Little John's end is one of the most horrible of all the dreadful tales of the Tower. It is enough to give the words of the Keeper of the Tower regarding his death. "*The man is dead; he died in our hands.*" A.D. 1606.—*Records of the English Province of the Society of Jesus*, vol. iv. J. R.]

The sixth Viscount Montague was chosen in 1732 Grand Master of the Free and Accepted Masons. The craft not having been at that date condemned by the Holy See, many Catholics belonged to it, and especially in Jacobite families. Masonry played a large part in Scotland, especially in the attempts for the Restoration of the House of Stuart. Pius VI. first forbade Catholics taking the Masonic oaths, in common with all other secret societies.

Of the seventh Viscount Montague we only know at first that he enlarged and beautified the park, improved the grounds, and added largely to the collection of works of art at Cowdray which two centuries of wealth and taste had accumulated there. By degrees he appears to have sought out the society of Protestants, and his marriage with the widowed Lady Halkerton, a Methodist of Lady Huntingdon's school and sect, set the seal on his defection from the faith. The accursed spirit of the eighteenth century, which preceded the French Revolution, was on him, and he at length followed the Duke of Norfolk, Sir William Gascoigne, and other Catholic noblemen and gentlemen in an open apostasy.

The reason he gave for it to his friends was the double land-tax imposed on Catholics at that time, and which fell heavily on his broad manors, the old inheritance of the monks of Battle and Shulbred, and of the nuns of Easebourne. It seems to have been suddenly decided on. On the Sunday after the legal communication of the Act, Lord Montague ordered his coach, and on stepping into it, desired his coachman to drive him to the parish church of Midhurst. The faithful servant turned, threw down the reins, and descended from the box. "No, my Lord," he said; "if you will, the devil may drive you to the devil, but not I."

The next step was to dismantle the household chapel, and Lady Montague was very anxious to hold evening services there. On more than one occasion this was attempted, but the lights could never be kept in above a few moments, and persisted in going out without any apparent cause, till even the Protestant servants introduced by Lady Montague took alarm at the omen, and the idea of services in the chapel was abandoned. Lady Montague, however, was in the habit of preaching in the park, and is said to have persuaded her friend and visitor the celebrated Selina Countess of Huntingdon to hold forth to an outdoor congregation under the trees near the house.

And so the faith was trampled out in the little town, two-thirds of whose inhabitants had been baptized into the Catholic Church. The old servants were discharged and dispersed, the chapel removed to a miserable cottage in Easebourne, where a priest yet strove to keep the altar on a wretched stipend insufficient for existence, and the Methodist propaganda went on unceasingly under the patronage of Lady Montague, who had full influence over her weak and wicked husband.

Time passed, and sickness long and sore brought Lord Montague an unhoped-for and undeserved proof of God's mercy. Unlike his companions in apostasy, he had time to repent; too late indeed to repair his sin, but in time at least to be absolved in his last hours and reconciled to the Church. He died in 1787, and ordered with his last breath that his recantation should be published after his death in the *Gentleman's Magazine*, as well as in the newspapers of the day. In it he asks pardon for the scandal given to his fellow-Catholics, and implores the mercy of God for the injury he had done to his dependants, and he declares that his apostasy was solely based on worldly motives, and not on any doubts as to the authority to the Church. A copy of the original document also exists in the registers of the Catholic Mission of Slindon.

THE FULFILMENT OF THE CURSE.

The Dowager Viscountess Montague continued to reside at Cowdray, paying only occasional visits to London. She seems to have devoted herself to the education of her two children in the most rigid principles of Evangelical Protestantism. With her daughter she succeeded; but her son, George Samuel, eighth Viscount Montague, was a wild careless young man, who chafed at his mother's authority, laughed at her pet preachers; and without evincing the slightest tendency to return to the faith of his ancestors, he yet never took kindly to the new lights of the Evangelical revival.

No sooner was he of an age to emancipate himself from his mother's authority than he started for the Continent with his friend Mr. Burdett and an old family servant. . . . They conceived the mad project of passing the Falls of the Rhine in a small boat. . . . The old Cowdray servant, Dickinson, tried to drag Lord Montague back, exclaiming, "Oh my Lord! it's the *curse of water!* For God's sake give up the trial!" But it was useless. . . . The first fall was passed in safety, and Dickinson standing on the shore saw the two young men rise up in the boat waving their handkerchiefs in triumph. They neared the second fall, and entered the cloud of spray that encircles this, the most terrible point of the passage. They were never seen again. . . . The old servant lingered for some time on the spot in the hope of recovering his master's body, but as days passed and the river gave back no sign or token of the dead, he departed sorrowfully for Cowdray to tell the tale of desolation to the widowed mother. Ere he reached England the other part of the curse—*the curse of fire*—had swept with devouring fury through the halls acquired and raised by sacrilege, and Cowdray, one of the stateliest mansions of the Tudor era, was a smoking and blackened ruin. . . . The flames, fanned to double rapidity by a fierce September gale, soon did their worst on the entire edifice. Never was a ruin more complete than that which stood bare and bleak beneath the light of the harvest moon when the fire had ceased to roar and crackle through the desolate halls of the Montagues.

Very few family relics were saved, and the few that were so seem to have been dispersed and uncared for in the deeper grief and desolation that fell on the house at the death of its heir. There was no thought of rebuilding the mansion; the curse had come home at last, though its avenging force was not yet all spent, and even the mourners seem to have recognised and dreaded it, and to have made no attempt to restore the pride and magnificence of the old Lords of Cowdray.

The title, but not the estates, devolved on a poor Friar of Fontainebleau, a distant kinsman of the house, who most unwillingly accepted a Papal dispensation from his vows in order to carry on the line. In spite of the marriage which he contracted and which only lasted a few months, he left no children, and with him the family honours became extinct.

Mary Browne, sister of the eighth Viscount Montague and heiress of the estate, was brought up by her mother, and was a beautiful, pious, and amiable woman, wanting nothing save the light of faith, of which her father's apostasy had deprived her, to have been one of the noblest types of womanhood. She was married

APPENDIX. 173

shortly after her succession to the estates to William Poyntz, . . . a very handsome and accomplished man.

On their marriage the old keeper's lodge in the centre of the park was completely renovated and added to, and it became the residence of Mr. and Mrs. Poyntz. Here old Lady Montague partly lived also, devoting herself to the exercises of piety of her sect, but constantly haunted by the idea that the terrible family curse would some time find out the two boys who had been, with three daughters, born to the young couple. . . . The children of Cowdray grew in strength and age, and were in the fulness of their boyhood when in 1815 they were taken as usual to the seaside at Bognor. . . . It was a lovely summer's day, and Mr. Poyntz, seeing how exceptionally bright and calm the sea was, proposed to go out boating. To this Mrs. Poyntz, who inherited her mother's vague terror as to the family prediction, strongly objected, but was at length persuaded into giving a very reluctant consent . . . The boat heeled over, . . . and the two boys sunk never to rise again.

What wonder that to their dying day the unhappy parents could never endure the sight of the sea, or that the bereaved mother, at least, carried to her grave the terrible conviction that her sorrow was the accomplishment of the curse invoked by the pious founders of Easebourne on the spoilers of their peaceful cloister! That this was her belief was borne ample witness to by the older inhabitants; and it haunted her through the childhood of her boys, and left its indelible mark upon her after life of prayer, retirement, and charity. Few will look on her monument in Easebourne church without tracing in the beautiful portrait due to Chantrey's genius the shadow of a more than common sorrow. . . .

In 1843 the Cowdray estates were sold to the sixth Earl of Egmont, a naval officer of considerable reputation at Navarino and Algiers.

It was in 1845, when I was on a visit at Cowdray Lodge, that I first saw the priest's hiding-hole. The Montague family had never allowed it to be shown, and were very chary of any reference to their Catholic forefathers. The rooms adjacent to it were said to be haunted by the Lord Montague who had died there, and Lord Egmont himself told me that it was difficult to get the servants to go into the corridor at night, and that one or two visitors had been so much frightened, it had become impossible to use the rooms.

The old Catholic mission lingered on at Easebourne till, on the death of its last incumbent, Father Boland (one of the last survivors of the ancient English College of Douai), it was removed into the town of Midhurst itself, and a very plain and modest building under the invocation of St. Francis was erected by Dr. Grant, Bishop of Southwark. For some years it was served from the neighbouring mission of Burton Park near Petworth, but it now possesses a resident priest, the Rev. James Carter, Chamberlain to his late Holiness Pius IX. As Midhurst has now easy and rapid railway communication with London and with the South Coast, there is some hope that in time Catholics may fix their residence in the beautiful environs and revive what was once a principal asylum and centre of English Catholicity. Of the original congregation there remain, alas! but very few traces, but one or two pious and zealous families connected by birth or marriage with Midhurst have returned to reside there. It is much that, after such vicissitudes, apostasy, repression, and adverse influences, the lamp of the sanctuary has never been quite extinguished.

To those who, like myself, remember the deplorable state of Catholicity in Sussex forty years ago, the great revival now spreading through the county is full of hope and interest. The re-establishment of the great Order of St. Bruno in the Carthusian monastery of Cowfold, of the Præmonstratensians at Storrington, and of the Servites at Bognor, the resurrection of the Mission of Our Lady of Consolation at West Grinstead, the staunch maintenance of faith and practice in the ancient Catholic parish of Burton, the Franciscan foundation at Crawley, that of the Theresian nuns at Chichester,—their venerable Prioress being the last of the Pendrels of Boscobel,—the establishment of missions at Liphook, Worthing, and Shoreham, and above all of that central radius of South Saxon Catholicity, Arundel, and its magnificent church (worthy of the best days of Christian piety): these and countless other religious foundations spreading along our sea-board and wherever new communications are opened, give assurance that the seed sown in persecution, confiscation, and martyrdom will prevail over the tares and cockle of sacrilege and self-seeking, and that fresh conversions to truth from among those separated from us so widely and yet in outward rite so near may here and elsewhere spread the faith, re-people the cloister, raise once more worthy temples of God and the saints, and draw down on the beautiful forest county the blessing of that unity of faith our forefathers rejoiced in.

In the meantime it is well to keep living the memory of old days, the sins and the good deeds of those who have gone before us. In times like the present, when the hand of retribution is becoming more and more visible among the spoilers of God's Church on the Continent, when the holy shrines of Rome and Italy are laid waste and the cloisters are made desolate, it is well to recall what in our own land has ever been the doom of sacrilege,—testified to by innumerable Protestant writers, of whom the learned Sir Henry Spelman and his annotators are among the principal.

Church lands have never prospered in the hands of impropriators, and many a family dates its decadence from a careless acceptance of the fatal legacy, or from a covetous acquisition of what has once been and should still be the patrimony of the altar and of the poor.

APPENDIX.

Wherever restitution cannot be made, a thinking Catholic will at least feel himself obliged in a special manner to make reparation to the Church, by aiding her needs in the locality from which he derives his confiscated wealth as far as he can, according to the intentions of the pious founders, in order to avert from himself and his heirs the curse which has certainly been incurred by the original spoliators, and which in many notable instances seems to have followed family after family with the avenging and mysterious scourge of God's inscrutable justice.

K. S.

INDEX.

ANNE of Cleves, 14.

BATTLE Abbey, 13, 34, 81, 87, 90, 98.
Betchworth Castle, 11.
Browne, Sir Anthony, K.G., 11–22; his portrait, 20, 92; his funeral pageant, 19.
Browne, Brother William, S.J., 25.
—— Stanislaus, 47.
—— Anthony, of Lings, 84.
—— Joan, 149.
—— Baronetcies, 11, 35, 105.
Blackdown, 157.
Book of household rules, 51–74.
Borough English, 147.
Burgage tenements, 150.

CLARENCE, Margaret of, Countess of Salisbury, 8, 92, 133.
Close Walks, 124, 139.
Cobbett, William, 133.
Commandery House, Midhurst, 151.
Copley, Anthony, 46.
Cowdray, description of, 111–126, 133–140.
Cowdray, fire at, 126–133.

DE BOHUN family, 2.
De Bohun, John de, 2, 3.
De Bohun, Mary de, 3.

EDWARD VI., visit to Cowdray, 23; procession of, 16, 97, 117.
Elizabeth, Queen, at Cowdray, 27, 38–45.
Easebourne, 2, 143–147.
Evelyn, John, 78, 81.

FITZWILLIAM, William Fitzwilliam, Earl of Southampton, K.G., 7–11.
Farnhurst, 154.
Fire-backs, 28.
Fire at Cowdray, 126–133.
Fair Geraldine, 18.
Fountain at Cowdray, 110, 138.
Fox, Charles James, 150.

GUY FAWKES, 48.

HEARTH-MONEY, 83.
Hiding-hole, 89, 168.
Huntingdon, Countess of, 93.

z

INDEX.

JOHNSON, Dr., 94.

KILDARE, Earl and Countess of, 26, 27.

LAMBE, Richard, 55.
Lanman, Father, S.J., 77.
Lodsworth, 151.

MIDHURST, 147-151.
Manuscripts at Cowdray, 135-139.
Montague, Sir Anthony Browne, K.G., first Viscount, 22-38; his tomb, 29-33; his portrait, 32; his possessions, 33.
—— Anthony Maria, second Viscount, 45-51; his household rules, 51-74; his imprisonment, 48.
—— Francis, third Viscount, 78-83; his estates sequestered, 78, 81; his steward's accounts, 82.
—— Francis, fourth Viscount, 87, 88, 123.
—— Henry, fifth Viscount, 89, 167.
—— Anthony, sixth Viscount, 90.
—— Anthony, Joseph, seventh Viscount, 92-99, 170; his recantation, 94, 95; his letters, 96-98.
—— George Samuel, eighth Viscount, 100-104, 128, 131, 172; his letters, 99, 103.
—— Mark Anthony, ninth Viscount, 47, 104, 105.

Montague, Magdalen, Viscountess, 34.
—— Frances, Viscountess, 107, 171; her letters, 98, 129

NORTH Heath gibbet, 152.

OWEN, Sir Davy, 3; his effigy, 4; his will, 5, 6.
Overy, St. Mary, 14.

POYNTZ, Mr. and Mrs., 106-110; death of their sons, 108, 109.
Poyntz, John, 12.
Puzzle-walk, 124, 139.

RIVER House, 36, 152.
Rules, book of, 51-74.

SHULBRED Priory, 155.
Southampton, Earl of, 7-11.
Storm of 1703, 88.

TOKENS, 147.
Todham, 35.

URBAN VIII., Pope, letter from, 74.

VERDLEY Castle, 153.

WALPOLE, Horace, 91, 47, 117.
Waller, Sir William, 79.

THE END.

PRINTED BY BALLANTYNE, HANSON AND CO.
EDINBURGH AND LONDON.

www.ingramcontent.com/pod-product-compliance
Lightning Source LLC
Chambersburg PA
CBHW020913230426
43666CB00008B/1444